THE ORIENTAL ADVENTURE

The Oriental Adventure

Explorers of the East

by

TIMOTHY SEVERIN

Angus and Robertson · Publishers

Angus and Robertson . Publishers
London · Sydney · Melbourne · Singapore · Manila

First published by Angus and Robertson (U.K.) Ltd 1976
Copyright © Timothy Severin 1976

Designed and produced by George Rainbird Limited
Marble Arch House, 44 Edgware Road, London W2
House editor: Penelope Miller
Picture research: Sarah Waters
Designer: Jonathan Gill-Skelton
Cartographer: Tom Stalker Miller
Calligrapher: Alison Urwick

ISBN 0 207 95699 5

Text set by Jarrold and Sons Limited, Norwich, Norfolk
Printed and bound by Dai Nippon Printing Company Limited,
Tokyo, Japan

PRINTED IN JAPAN

Facing title page *Seventeenth-century Europeans bearing gifts at the court of Shah Jehan*

CONTENTS

COLOUR PLATES

MAPS

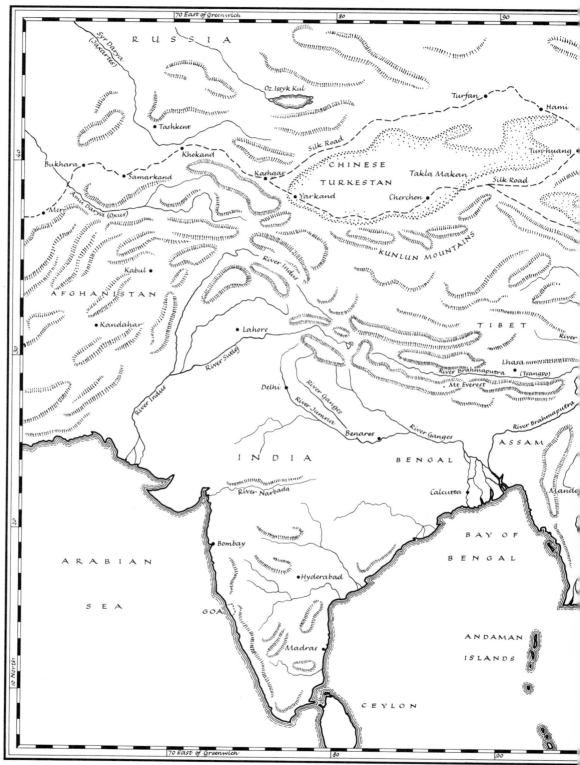

Scope for the Oriental Adventure

MONGOLIA

GOBI DESERT

KIANG

Great Wall

Silk Road

Yellow River (Hwang Ho)

Great Wall

Harbin •

MANCHURIA

• Peking

KOREA

YELLOW
SEA

JAPAN

Yellow River (Hwang Ho)

• Loyang

Grand Canal

C H I N A

River Yangtze

• Chengtu

River Yangtze

Hangchow •

EAST

CHINA SEA

• Tali

Red River

Amoy •

Canton •
• Hong Kong
Macao

Hanoi •

Gulf of
Tonkin

HAINAN

TAIWAN
(Formosa)

RMA

INDO-CHINA

River Mekong

SIAM

goon

• Bankok

SOUTH

CHINA SEA

Gulf of Siam

THE ORIENT

CHAPTER ONE

BEYOND THE STONE TOWER

OUTSIDE THE GREAT WALL OF CHINA begins the Gobi Desert. To the eye it is only a gentle change of landscape as the fields of the Chinese farmers give way to the thin grasses of the desert margin and these surrender in turn to the camel sage and thorn bush of the Gobi proper. The naturalist may notice a sharper boundary where creatures of the grassland are replaced by typical animals of the Gobi life-zone, long-tailed Gobi antelope, pale rat-like jerboas which can jump eight or nine feet in a single leap, venomous brown pit-vipers, and whirring flocks of sand grouse. To the geologist the edge of the Gobi is most obvious of all when he can identify the sharp ridge of the continental divide which sends the rivers either draining freely into the Yellow Sea and the Sea of Japan or inland to be swallowed up in the huge sink of the Gobi. For the Gobi is nothing so much as a vast, dried-up moat laid along the foot of China's Wall. It is one of the great geographical facts of Asia, an immense land-locked trough a thousand miles long and up to six hundred miles wide, which has hindered invader and explorer, diplomat and trader throughout the whole of Asia's history.

Of course, the Gobi can be, and is, crossed. Much of its surface is only semi-desert, and there is enough pasture for the flocks of sheep and goats and the camel herds of the Mongol nomads. Even when the land runs out into barren gravel flats, the caravan trails are marked by lines of wells, ten to fifteen miles apart, which reach down to the water-table not far below. Yet very few people actively relish the prospect of crossing the Gobi, for the desert is too strange, too incomprehensible, and too full of surprises. It is a place where in the 1920s a scientific expedition found dinosaur eggs lying exposed on the ground like the fossilized clutches of monstrous chickens; and while trying to map one of the Gobi's famous 'moving lakes', the scientists watched as a lake writhed and changed shape, and finally vanished into thin air as its water evaporated and its feeder streams choked to death in the sand. Camping overnight on the shore of another lake, the same expedition woke up when the wind, which had been steadily heaping up the water on one side of the lake, suddenly changed direction and, blowing out of another quarter, drove the water away so that hundreds upon hundreds of small silver fish lay stranded on the damp ground. No one could imagine how these fish had got to this remote inland pool, and in the moonlight of the desert they watched in awe as the fish lay and flapped. The noise of the doomed shoal was like the sound of a crowd softly applauding.

The great scourge of the Gobi is not its heat, though temperatures can reach well past one hundred degrees Fahrenheit, nor is it the dry season when no drop of rain falls for eight months. Rather, it is the wind and cold of the Gobi which appals the unwary visitor. The winter wind is the *buran*,

Portiuncula Muri Sinensis, qua structura ejus exprimitur.

12. Cubit.

30 Cubit.

Porta Tartarica

Cracaus fluvius

a howling blizzard out of Siberia which slashes across the flatlands of the Gobi with numbing cold, drifting snow against every obstacle while the temperature slumps to ten degrees of frost. In summer the wind can be even more disastrous because it comes so suddenly that it catches the caravans unprepared, and produces havoc in the travelling season. Out of a clear calm sky a summer storm begins to gather. The camels of the caravan start to fidget and grumble; dogs howl; and the men hurry frantically to tighten saddle-straps or to double-peg their tent ropes. Clearly visible, the storm is a yellow-grey cloud soughing across the desert and spawning small dust devils which whirl and skitter at its leading edge like acolytes. Then with a shriek and a crash which has been compared to a burst of artillery, the storm strikes. A fog of whirling dust blots out the sun, and a man can no longer see as far as his feet. Through the dust comes a tearing rattle of sand and gravel hurled along by the force of the gale. This shrapnel lacerates an unprotected face until it bleeds, and has been known to strip thin clothes from a man's back. The only defence is to lie prone on the ground, head covered in a towel, and wait for the storm to blow over. The slightest movement is difficult, and even cars find it awkward to make headway against the full force of the wind. Every item is quickly saturated in a choking haze of fine dust which penetrates the most carefully sealed containers and boxes, and ruins fine instruments. Then, just as suddenly, the windstorm moves away; the tent flaps, which have slatted and cut themselves into tatters, hang straight down in the absolutely still air; and the grime-covered men rise to their feet to clean off their clothes, reassemble baggage, and begin again their journey.

Left *Gateway in the Great Wall of China, facing the Gobi, drawn by a Jesuit surveyor in the mid-seventeenth century.*

11

The classic Silk Road along almost half its length either skirted or crossed the Gobi and its adjacent desert regions, and most of the exotic wares, lustrous silks, and even more colourful fabric of rumour, which reached Europe from China by land for centuries, was carried across the heart of Asia by this route. And yet the Gobi remained virtually unknown to anyone in the West. Partly this was because the Gobi lay within High Asia, that vast uplifted core of the continent which has played such a central role in world history that the pioneer geo-politician Sir Halford Mackinder pronounced it to be the 'geographical pivot of History', and claimed that whoever ruled this area would also control the world. Certainly the heartland dominated the lives of the settled peoples of the great civilizations who lived on its lowland fringes. They suffered, one after another, the great cataracts of migration pouring out of High Asia in the form of the armies of Scythians, Sarmathians, Huns, Mongols, or Turks. Like locusts, these invaders seemed to breed and strengthen in the far wastelands until they felt themselves ready to migrate, and then suddenly appeared in voracious clusters, alien, insatiable, and exceptionally destructive.

Pure geography also had much to do with the West's ignorance of farther Asia. Whereas the Chinese looked across the Great Wall and saw mostly the Han Lai, the Dried Sea, the Europeans looking in the opposite direction had their view blocked by the second great geographical barrier of interior Asia: its colossal ranges of mountains. Three months' journey by caravan eastward from the seaports of the Mediterranean or the Black Sea rose the plateau of the Pamirs. Like the upheaval left by the blow of a gigantic fist striking the underside of the earth's crust, the Pamirs formed a series of finger ridges with their intervening valleys and the projecting knuckles of higher peaks. Exposed wild places, the Pamirs are softened in summer by lush meadows along the watercourses and by clumps of tamarisk where the forest rose and the familiar blue gentian grow. In the great days of the Silk Road small watchtowers were built of stone to guard the network of pathways by which men crossed the Pamirs, and looking up the tributary valleys the traveller could see the blue-green bulk of the small glaciers which foretold the snows and ice of an Asian winter. Near the very centre of the Pamirs they passed the lake which was recognized as a source of the classical Oxus river, and which was inevitably called Lake Victoria by the first nineteenth-century Englishman to survey it, a Lieutenant John Wood. The same discoverer also found that the air at such altitude was so rarefied that breathing was difficult, and that a run of only fifty yards exhausted him, while a musket shot sounded as if the gun-barrel had been filled with water, and the whizz of the ball could be heard distinctly as it flew through the thin air.

The Kirghiz who fattened their flocks in the remote plateau in summer, had called the Pamirs the 'Roof of the World', but the plateau is more accurately described as its gable end. On the Pamirs converge four huge mountain ranges, breath-taking in their size and splendour: the Hindu Kush running down into Afghanistan; the Himalaya-Karakorum; the Kunlun range which encloses the north side of Tibet; and the Tien Shan or Heavenly mountains curving in an arc round the border of Chinese Turkestan. Some idea of their immensity can be gained from the fact that all but two of the ninety-four highest peaks in the world are located in this mountain complex, and those other two are located also in central Asia, in the trans-Altai; while in Tibet more than half a million square miles lie over thirteen thousand feet high. By comparison the Alps are little more than flying buttresses, and the Andes stand nearly a mile shorter.

To the Romans the barrier of the Pamirs marked the beginning of *terra incognita*. In the early second century A.D. Maes Titianos, an enterprising Roman merchant, paid his agents to trace the Silk Road to its ultimate source, but his spies got no farther than the mysterious place they called the Stone Tower. Quite where this particular stone tower was placed, was never precisely determined, but it seems to have been on the flanks of the Pamirs or perhaps high in the middle of the tangled plateau. This Stone Tower was the great rendezvous of the Eastern caravans, the place where they prepared for the long ordeal ahead, gathered together to rest their animals and exchange merchandise, and formed up into travelling parties for mutual protection. The Stone Tower was the point of balance of the Silk Road, the fulcrum between East and West. Beyond it began the great desert marches of High Asia where no one could falter and still hope to complete his journey, and where all roads eventually led through the Gobi to China. The Stone Tower was a psychological boundary, too. It was the zone where hazy fantasy began to take over from fact, and a medieval traveller began to think that he might see in the flesh the famous Uniped lying on his back in the desert and sheltering from the sun beneath a single foot as broad as a parasol; or perhaps he might meet the giant ants who, according to Herodotus, burrowed in the earth for gold and tore to pieces any stranger who ventured among them.

In short, the Stone Tower was where the Oriental Adventure began; and with it the process by which European travellers gradually involved themselves in the East, dismantling its legends, exploring its realities, and substituting facts and opinions of their own, usually precise but sometimes as fabulous as their predecessors. This was the Oriental Adventure and it was an experience which lasted more than six hundred years at the most conservative estimate, from the time when Marco Polo became the first European to record his experiences as he crossed over the Pamirs and passed by the Stone Tower, right through to the twentieth century when Europeans were barred from travelling freely in a large portion of farther Asia. The account of the Adventure which follows is only a tiny and personal selection of its main episodes and themes. Yet it is a deliberate selection which tries to describe those people and incidents which were either typical of their time or shed some useful light on special facets of the Oriental Adventure, whether its motives, directions, or human actors. Also it is an attempt to cover as much as possible of the territory itself, taking examples from all the major regions of Asia, ranging from Siberia to Indo-China, and in every case concentrating on the particular episode which appears to be the most characteristic or to have produced the most far-reaching effect.

Certainly an overall history of Asian exploration is not intended, because the very idea of Europeans 'exploring' Asia is something of an impertinence. In most cases the Asians knew very well where they lived and they had a shrewd idea of who their neighbours were, long before the Europeans arrived and put them in another perspective. The Chinese, for example, dispatched regular trading fleets to Southeast Asia, imported fine horses from Turkestan, had once built a garrison post in the very centre of the Pamirs, and Chinese pilgrims had written widely read books describing how they had walked the sacred way along the Ganges.

Nor did it matter that Asiatic geographical notions differed from European ideas. Hindu scholars preferred to believe that the Himalayas were the vortex of four great rivers which watered the world, and the Chinese often drew their maps like chessboards, the stylized squares growing larger and emptier the farther one got from the centre at Peking. Instead, it must be accepted that the idea of Asian exploration was a European conceit, a description of the process by which the Europeans themselves got to know about Asia, and even then there was no guarantee that their knowledge was accurate. Far too often the story of Europe's discovery has been given a maritime bias and seen as the opening up of the sea route to the Indies and the establishment of the great seaborne empires. But this was a process which only touched the fringe of a continent whose coastline is notoriously short for its bulk. Far more impressive were the land journeys of Europeans within the Orient when, far from the comforting security of their ships, they encountered Asiatic peoples and cultures, reported on their own experiences and ambitions, and in the process created our picture of Asia.

So the Oriental Adventure has been treated as a landsman's tale, deliberately excluding the Japanese islands and the Southeast Asian archipelago as belonging to the maritime phase. And although the accumulation of pure geographical knowledge was a vital part of the process, just as interesting was the way in which Europe's view of Asia changed shape, as the travellers altered and enlarged the sum of knowledge, and at the same time revealed their own natures. It was a long-drawn-out process, utterly unlike the opening up of underpopulated Africa, America, or Australia, because Asia was not only the more overwhelming experience in size, variety, and sophistication, but it was also a place where Europeans as a general rule approached the indigenous cultures with much greater respect, and this often changed to awe or, equally sharply, to disillusion. It was this interaction between Europeans and the Asiatic experience, as much as the pure exploration of the land mass, which gave the Oriental Adventure its special texture, whether narrated by the explorers and travellers or reproduced in the pictures they drew to illustrate their experiences.

THE MERCHANT AND THE KHAKHAN

MARCO POLO PASSED NEAR THE STONE TOWER at the extreme limit of the caravan travelling season when the combination of cold and high altitude meant that his camp-fire burned feebly and scarcely cooked his food at all. Even the bird life, normally so abundant in the highlands, had migrated away from the bitter weather, abandoning the plateau to utter desolation and silence. To Marco the Pamirs seemed the highest and most forlorn place in the world, and during the whole of his forty days' crossing he saw not a single living creature, finding only the remains of cattle-pens left behind by the summer nomads who had twined together the discarded horns of wild sheep to form their makeshift corrals. One day the same wild sheep would be identified as a separate species and named *Ovis poli* in Marco's honour, but in the early 1270s their magnificent curled horns had a more practical use: the nomads carved horseshoes from the horn to prevent their ponies from slipping on the ice, and here and there they had been heaped up into cairns to serve as signposts, guiding the stranger across the featureless snow-shrouded barrens.

Marco Polo was himself a rare creature to be venturing out on this historic plateau at such a time. No European had ever been known to have crossed the Pamirs before, and he stood on the threshold to the Orient at an extraordinarily lucky moment for his journey. Virtually the whole of the continent, excluding only India and Southeast Asia, lay under a single political heritage exercised by the princely heirs to Genghis Khan and his Mongol cavalry armies. Four great Mongol Hordes – in Persia, China, Siberia, and on the Volga – had divided up the bulk of Asia between them, and still maintained political relations with one another so that a traveller armed with the proper credentials could be handed on from the Don river in the west as far as Peking in the east. The khans, the Mongol chiefs, maintained regular courier routes between their encampments, and obliged the local populations to maintain way-stations for horse-riders and to provide crews and boats at ferry points on the large rivers. In northern Siberia there was even an organized dog-team service, so that across the ice of winter and the mire of spring the traveller could be transported aboard a light sledge pulled by a team of half a dozen dogs, trained to take the correct route to the next relay station. This sophisticated network of routes was mainly for the use of official Mongol couriers passing between the Hordes, but anyone who had official permission could take advantage of the system and could also claim Mongol protection if he displayed the passports which the great Mongol lords issued as symbols of their patronage. These passports were the famous *paizahs*, the 'tablets of command' copied from the Chinese. Each *paizah* was a flat plate of metal, usually of gold or silver, about a foot long and some four

*Nomads at their daily chores
in camp*

inches broad, and in special instances set with a semi-precious gem. On them were engraved a few lines of writing authorizing the bearer's safe conduct in the name of his Mongol sponsor, and usually, too, there appeared the semi-sacred figures of birds and beasts. Anyone who harmed or dared to flout the safe conduct of the traveller who carried a *paizah*, was punished as if he had damaged the Mongol khan himself.

Very probably Marco Polo had the protection of a Mongol passport, for he was travelling eastward with his father, Nicolo, and his uncle, Maffeo, who had already been to Cathay and were now returning there at the express invitation of the khakhan or supreme chief of the Mongols, Kubilai, the Emperor of China. Of the elder Polos' earlier trip very little is known, except that it had been a merchant venture by a more northern route, probably to trade in jewels with the Mongol khans of the Golden Horde on the Volga. It seems that a civil war had cut off their return road, and so, like the ambitious Venetian traders they were, they had pressed forward to try their fortunes with Kubilai, who had been sufficiently impressed with them to ask them to carry a message back to the Pope in Rome, tentatively opening diplomatic communications and asking for more information about the Catholic Church.

When Marco Polo set out he had his uncle and father to supervise the day-to-day running of the caravan, and he was left free to make notes of his own observations across the width of Asia. Thus the first really widely known participant in the Oriental Adventure was also the man who had the most time and opportunity to record in detail all that he saw, and the result was a portrait of Oriental peoples and places, unparalleled for colour and accuracy.

On the far side of the Pamirs Marco found that the Silk Road descended to the frontier town of Kashgar, renowned for the excellence of its orchards and vineyards and the villainous miserliness of its people. From there the road swung south in a great curve, skirting round the bleak sand-drowned basin of the Tarim river and linking together the towns which lay along the foot of the Kunlun mountains. Each town depended upon water brought down by streams flowing from the mountains, and there were bright irrigated

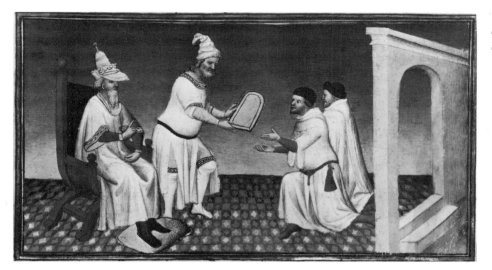

patches of cotton and fruit. Occasionally one also came across the huts of
the jade-miners who spent their lives scouring the gravel of the jade-
streams, looking for the green and red, sometimes gold-flecked, stone for
which the Chinese would pay astronomical sums. In Marco's day this was a
dangerous stretch of the Silk Road, for the region was being contested by
Kubilai and a rebellious Mongol warlord named Caidu, and here Mongol
fought Mongol. When they had any warning of trouble, the townsfolk wisely
gathered up their belongings and trekked into the sanctuary of the desert
with their cattle, relying on the wind to blow sand over their tracks.

At Charkhliq, a city which Marco Polo called Lop, the Silk Road met the
edge of the Black Gobi, the shortest but also one of the most difficult cross-
ings of the Great Desert. Even those who had already struggled across the
Pamirs or seen the empty wastelands of the Russian steppes, had a peculiar
revulsion for this region which the Chinese called 'the Flowing Sands',
because the great whispering dunes were never entirely stationary but
humped and twisted and changed their position as the wind blew over them.

To Marco Polo, with his background of European geographical super-
stition, the Black Gobi was a positive evil, a malignant horror set to snare
the intruder, and he described it in such terms, as if it had a grim life of its
own. Caravans, he said, took at least a month to cross the desert, and all the
way the water from the wells was enough only for small groups of fifty or a
hundred men with their beasts, and so the larger caravans had to split up
into smaller segments. These small groups felt isolated and vulnerable in
the vastness of the Gobi, and Marco sincerely believed the old travellers'
tale that baleful goblins and malicious spirits roamed the desert, tormenting
the visitor and seeking to destroy him. If a traveller fell behind his companions at night, perhaps by falling asleep in the saddle, he would awake to
hear the noises of the demons and, thinking to rejoin his friends, wander
away from the main party and out into the trackless wilderness where he
would surely lose his way and perish from thirst. The demons played other
tricks on men's senses, and in Polo's day the caravan leader made sure
every night, before the caravan went to sleep, to plant an arrow in the sand

*Kubilai Khan gives the elder
Polos gold paizahs to ensure
their safe passage through his
empire, an illustration from
one of the many European
manuscript versions of the
Polo story*

17

Portraits thought to be of the
Polos. Centre row, facing
forwards, from left to right:
Maffeo (in dark Eastern garb),
Nicolo (with white beard) and
Marco (holding the bestseller
he eventually wrote about his
Oriental Adventure)

pointing in the correct direction they should take in the morning, otherwise
the demons would confuse their judgment and send them astray next
morning. Entire caravans were alleged to have been drawn off course by
eerie noises coming from behind the dunes, the sounds of ghostly companies
who could be seen riding directly across their path, or scattered in terror by
phantom armies of raiders which came sweeping down on the column in a
cloud of dust, driving them helter-skelter into the desert. Such a terrifying
ordeal as the crossing of the Gobi acted strangely on the medieval European
mind. It was a traumatic experience which dislocated a traveller's previous
terms of reference, sharpened his anticipation for the entry into China,
and presented him compliant at the Jade Gate through which the caravans
entered the Middle Kingdom. In a sense, the Gobi had already stunned him
before he met the cultural shock of China's advanced civilization.

Su-chau, the ancient oasis of Tun-huang, was where the Silk Road finally
emerged from the Black Gobi, and here Marco Polo found a totally different
countryside from anything he had previously experienced. It was dotted
with lamaseries and temples where the Tibetan-speaking inhabitants of the
province offered sacrifices of roast sheep before great stone idols, and
practised weird devotions to their gods. On the public highways funeral
cortèges dolefully shuffled along behind bands of wailing musicians, and
carried coffins made of boards incongruously painted in bright colours
and covered in dazzling silk shrouds. Each coffin was tightly sealed with
pitch and lime to keep in the stench of putrefaction, for the natives refused
to bury their dead except on the auspicious days selected by their astrologers,
and might keep the corpse rotting for months on end. They always outfitted
the body with a strange trousseau of doll-sized furniture and baggage and a
complete set of miniature houseware, painstakingly cut from tiny pieces of

paper, all of which they believed would be transmuted into solid gold during the after-life; and then they closed the coffin, leaving it lying around the house until burial day, like some macabre item of furniture.

Forty days' distance from their destination the Polos were met by imperial messengers from Kubilai Khan himself who had heard of their arrival, and directed to meet him at Chemeinfu, the 'City of Peace'. This was Kubilai's summer residence north of the Luan river which he had erected as a retreat from the heat and dust of summer-time Peking, and it was at the 'City of Peace' that Marco Polo was presented at court and met for the first time the man who, after holding the throne of China for fifteen years, was generally acknowledged as the most gifted of the Tatar emperors since Genghis Khan himself.

Kubilai overawed Marco Polo. According to the Venetian, the Emperor of China was a well-set-up man, moderate in height and girth, with a fair skin, black eyes, and a well-shaped nose set squarely in place. But contemporary portraits show that Kubilai was much more than this. A few months short of his official sixtieth birthday, which was due to be celebrated according to custom on the twenty-eighth day of the lunar cycle of September, he had the lined and world-weary face of a man who had not only gathered power but knew how to wield it skilfully and without remorse. For half his lifetime Kubilai had been steering a delicate course between the interests of the traditionally minded Mongol warlords of his homelands and the hostile Chinese of the kingdom he had chosen to rule. On one side he was still fighting a running battle against the Mongol rebel Caidu in the west; and on the other, he had only just subjugated the rump of the indigenous Sung empire in the south. Nor could his palace be called a safe haven. He had survived several insurrections, and at least one high-born rebel had been wrapped in carpets and trampled to death by horses. All this had left Kubilai a cautious, scheming and, when the occasion demanded, ruthless despot. Well past the full activity of his youth when Marco Polo first saw him, he had become a manipulator, a clever director of his kingdom, rarely leaving his chain of palaces or breaking his court routine, but content to work through agents, commissioners and loyal generals. His portraits, therefore, showed him as bland but alert, solidly powerful, and with the calm self-confidence of his imperial position. In short, he was the archetypal Asiatic potentate.

The 'City of Peace' was essentially an allegory of Kubilai's Mongol pastoral background. It was the place where he indulged his nomad love of open spaces, field sports, and personal freedom. His court architects had built for him a special mobile palace, an ingenious pavilion made entirely from huge bamboo canes split down the middle to provide the cladding for the walls, as well as lightweight shingles for the roof. Held in place by two hundred guy-ropes of pure silk, it could be dismantled at whim, moved, and swiftly re-erected at a new location. Elevated off the ground on pedestals of cane, its main pillars were surmounted by capitals carved in the shape of dragons which carried the roof; its interior was delightfully painted, and the whole edifice was varnished on the outside to make it waterproof. The favourite site for this extraordinary structure was the great animal park of Chemeinfu, a huge enclosure within a sixteen-mile wall which had been

built to surround the game preserve where Kubilai kept his hunting hawks and other birds of prey, including his renowned mews of two hundred gerfalcons. Kubilai himself could sometimes be seen riding out in the park on a horse, a hunting leopard on the crupper so that when he felt inclined he could release the leopard to pull down a deer, and then feed the venison to the hawks in the mews.

Kubilai was obsessed with hunting, like all his Mongol ancestors. Besides the game park at Chemeinfu, he maintained imperial game reserves all over the north of China, including one entire valley sealed off as a partridge-rearing farm, and he paid for a huge establishment of kennelmen and hawkers to look after his menageries. He had leopards and cheetahs to run down wild deer, eagles trained to attack wolves and, most difficult of all to handle, several tigers bred to the chase which were carried to the hunt in special cages loaded on light carts, keeping company with small dogs which, for some strange reason, had a soothing effect on the great cats. Particular care was needed when bringing these tigers near their prey, for if they caught the scent of game prematurely, they became dangerous and uncontrollable. Every spring and summer this entire hunting establishment, nearly twenty thousand men in all according to Polo, trekked down to the coast to spend several weeks in vast organized hunts which were virtual campaigns against the wild life. They were separated into two divisions, each with its own livery, scarlet and blue, and were commanded by two senior Mongol barons known as the 'Keepers of the Mastiffs'. On the march, the line of huntsmen extended across a front a day's journey in length, and Kubilai himself occupied the centre of the line, travelling luxuriously in a special wicker palanquin decorated with cloth of gold inside and tiger skins outside, and carried between four elephants. When his master huntsman saw a quarry worthy of the imperial hawks, Kubilai could order the lid of his palanquin to be thrown back, and he himself released the gerfalcons, and then sat back to enjoy a full view of the contest between the hawk and its prey.

Kubilai's personal retinue was equally massive. He had four chief wives, each of whom held the title of empress in her own right and maintained her own separate court with three hundred ladies-in-waiting and several thousand servants, courtiers, eunuchs, and other attendants. Then there was his heir apparent, Prince Temur, who occupied a special position at court with his own entourage, and had a strong military contingent, since Kulilai employed him as a field marshal and sent him to command the imperial armies in battle. In addition, Kubilai had at least another twenty-four legitimate male children, besides an uncounted total of offspring by a flock of concubines.

Supplying the royal bed was a highly organized business, and every second year, Marco Polo reported, teams of imperial commissioners were dispatched to arrange beauty competitions among the young women of the Ongurat tribe which was renowned for the physical excellence of its women. All the village maidens were obliged to appear before the imperial commissioners and be examined by specially appointed valuers who awarded the girls points for the quality of every physical feature whether hair, face, eyebrows, mouth, lips, or body, as well as for their deportment and general manner. Kubilai himself laid down the minimum requirement for selection,

*A Chinese beauty crossing a
river in her carriage escorted
by Mongol soldiers*

usually twenty or twenty-one points, and all the girls who exceeded this level
were sent on to the imperial household. There they were examined a second
time in order to select the thirty or forty most beautiful. The rejects became
tirewomen and were trained in such skills as needlework and glove-making,
while the chosen few were assigned to the households of high-born Mongol
ladies who instructed them in court procedure and kept a careful watch over
them to make sure that the girls were virgins, unblemished in every way,
and did not reveal any personal drawbacks such as snoring in bed or bad
breath. Finally this last group was divided into teams of six and placed to
attend Kubilai. Throughout the year they worked in rotation, three days
and nights at a time, some staying at the emperor's side while others waited
in an ante-chamber on call to supply food or wine or to enter his bed. When
Kubilai was finally bored with them, they would be furnished with substantial dowries and married off to his Mongol courtiers, happily assured of a
wealthy retirement.

The summer idyll at Chemeinfu, the Xanadu of Coleridge's poem, ended on
precisely the same day every year, 28 August. On that day Kubilai held a
solemn ritual when milk from the snow-white mares of the imperial stud-
farm was flung in the air and sprinkled on the ground in the traditional
Mongol rite to bring good fortune and fertility to all those living within the
emperor's possessions, whether birds and beasts, men or women. And then,
on that same day, the entire court began its march back to Peking where, like

a mirror pivoting on its hinge, Kubilai's court met its own reflection of its Chinese counterpart.

Khanbaliq, the 'Royal City' adjacent to Peking, was a much more serious place than Chemeinfu. It was a Chinese creation, a carefully devised and meticulously run hub of imperial administration whose concept and function owed much to previous Chinese dynasties, and was staffed at many levels by Chinese civil servants whose efficient management, in the last analysis, allowed the Mongol emperor to enjoy himself hunting in the countryside while his bureaucrats ran the intricacies of his government. The nerve centre of this bureaucracy was a new town, Ta-tu, the 'Great Court' which Kubilai had ordered to be built about half a mile to the northeast of the old capital of Peking. Its construction had begun in 1272, the year the Polos left the Mediterranean, and although twenty thousand workmen were employed on it, Ta-tu was still only partly finished when the Polos arrived there and Kubilai Khan had already moved in, ignoring the ten thousand labourers who were kept working on the site. Fourteen square miles in area, Ta-tu was larger than seventeenth-century London would be, and had been laid out as a strictly functional parallelogram, its streets crossing at right angles, orderly lines of dwellings on each side, and in the centre a large watchtower where sentries kept a look-out for fires and civil commotion.

Monkey on a stick, Chinese style

To enter Ta-tu, the visitor was obliged to pass through a massive, white-washed outer wall strengthened with heavily fortified gates and loopholes for archers. At each corner stood fortress towers which held the imperial armoury, containing sufficient weapons to equip an army, together with saddles, bridles, and other munitions. Inside, a second and equally well-defended wall surrounded the royal residence itself, and typically of Kubilai, the intervening space between the walls had been turned into another park, complete with tame animals, a magnificent horticultural garden which contained trees brought by elephant from distant parts of east Asia, an ornamental lake stocked with fish penned in by bronze grilles, and a land-scaped extravagance known as the 'Green Mount'. The latter was planted in Chinese style with a whole range of evergreen exotic shrubs, and decorated with fancifully shaped green rocks. On its summit stood a small green pavilion. The great central entrance to the inner wall was reserved exclusively for Kubilai himself, and the visitor had to pass through one of the smaller gates on the side where he found himself in an open plaza, filled with courtiers, petitioners, and imperial retainers. Before him rose the Winter Palace itself. Though only a single storey in height, it was nevertheless a lofty building, for it was raised on a marble platform, and its roof was brightly covered in yellow, vermilion, green, and blue paint, and then varnished over, making it seem like an enormous glittering coffer of enamel.

The inside of the Summer Palace was equally brightly decorated, the ceilings with gold and silver leaf, and the walls covered with the figures of dragons, birds, and men. The emperor's private apartments lay at the rear of the palace, cordoned off by his lifeguards, and it was in the great assembly hall near the main portals that privileged visitors like the Polos were invited to see Kubilai hold court. Thirteen times a year he gave a great banquet attended by his courtiers in a style no European monarch could

23

match. Every man was required to wear a tunic of matching colour provided by the emperor, and on his feet soft white slippers so as not to dirty the superb rugs strewn across the floor of the great hall. For the same reason the courtiers had to carry with them, and use, small spittoons. Kubilai himself sat on a special dais raised at the far end of the hall where he could look out over the assembly. On his right, and a little way down the hall, were arranged the male members of his family as well as the ranking Mongol barons. On his left in the foreground were the imperial women, ranged by seniority and superbly coiffed in the traditional Mongol headgear of crescent-shaped frames, from which silver ornaments dangled and tall feather plumes sprouted so that one observer compared the sight to the bobbing lances of a troop of cavalry at the trot. On the dais Kubilai was attended by lords-in-waiting, their mouths covered with silk scarves lest their breath fall upon the royal food; and every time the emperor took up his goblet, the imperial orchestra would strike up, the royal cup bearer retired three paces and dropped to his knees, and every person in the hall was required to kneel and make a show of humility while Kubilai drank.

Major-domos constantly circulated throughout the hall to ensure an endless supply of wine and *koumiss*, the favourite Mongol drink made from fermented mare's milk, fizzing slightly and tasting of almonds, and a great chest of gold, nine feet by nine feet sitting squarely in the middle of the hall, served as table and reservoir for the liquor. Its top was piled with spare gold basins, each big enough to satisfy eight or ten men, and from spigots on each side was drawn the selected beverage. The major-domos would fill the basins, carry them to the waiting guests, and return with empty bowls. When the guests had drunk themselves into a semi-stupor, the carpets were rolled aside to allow space for jugglers, clowns, buffoons, and acrobats, some of them brought from as far afield as Malaya, to entertain the crowd with their special tricks and sleight of hand. Among them, according to Polo, were magicians who could make cups filled with drink fly through the air from the hall to land on Kubilai's own table. And as a climax, a trained tiger was brought in, ceremoniously unchained, and allowed to pad its way up the hall until it reached Kubilai's feet where the great beast would drop down in obeisance and fawn. By the end of most banquets the guests would be so befuddled that they would have to be half carried out across the palace threshold lest they offend their Mongol host by tripping on it and bringing bad luck upon the house.

Life at the Great Court blended this barbaric splendour with urbane efficiency and tried to superimpose the mixture on the shifting base of Mongol ferocity, Chinese resentment, and common ambition. Ambassadors and foreigners like the Polos were specially privileged – indeed imperial edict gave the ambassadors the free services of Ta-tu's considerable community of prostitutes who thereby remitted their taxes – but anyone who became closely involved in imperial politics ran the risk of corruption, violence, and possible death. In Marco's own time at court, Kubilai was nearly toppled by the assassination of his chief minister, a Muslim named Achmed, whose death was meant to have been the signal for a general Chinese uprising. Achmed's behaviour had been scandalous. For years he had been duping Kubilai, stealing tax money from the imperial treasury, filling Government

اهل ملک را بطریق طلوع است و مقصود که خواستیم که از سرحیت وجبروت درین حرکاه و بارکاه زوم می باشد که این زبان حاکم و
حکوم ما وشما با معاف در سرهور ونیار امرشت کاهان خواسته حسنع وخضع ان حرکاه درام واسد ابلا و تیعران مجید وطاعت
وعادت کنیم انکاه حرکاه وطرب استعال غام ان علان کم یازه ام خدای تعال و رسول عدالم نرده بای حبار کد حرکاه حلای و بشت

حكايت

احكامي كه الماطان بعد از طوس دربارئ كليات مصالح ممالك فرمود

دبعد از ملك از طوس عمارت غارغ شده بشيرنا . علاغل باطراف ممالك روانه كرداند بدین بساب سماست رعیت اجان فرمین آرام مانفا اکاه شا . زادکارا

ولقد بارفنه

posts with his relations and friends, and squeezing the Chinese mercilessly for bribes. He had even built up a harem to rival Kubilai's, and sent gangs of thugs to demand the prettiest girls from Chinese families, adding them to his household. Because Achmed virtually ran the civil service in Peking, it was almost impossible to ignore his demands, until finally a group of Chinese decided to murder him. Taking advantage of Kubilai's absence from Ta-tu, the conspirators appeared one night before the walls of Ta-tu pretending to be the escort to the heir apparent. The gates of the town were thrown open, and as Achmed rode forward to greet the supposed prince, he was dragged from his horse and stabbed to death. Marco Polo's version of the killing was more bloody. He claimed that Achmed was summoned in the middle of the night to Temur's audience chamber where an impostor prince was seated on the royal dais surrounded by dozens of candles. Dazzled by the blaze of lights, Achmed failed to spot the deception, and as he knelt humbly before the impostor, his head was struck off by the sword of one of the conspirators. At that moment the Mongol garrison commander of Ta-tu happened to enter the chamber, realized what was happening, and drawing his bow shot and killed the leading Chinese conspirator. The Mongol garrison was immediately called out, and a curfew imposed so that anyone found on the streets was executed on the spot. This swift action, typical of the Mongol army, scotched the Chinese rebellion and gave Kubilai time to hurry back to the capital to investigate the affair. When he uncovered the extent of Achmed's misconduct, he promptly ordered that the minister's body should be exhumed and flung in the streets to be torn to pieces by the dogs. Achmed's fortune was confiscated; and those of his sons who had connived in the minister's misrule were also put to death.

Opposite *The wives of a Mongol khan wearing their crescent-shaped hats (bokhtas) and seated at a banquet in order of precedence*

Two annual festivals neatly symbolized the dual nature of Kubilai's dominion over both his Mongol and Chinese subjects. In accordance with ancient Tatar custom, the emperor held the single greatest feast of the year on his birthday. It was a colossal banquet at which he appeared in a magnificent robe of beaten gold; his courtiers wore costumes of embroidered silk, and all the Tatar nobles displayed the gold and silver belts which were the mark of Mongol nobility. From all over the empire tribute and presents poured in from the emperor's vassals and liegemen; and the collective corps of royal soothsayers, astrologers, necromancers, and shamans made sacrifices and orchestrated their chants to their various deities to call down blessings upon the emperor. By contrast, Kubilai's second great festival of the year was the Chinese New Year, reckoned to start in December, when he and his court would appear dressed in white, the traditional colour of good luck. This was the formal state occasion, when he was expected to display the imperial wealth and prestige, and so it began with a march-past of the imperial elephants, each draped in an embroidered saddle-cloth and slung with two strong-boxes filled with plate and valuables. Behind swayed a long array of sumpter camels loaded with provisions for the evening's feast to which all the imperial officers were summoned, bringing with them the traditional New Year gifts of jewellery, white horses, and white cloths to be presented to the emperor with their felicitations for his health and good fortune, while those men who were particularly ambitious, took the chance to attach to their gifts petitions for favour, which were scrutinized by the chancellery.

THE MERCHANT AND
THE KHAKHAN

*Hustle and bustle in a thriving
Chinese town, part of a study
by Chang Tse-tuan, from the
scroll 'Going up the River for
the Ching Ming Festival'*

On that day, more than any other, the true nature of Kubilai's rule over the Chinese was apparent. He and his Mongol barons were an alien élite, superimposed by military force upon the native Chinese who privately mocked them as uncouth barbarians, lampooned them in their Chinese theatres which the Mongols could not understand, and joked that when the Tatars arrived they used palaces for their horses and tents for themselves. In fact, other Chinese ruling dynasties had also come from outside the Great Wall, just like the Mongols, but Kubilai's regime was different in the sheer scope of his alien arrival. This was not simply a Mongol regime, but an international one. Uighur, Mongol, Arabic, Persian, Tangut, and Chinese were all recognized as official languages at court; and Kubilai's officers and administrators were drawn from all over the huge Tatar empire. He had secretaries and ministers from the great Uighur culture in the west, historians and scribes from Persia, wild holy men with naked bodies and tangled beards from the Himalayas, Nestorian Christians employed as privy councillors, and, of course, the Chinese civil servants who calmly made the transition to working in the new bureaucracy. Kubilai's new chief minister was a Tibetan; his finest mining technicians were Alans from near the Black Sea; and a handful of unfortunate German refugees had been kidnapped from their homes by Tatar raiders and bundled across half the world to work the essential iron-mines of the Gobi frontier. Even Kubilai's siege-train, with which he terrorized the huge Chinese cities, was directed by artillerymen specially brought in from the Levant.

In this polyglot company Marco Polo and his father and uncle were only mildly exotic, and with typical skill Kubilai's administrators soon found a niche for them. Nicolo and Maffeo were allowed to trade and travel in the western provinces, while Marco was drafted into the imperial civil service. At one time he seems to have been appointed as a superintendent of salt taxes and, more important, as a royal commissioner, second class, attached to the privy council with the job of travelling within China and reporting back upon its condition. It was in this capacity that he had his chance to make the two great journeys within China which gave him a unique insight into the richest and most populated civilization of his day.

The first thing he noticed was the iron efficiency of Mongol rule. At key points throughout China Kubilai had stationed crack Mongol cavalry regiments which were maintained in a constant state of readiness to move in and crush any trouble. To facilitate this work, the Chinese cities had been forbidden to maintain walled defences, and in some cases the paving-stones of the city streets had been torn up to make it easier for the Mongol cavalry patrols to operate. Backing up the horsemen was an immense standing army of Chinese levies, foot-soldiers who were required to serve garrison duty throughout the empire and were carefully allocated by Kubilai's war office to distant provinces where they, too, felt like strangers. Rapid communication was the essence of Kubilai's reign. It meant that he could gather intelligence quickly, dispatch his civil servants to deal with regional problems, and in the event of real trouble bring troops on the scene with astonishing speed. So Kubilai had improved and updated the communications network which the Mongols had inherited. Every Chinese province was obliged to maintain a proper road network, even if this meant throwing causeways across swampy ground, running the roads along the river levees, or building huge bridges, sometimes twenty-four arches long, across the great Chinese rivers. In the mountainous southwest of the country, they had to construct their roads on makeshift ledges of bamboo and logs, jutting from the mountainside like rickety shelves.

To Marco Polo as a second-class imperial commissioner, the roads of China became the familiar backdrop to his accompanying group of civil servants, the escort of a handful of Mongol soldiers in their leather armour, a creaking cartload of documents and ledgers, and, tucked away in his baggage, a few trade items from which he could make·a profit on the side. Shaded by trees planted at Kubilai's command, the roads were busy with local farmers taking produce to the nearest market town, small caravans of local traders, itinerant hucksters, and every now and again the running figure of an imperial postman, trotting along his stage of the route, a belt of bells jangling round his waist to warn passers-by to give him a clear run so that he could deliver his packet of letters to the next relay post three miles down the road. There one of the vast army of postal scribes scattered throughout the kingdom would note the time and the performance of every messenger, the condition of the station house, and the functioning of the entire system which brought Kubilai not only his state news but also partridges for his kitchens and fresh spring fruit carried up from the south so as to arrive ready on his table in wintry Peking. Very occasionally, too, there would be a sudden commotion and a hurried scattering away from the soft track at the side of the road to allow a mounted state courier to come galloping full tilt up the road, bearing urgent dispatches under the imperial seal. At full stretch these horsemen could cover up to three hundred miles in a day and a night, galloping through the dark by torchlight like weird jockeys, their torsos strapped up in huge belts to keep them upright in the saddle, their heads heavily bandaged against the wind and the flying stones, and a post horn which they sounded as they approached the special horse relay stations, twenty-five to forty miles apart, to alert the station manager to have fresh mounts ready and saddled so that the messenger could fling himself from one horse to the next, and go thundering up the road.

But to Marco Polo the imperial road system meant comfort rather than speed because the larger post houses were also designed as inns and, as an imperial employee, he was entitled to use them and receive free food and lodging. At times, too, he would have been able to make use of the imperial barge service which moved sedately along the canals so that the leisurely traveller could tie up comfortably for the night and use his barge as a floating hotel. The Venetian took a very practical approach to his job: he measured the length of the bridges and counted the number of their spans; he inquired about the prices of goods in the markets, from fresh fish to ginger; and he noted how travellers in desolate jungles threw lengths of bamboo on the fire so that the explosion of air bursting from the hollow tubes scared away wild beasts. He was an exceptionally alert observer and the emperor's privy council sent him as their eyes and ears in some of the more exotic countries of the southwest fringe of China which had only just passed under Mongol control. He visited the wild country on the borders of Burma, journeyed across a corner of Tibet, and in such places found tribes who wore gold

*A unit of Kubilai's expertly
trained Mongol soldiers would
have accompanied Marco Polo
during his term as a travelling
Chinese civil servant*

casings on their teeth; others who tattooed every inch of their bodies with
fanciful designs of lions, birds, and dragons; and one settlement whose
women counted prestige by the number of times they prostituted themselves
to travellers, thereafter displaying the foreigner's gifts as evidence of their
prowess.

Polo calmly described some of the people he met as treacherous brigands,
others as murderers who ate their victims, but he himself was in no way
perturbed. He had an eye for natural history, remarked on the yak, the musk
deer, and even on the behaviour of crocodiles which the Chinese caught so
as to use their gall as medicine. But he entirely ignored painting and litera-
ture, and among the arts only architecture seemed to interest him. Of some
matters he made no mention whatever, and a reader of his travelogue would
have learned nothing of the Great Wall, nor of Chinese pictograph writing,
nor that they drank tea and the women bound their feet.

Part of the difficulty seems to have been that Marco Polo never learned
either to speak or to write a Chinese language. As an imperial servant he
could get along well enough with Persian and Turkish, and to judge by his
accurate translations he also knew how to read the official Mongol script in

which Kubilai's edicts were published. But Chinese remained a mystery to him, and he was forced to rely on his interpreters. As a result he gained a strangely detached view of the Chinese as though he was watching them in a dream, and he himself was set apart as a disembodied observer. For example, he never used a single word to describe the Chinese people as a whole, but clearly thought of them as separate groups, each group particular to its city or province; and as a result the Chinese of his narrative remained blandly impersonal, lacking the human touches which would have brought them to life.

Yet there is no doubt that Marco admired the Chinese enormously. He praised them as peaceable, industrious, and exceptionally cultured, and he felt there was much that could be learned from them in good manners, artistic sensitivity, and honesty. Some of their behaviour was downright curious, of course. He was queasy about their gourmet delight in eating the flesh of all manner of strange animals, even snakes, and often raw: and he was mystified by the peculiar custom of a wronged man's taking revenge by hanging himself outside his enemy's door in order to bring shame on his tormentor. Also the Chinese seemed to him to be ridiculously superstitious.

35

They never began a new venture unless their soothsayers said it was an auspicious day, and when Chinese sailors were about to embark on a voyage, they took some hapless mariner, either a fool or a drunk by Marco's sour judgment, and tied him to a hurdle which they then suspended beneath the tail of an oversize kite. If the kite flew well and carried the man up with it, the sailors put to sea; if not, they obstinately stayed in port.

Yet this same superstitious race used coal for heating their houses, provided hot water at public baths, and were superb technicians whether in the manufacture of delicate porcelain or the way in which they obtained high-grade salt by pouring water over saline soil and then boiling the brine. The use of paper money really summed up for Marco Polo the admirable quality of the Chinese. He described how all the gold and silver and jewels of China were an imperial monopoly, and that, in exchange, Kubilai's treasury issued notes made of mulberry paper over-printed with the signatures of the bank officials, the value of the note, and the imperial seal. It was remarkable, he thought, that everyone throughout the kingdom calmly accepted these banknotes at face value, and when the notes were badly worn, dutifully returned them to the treasury to be changed for fresh money at three per cent discount. The whole system struck him as being almost a conjuring trick, and he pointed out that as an example of civic obedience it could scarcely be excelled.

The centre of all these Chinese virtues, as far as Polo was concerned, was to be found in the huge Chinese trading city of Hangchow. It lay on the tidewater, a short distance south of the mouth of the Yangtze, and to approach it by water one passed one of the great wonders of China, the Marine Wall, begun about AD 915 by Prince Ts'ien Wu-su. Designed to stabilize the river's course, the Marine Wall was a stupendous endeavour, a dike 180 miles long and rivalling the Grand Canal and the Great Wall for the engineering difficulties involved in its construction, not least of which was the famous tidal bore of Hangchow's river, a wall of water which came racing up the estuary every tide as fast as eleven knots and regularly capsizing fishing-boats, ripping away the bank, and flooding the sandflats of the estuary. By the time the bore reached Hangchow itself, its force was nearly spent, though to contain unusually high tides the Chinese architects of the city had cleverly designed a vast reservoir, controlled by sluice-gates, which served both as a cistern and as a moat for Hangchow. Excess floodwater was diverted into the reservoir by gates and held there until low tide, when it would be released through sluices into the canals which criss-crossed Hangchow itself, flushing out the debris of the city.

Hangchow, the 'City of Heaven' in Marco Polo's words, stood between the river on the east and an artificial lake on the west. Its outer walls had a perimeter of about eighty miles, and there was an immense second rampart of earth faced with limestone nearly thirty feet high and ten feet thick. Under Mongol rule Hangchow's thirteen barbican gates and five fortified water-gates had been deliberately allowed to fall into disrepair, yet its moats and the surrounding maze of waterways, rivers, and lakes still made the city almost impregnable. Inside Hangchow the houses of the Chinese were packed together in indescribable confusion, eave touching eave, and the narrow lanes and alleyways so congested that to control the crowds, the civic authorities had to place sentry posts every two hundred yards along the streets leading to the government quarter. The fire risk among this tightly packed mass of wooden buildings was appalling, and at strategic positions within the city there were tall watchtowers manned by a permanent task force of fire-watchers. If they saw a fire starting, they would signal its position by flags, or at night by raising lanterns in pre-arranged patterns, to alert the city brigade of nearly three thousand men who were trained to extinguish fires within Hangchow itself or among the suburbs which lapped round its walls. The spine of the city was the magnificent Imperial Street, nearly three miles long and paved with thirty-five thousand stone slabs laid so evenly that the grand carriages of the governor and his officials and the merchant princes flowed smoothly along it in an unending stream, creating enormous traffic jams on public festivals when swarms of holiday-makers tried to leave the city for their favourite excursions – to spend the day at the neighbouring pleasure gardens, or visit the city burial-ground to honour their ancestors, or take the well-worn excursion of a stroll along the Marine Wall at high spring tides to watch the river bore tumbling upstream in a streak of white foam.

The commercial bustle of Hangchow exceeded anything which Marco Polo had seen before, even in Venice. Most of the city's trade was controlled by great merchant families who owned the enormous emporia built at one end of Imperial Street. These emporia, often eight or ten storeys high, were vast rabbit warrens, part warehouse, part residence, divided into hundreds of small rooms in which merchandise was stored, bought, and traded, and where the employees of the great families lived. Hangchow was renowned throughout China for its silk and furniture industries; and the sheer volume and variety of commodities bought and sold within the city made it the greatest single revenue producer in Kubilai's kingdom. Each day ninety tons of rice were brought into the city for consumption by ordinary families, excluding the great households, and in different parts of Hangchow were found the headquarters of dozens of guilds and crafts, leatherworkers, silversmiths, jade-carvers, and so forth. By imperial regulation every artisan, however successful, had to be followed into the same trade by his son, and sometimes the descendants of wealthy craftsmen, rather than work for themselves, employed platoons of apprentices so that a man who was officially a mere leatherworker, might in fact be a millionaire.

Some of Hangchow's courtesans were so prosperous that they owned splendid apartments and had retinues of trained handmaidens to follow them as they paraded through the city, exquisitely dressed in silk, jewelled and perfumed. Civil government was conducted from a number of city halls located in each district, usually in twin buildings overlooking the main square, and here the panels of local judges would sit to settle disputes and organize the town watchmen who were posted on each of Hangchow's 418 bridges, every unit equipped with its wooden drum and metal gong to raise the alarm if necessary, and a water-clock so that they could cry the hour regularly to the citizens. Threaded along Imperial Street itself were the ten great squares, each of which contained a thriving food market where wine, meat, spices, and groceries of all kinds could be bought at prices which Marco Polo considered astonishingly low. Nor did the food markets ever shut, for when the day-time traders had sold their wares, they were immediately replaced by the stalls of the night vendors who continued to sell their goods by torchlight right through until dawn.

To the Chinese themselves, however, Hangchow was most renowned for its Hsi Hu, the West Lake, artificially constructed by an unknown governor many years before. The lake was the gem of Hangchow, surrounded by monasteries and pagoda towers, the splendid homes of wealthy inhabitants, and on holidays alive with such vast crowds of free-spending citizens that its nickname was the 'Gold-lined Pan'. Two causeways crossed the lake to give access to small islands on which public restaurants had been built and furnished with crockery, linen, and plate; these could be hired for private weddings and banquets. On the shallow waters of the lake floated an armada of luxury barges and sampans. Grandees kept their own vessels, and the barges of the city magistrates were recognized by their official blue awnings, but the majority of the vessels were for hire, and here one could rent anything from a small skiff to an enormous balustraded barge under whose striped sunshades thirty or forty guests at a time sat down on silk cushions and enjoyed a magnificent feast while the vessel glided along, propelled by teams of boatmen with punt poles. It was scarcely surprising, Polo noted, that before public holidays, the entire fleet of rented boats on Hsi Hu was booked up for weeks in advance.

Hangchow's canals and bridges, and its coteries of merchant families, must have made Marco Polo homesick for Venice, for it seems that not long after his visit to the 'City of Heaven', he and the elder Polos applied to Kubilai for permission to return to Italy. By then Marco had been in the emperor's service for seventeen years, and Kubilai was in his late seventies, suffering increasingly from gout, and exhausted and weary of his rule. He arranged for the Polos to start homeward with a Chinese fleet leaving for Persia, and early in 1292 Marco set out to complete the circuit of Asia, lumbering round the rim of the continent in a great four-masted Chinese junk, its double hull rendered virtually unsinkable by a coat of lime and hemp, and then prudently subdivided into watertight compartments.

Once again, the Polo family were miraculously lucky as travellers, because they were among the twenty or so men who landed in Persia from the original six hundred who had sailed from China. The rest either deserted, turned back, or died from fever. An unfortunate encounter with robbers in Asia Minor cost the Polos some of their Oriental profits, but all three reached Venice safely in 1295, looking so travel-worn, it is said, that the gatekeeper at the Casa Polo on the Canal San Grisostomo, failed to recognize them and refused to let them enter until other members of the family had vouched for them. Legend has it, too, that they celebrated their happy return with a grand banquet given in the style of Ta-tu. Each of the guests was sent splendid robes to wear at the meal, and between every course the three Polos left the hall in order to reappear dressed in new and yet more gorgeous clothes. Finally, when the tables had been cleared, they came back with their stained and shabby travelling cloaks, and holding them up before their astonished guests, slit open the seams to release a cascade of gems and brilliants, hidden during their return.

More prosaically, Marco was called up to serve in the Venetian forces in a disastrous war against Genoa and was captured in a galley action. As a prisoner of war he was interned in Genoa, and there had his last, and in some ways most far-reaching, stroke of luck. In prison he met a professional ballad-writer and singer, Rustichello of Pisa, who collaborated with him to write a popular version of his travels, grandly called *The Description of the World*. The success of this book was so rapid that even as Venice and Genoa were making peace and exchanging prisoners, the fame of Marco Polo's travel-book began to surge across Europe. Italy was soon buzzing with it; translations started to appear in different languages and dialects including, eventually, Irish; and Marco himself received the somewhat ambiguous nickname of 'Il Milioni', either because he was supposed to have become a millionaire from his trading in the East, or because he always used such vast and inconceivable numbers to describe the marvels of the Orient that people made a joke of it. Yet he and Rustichello had succeeded in writing Europe's first – and for that reason all the more important – bestseller of the Oriental Adventure. Previously there had only been scholarly accounts of the Mongols written by churchmen, and although missionaries would soon be going to China and writing their descriptions of the country, nothing would equal Marco Polo's tale for its scope and popular appeal. It dealt a mortal blow to many of the old fears and legends of Asian monsters and myths, substituted new and prosperous lands which few had ever imagined, and raised above everything the glittering spectre of the great Khan of China ruling over his teeming subjects. It was a vision of farthest Asia which was to remain unchallenged for almost two centuries until the first European seamen arrived on the Chinese coast, and even then Polo's word was still so strong that it was another 170 years before it was confirmed that the new China of the seamen was the same as Marco's Cathay. For far longer than that, folklore would accept the Great Khan or Grand Cham as a supreme expression of power and fortune, and, right through until the nineteenth century, students of geography would still be depending on Marco Polo's descriptions of the high mountains of central Asia. As the first European traveller to draw a line right across the heartland of Asia from one side to the other, and to tell the tale, Marco Polo had blazed such a searing trail across popular vision that he was to remain indelibly on the public consciousness, the popular pioneer of the Oriental Adventure itself.

As for Marco himself, legend far outstripped the man. He spent the rest of his days in Venice, the most widely travelled European of his day and its most famous living author. Yet he reaped little advantage from his fame. The tale of his fabulous home-coming banquet seems to have been a pleasant myth, for in reality he had only a modest fortune, perhaps because of the robbery in Asia Minor. He turned crabby and mean in his old age, and remorselessly sued business associates and members of his own family for small debts. Yet he also nursed an affection for his days in the East and treasured the mementoes of the seventeen years he spent in the service of the man he considered the greatest ruler on earth. When Marco Polo died in 1324, among his personal effects were found two *paizahs*, several examples of Mongol women's headgear, and the silver belt of a Tatar knight which Marco would have earned in the service of Kubilai Khan.

CHAPTER THREE

CONQUISTADORS OF SIBERIA

IF THE SUCCESS OF AN EXPLORER is judged by the size and permanence of the territory he wins for his country, the most effective European explorer the world has known would not be Columbus nor Captain Cook but a sixteenth-century brigand-adventurer with the simple name of Yermak, who changed the map of Asia when he made Russia an Oriental power and set afoot a series of events which added one-tenth of the world's land surface to her empire. It was an enterprise in conquest whose scale still beggars the imagination. In the beginning Russia was only a fledgling state, just growing accustomed to the idea of calling the prince of Moscow its tsar, and no more important than either Poland or Sweden. Yet within the span of a single lifetime Yermak and his successors had explored and staked a claim to a quarter of Asia, and carried the Russian flag three thousand miles from the Urals to the Pacific so that its shadow would eventually fall as far away as Alaska and California. It was the largest and most enduring land grab ever made by Europeans, and yet – curiously enough – it was scarcely noticed in the annals of discovery.

There were two main reasons for this oversight: firstly, Yermak and his heirs were semi-literate adventurers who lacked an outstanding chronicler to record their achievements; and secondly, their exploits fell outside the traditional area of European maritime discovery. To a certain extent, too, they were overshadowed by the Spanish conquistadors in the New World whose exploits they so closely mirrored and followed by only half a century. Yet, much like the conquest of Mexico and Peru, the opening of Siberia was land exploration equally aggressive and self-confident, a *Drang nach Osten* of the Oriental Adventure which eventually brought Europe face to face with China.

The chief actors in this extraordinary campaign were themselves suitably dramatic and highly charged. At the hub in Moscow ruled the ageing half-mad Tsar Ivan the Terrible, worn out by nearly half a century of despotism, distrustful after scheming and plotting to stitch together his kingdom, and, like Kubilai Khan three hundred years earlier, still threatened by a treacherous nobility within and foreign rivals without. Six months' journey to the east lay Kuchum Khan, the blind ruler of Siberia, who had also come to his throne in a welter of dynastic murder and dreamed that the mantle of Genghis Khan had fallen upon his shoulders so that one day the Russians would again pay tribute to a Tatar overlord. Between the two in 1577 there suddenly appeared the bloodstained figure of Yermak, part mystic, part robber-baron, and seeming to spring from the soil like the crop of the dragon's teeth, ready armed with a host of warriors at his back.

Quite where Yermak came from, no one has ever been sure, and this

mystery has only added lustre to his legend. Tradition has it that his grand-father was a renegade coachman from Suzdal near Moscow, who ran away to join the Cossacks of the Lower Volga. If so, his grandson was born a Free Cossack, changing his birth name in Cossack fashion from Vasili to the anonymous Yermak, thus breaking all ties with his past. These early Cossacks were themselves an enigma. Even their name, the Russian *kasak* of Turco-Tatar origin meaning 'freebooter', was applied indiscriminately. Sometimes it referred to the posses of vigilantes who defended the south Russian frontier towns; and at other times it was applied to bands of Tatar irregular cavalry who hired themselves out as *condottieri* to the larger state armies. In Yermak's case, it probably referred to the independent communities of Free Cossacks who lived in the Crimea and on the banks of the Don and Volga. The Free Cossacks were, in effect, both caste and out-

The roving Free Cossacks terrorizing and plundering peaceful Russian settlements; from the Remezov Chronicle – a rare example of Russian seventeenth-century illustration – which depicts Yermak's career episode by episode

41

casts. Those who had not been born Cossack, were mostly runaways, either from Russian service, from the Tatar tribes, from the law, or even from the slave benches of the Turkish galleys. They lived in loose military-style communes which they called 'hosts', recognizing no master but their own elected leaders or *atamans*. A heterogeneous group, the Free Cossacks occupied a twilight zone between nation, culture, and frontier. They spoke Russian spiced with Turkish and Mongol words, and earned their keep by trade, mercenary hire, and a good deal of protection money from the caravans. Even their settlements had an air of casual impermanence. They were called *stanitsas*, a term usually applied to a flock of migrating birds resting on the ground but always ready to take wing.

Tsar Ivan lost his temper, never much restrained, with the Free Cossacks in the summer of 1577. Previously they had been useful to him as occasional mercenaries, but now they had grown impudent and were openly attacking Russian settlements and plundering Russian traders; they even had the daring to molest a Russian embassy on its way to the Shah of Persia. The tsar could no longer tolerate the effrontery and so he sent an army of his new professional soldiers, the *streltsy*, to put down the Cossacks. They promptly scattered 'like wolves', it was said, and one war band of about five hundred men who had been making a fat living as river highwaymen on the great bend of the Volga, beat a hasty retreat northeastwards up the Kama river and suddenly reappeared in Russia's most eastern frontier province under their *ataman*, Yermak.

In this area the Russian frontier was held not so much by the tsar himself as by the powerful merchant family of the Stroganoffs. Rich and successful pioneers, the Stroganoffs had made their money by leasing and developing vast tracts of frontier land from the Crown. Their fief had grown to be almost a state within a state. They built their own towns, imported their own labourers, held their own law-courts, and raised their own troops for whom they even manufactured their own cannon. Immensely experienced in frontier ways, the Stroganoffs knew that to attempt to settle a Cossack Host was to try to pen the wolf. Sooner or later, five hundred heavily armed Cossacks were likely to revert to their old vices and go on the rampage. So, after hiring them briefly as guards, the Stroganoffs offered to supply and equip Yermak and his men if they agreed to march eastward across the Ural mountains into unknown territory.

Once again, no one knew where this idea of an eastern expedition originated. It might have been proposed by Yermak himself, eager to plunder virgin lands, or by message from Tsar Ivan with plans to test the strength of the Siberian khan, or, more likely, by the Stroganoffs intending to be rid of their unwelcome guests, and with the added attraction that if Yermak did not get himself killed, he might open up more territory for Stroganoff settlers. But whoever devised the plan, it was readily accepted and in July 1579 Yermak with 540 Cossacks reinforced by 300 Stroganoff soldiers set out across the Urals to challenge the peoples and hazards of Siberia.

As Russian historians have noted, the comparison with Pizarro's assault on the Inca empire of South America is remarkable: Yermak's venture set out with the same reckless air of make-or-break audacity, the same swashbuckling romance corrupted with an odour of earthly greed, and the same high gloss of sanctity. Where Pizarro claimed to take the word of God to the heathen Indians, Yermak's brigands carried icons on their shoulders and embroidered the figures of Russian saints on their war banners which they proposed to raise aloft against the pagan Siberian tribes and the Muslim Tatars of the Siberian khanate. And instead of Inca gold, the Cossacks sought a harvest of costly Siberian furs.

To the contemporary Russian mind the Ural mountains were as great a psychological barrier as the Andes had been to the conquistadors. The Urals represented the limit of habitable Christian land; they were the official frontier of Europe, and by tradition the Iron Wall which Alexander the Great had raised to fend off the ungodly hosts of Gog and Magog and the Legions of Hell from beyond Tartarus. A handful of fur-traders had penetrated across the Urals, and spoke with revulsion of the natives as Samoyeds or 'Self-eaters', so wretched and poverty-stricken that they turned cannibal and ate one another to sustain life in the depths of winter. It was said that when a visitor arrived in their camps, they either devoured him, too, or, eager to please, slaughtered their own children and served them up as a banquet. With more truth the Cossacks were to find that the Samoyeds kept strings of slaves, strangled reindeer over their graves in their death rites, and scalped their enemies, though they did not, as was also claimed, die every winter by falling into a frozen trance until revived by the return of the sun on 24 April each year.

Yet Kuchum, the Khan of Siberia, was a real enough Goliath for Yermak's David. Though far from an Inca in power or magnificence, Kuchum was nevertheless the battle-tried leader of a warrior people which had terrorized Russia for two hundred years, exacted tribute annually, and whose cavalry regiments had more than once sacked Moscow itself. Kuchum was a steppe warlord in the old Mongol tradition. Stone blind, he ruled with an iron grip over the central segment of the former Golden Horde whose horses had once cropped the pastures all along the Volga. His people remained a formidable fighting force, trained to the saddle and accustomed to harsh nomadic ways. They lived cheek by jowl with their herds of cattle, and dwelt in smoke-filled tents of felt-covered lattice-work like inverted poultry baskets. They had no more possessions than a few sacks of provisions, rugs and skins, and their weapons. Their culture was based on iron, flesh, and felt, and nothing was ever wasted. A European visitor among the Nogai Tatars some years later reported that when the natives found a dead horse,

a young man, naked, of about eighteen years old, received on his shoulders the skin of the animal. A woman who performed the office of tailor, began cutting the back of this new coat, following with her scissors the shape of the neck, the fall of the shoulders, the semi-circle which joins the sleeve, and the side of the habit, which came down below the knee. It was unnecessary to support a stuff which from its humidity already adhered to the skin of the young man. The woman tailor proceeded very smartly to form the cross lapels and the sleeves, after which the mannequin who served as a model, sitting down squat, gave her the opportunity of stitching the pieces together; so that, clothed in less than two hours in an excellent brown bay coat, nothing remained for him but to tan his leather by constant exercise which was accordingly the first thing he did, and I saw him presently mount a horse bare backed to join his comrades who were employed collecting the horses.

This, then, was the breed of warrior cavalrymen, estimated at thirty thousand strong, whom Yermak's Cossacks would have to face, and curiously enough, it was a reversal of the conquistador pattern that it was the men on foot who this time set out to challenge the native on horseback.

The Cossacks had long ago paid their enemies the compliment of copying the Tatar military structure. In overall command of the Cossack expedition was Yermak as its senior *ataman*. He could maintain discipline by the traditional Cossack method of tying anyone who disobeyed his orders in a sack weighted with sand and throwing him into a river. Beneath Yermak were two other *atamans*, Ivan Kol'tso and Ivan Grossa, and under them in turn four *esauls* or captains. The rank and file of the expedition were organized into *sotnias*, or companies of one hundred men, each with its own *sotnik* or commander, and there were further subdivisions of fifties led by petty officers. It was a simple enough arrangement, and it needed to be, because besides the problem of controlling the unruly Free Cossacks, the Stroganoff levies included Lithuanians and Germans who had been taken prisoner of war by the tsar and redeemed as labourers by the Stroganoffs. These foreigners, together with a smattering of Tatar renegades, made the expedition a very mixed force, and the best they managed for a secretariat were three priests who accompanied the venture as spiritual advisers, and a runaway monk, who was more noted for being a good cook. For weapons they carried old-fashioned flintlock muskets, pikes, swords, battle-axes, and even bows and arrows. Three small cannon were also part of their original armament, but apparently these were abandoned *en route* as too heavy to drag across the mountains, because they were never mentioned again. For the same reason the commissariat was very slim. Each Cossack carried only three pounds of powder and three pounds of lead, together with a basic supply of rye flour, oats, salt and biscuit, butter, and half a salted pig's carcass between every two men. It was said that Maxim Stroganoff was so stingy in providing even this pittance that Yermak had to threaten to kill the great landlord and plunder the Stroganoff estates if he did not receive his rations.

Setting out in July, the Cossacks' route lay up the Serebrianka river to bring them into the mountains. It was slow work because the brigade was travelling by boat and the water was so low that the Cossacks had to man-handle their craft over the shallows. Also, Yermak was relying on native guides to find his road for him and he needed to proceed cautiously because the Cossacks were in territory where their reputation for ferocity had already preceded them. The local natives, the Voguls, were hostile, and one Cossack patrol was taken unawares and mauled by a Vogul war band. So Yermak's first season ended badly. He and his men were still clambering up the western slopes of the Urals when the cold weather caught them, and they were forced to build their winter camp and settle in for a long hibernation behind the stockade. Small parties of Cossacks went out to plunder supplies from the Vogul settlements, and the Voguls launched half-hearted attacks against the intruders.

*A Samoyed woman with her
baby and cradle*

In the spring of 1580 Yermak gave orders for his men to break camp, and
the advance was renewed over the Ural ridge so that by May his Cossacks
had crossed the mountains by a newly found pass and reached the upper
waters of the Tagil river, and there they began to build themselves rafts to
take them into Siberia.

Knowingly or not, Yermak was now on the point of taking advantage of
Siberia's most convenient geographical feature: its remarkable network of
rivers and streams which virtually interconnected to form a great corridor
across the country. Over the width of Siberia three great rivers, the Ob, the
Yenisei, and the Lena, ran north and south, and between them spread a
tracery of tributaries separated only by low rolling hills so that the traveller
could transfer from one river basin to the next by easy portages. Thus it was a
relatively simple matter to make and launch a boat on a mountain stream
in the Urals, float down to the Ob, ascend a tributary on the opposite bank as
far as its head of navigation before abandoning one's boat, and then cross the

45

Opposite *Kuchum Khan
seen as the warrior king by a
Venetian artist in 1598*

watershed in order to repeat the process in the adjacent river basin. Making this progress even more effective was the curious phenomenon that all of the three great Siberian rivers were shaped like huge wishbones due to the addition of major tributaries, the Irtysh joining the Ob, the Lower and Stony Tunguska rivers running into the Yenisei, and the Aldan into the Lena. The area embraced by these expanded river systems covered almost the entire distance from the Urals to the Pacific, and to the southwest lapped against yet another wishbone river, the Amur, which flowed past the borders of China to the sea. Thus, when Yermak and his Cossacks launched themselves on the upper headwaters of the Tagil, it was as if a new virus had been injected into north Asia's circulatory system. Unless they were met and stopped by existing forces, they threatened to spread through the river system like a deadly contagion, reaching into every corner of north Asia.

It was not long before the first counter-reactions to the invasion were felt. It had taken the Cossacks several weeks to build their rafts and then, once the water was deep enough, to transfer to proper river boats. In the interval the Voguls, who were under Tatar domination, had time to prepare an ambush, and Yermak and his men were floating downstream when they were met by a flight of arrows. To the delight of the invaders, a single volley from the Cossacks' flintlocks was enough to terrify the natives into flight, as the Voguls had apparently no experience of fighting against massed fire-arms. To teach them a lesson and repay themselves for the trouble, the Cossacks promptly located and looted the Vogul camp before returning to their boats and continuing down the river.

The Tagil led them into the Tura, and in turn into the much larger Tobol river, and there near the river junction they decided to set up their next winter camp close to an old Tatar camp site, from which they could sally forth easily among the local tribes to demand their fur tribute, the famous *yasak*. It was this *yasak*, the annual tax levied by the rulers of Siberia, which was to make Siberia an El Dorado for the Cossacks. The enormous Siberian forests were fur-rich with sable, marten, fox, and squirrel, and the harvest of fur was beyond a poor man's dream. In Russia just two black fox skins sold for enough money to buy a new cabin, fifty acres of land, five good horses, ten cattle, twenty sheep, and a flock of chickens, and still have more than half the capital sum left over. Little wonder, therefore, that Yermak's Cossacks went about the task of terrorizing the Siberian natives into paying *yasak* with a ruthless efficiency that left native villages in smoking ruins and the local headman hanging upside-down by one foot from a tree so that in future he remembered to pay his *yasak* without question.

That autumn, too, Yermak's luck turned. His scouts captured one of Kuchum Khan's *yasak*-gatherers, a Tatar chief named Kutugai, who was taken to see Yermak. From Kutugai Yermak was able to gather useful intelligence about Kuchum before he released his prisoner unharmed and sent him back to his master dressed in a new brightly coloured Russian costume and loaded with gifts and compliments from Yermak to Kuchum, his wives, and his counsellors.

The ruse was too flimsy to lull Kuchum's suspicions, and in May of the following year when the rivers had unfrozen enough for Yermak's advance by boat to continue, the Cossacks began to run into stiffer opposition. On the

47

Tobol Yermak's brigade was attacked by a coalition of half a dozen Tatar princes who were defeated only after a sharp skirmish, and at the hamlet of Berezof the Tatars sprang yet another ambush from positions among the birch trees of the river bank. Then on 16 July 1581 Yermak's advance was brought to an abrupt halt by a heavy iron chain which the enemy commander had hung across the river. According to Cossack lore, it was Yermak's own boat in the van of his flotilla which ran into the chain and was forced to turn tail, with Yermak's crew rowing for their lives under a rain of arrows. Luckily he had been so far in advance of his main force that he had time to prevent them from blundering into the barricade as well, and since there was no question of scaring off the attackers with a single volley, or of breaking through the chain, he decided to trick his opponents instead. When his flotilla had regrouped out of sight of the enemy, he put most of his Cossacks ashore with instructions to outflank the enemy position, while he and skeleton crews on the boats drew the enemy's fire by pretending to force the barricade in a frontal assault. To deceive the enemy Yermak ordered his men to cut down bundles of birch poles and dress them in Cossack clothing, and these dummies were arranged in the boats to appear as oarsmen. The total success of this trick became one of Yermak's legends. The Tatars were duped into concentrating their fire on the invader's half-empty boats as they rowed towards the chain, and when the Cossack landing force suddenly smashed into their positions from the rear the Tatars were utterly routed.

It was now obvious to Yermak that he had pushed dangerously close to the heart of Kuchum's territory, and that the Tatar khan would soon be obliged to turn and fight a pitched battle. Wisely, therefore, Yermak proceeded very carefully. For eight days at the mouth of the river Tawda he waited in order to rest his troops and to learn more about Kuchum's position. From spies he heard that Kuchum was entrenching his capital at Sibir, the town from which Siberia was to take its name, and that he summoned to his standard all his allied tribes including outlying bands of Tatars, Voguls, and Ostiaks. More important, the Siberian khan had also ordered a defensive position to be prepared beside the river Irtysh at a point overlooked by Mount Chuvash, and here the main Tatar army was assembling at a bottleneck which the Cossacks would have to force.

Kuchum's strategy and tactics had been faultless. Having slowed down the Cossacks' advance with his river blockade, he now intended to draw the Cossacks away from the river and into open ground where his Tatar cavalry could be deployed against the invaders. He knew that control of the river system, in particular the Irtysh, was the key to the whole campaign and so he intended to fight this decisive engagement on its banks. Years later the legend would arise that in the year of Yermak's great advance into Siberia, the natives living at the junction of the Ob and the Irtysh saw every evening a small black hound appearing from the west to meet a great gaunt white wolf from the east, and they watched as the two animals fought on the banks of the river. Despite its smaller size the black hound was always the victor, driving back the old wolf and forcing him to flee into the forest.

So it was at the battle under Mount Chuvash. The contest lasted for five days, and it was claimed that as many as ten thousand cavalry took part on the Tatar side commanded by Kuchum's nephew and most experienced

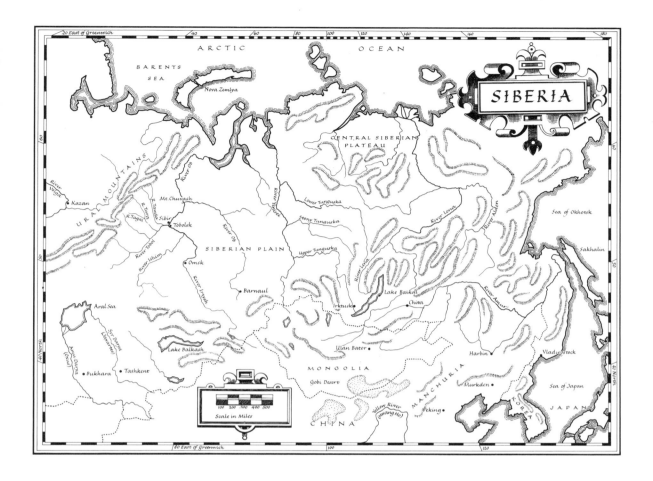

general, Mehmetkol. The blind khan himself took up station at a vantage point on the slopes of the mountain so that he could hear from his accompanying nobles, the *murzas*, of the progress of the battle. It was a long-drawn-out and bloody contest as time after time the Cossacks hurled themselves at the breastwork the Tatars had built, but failed to break through. In their turn they managed to beat off the counter-attacks of the Mongol cavalry sallying from the three gates in their defences. Finally, in a pitch of near exhaustion the Cossacks launched a grand assault, brandishing the standards of their saints and calling upon God to help them. An arrow storm from the Tatar abatis knocked down so many Cossacks that the Tatar defenders were encouraged to come out from their positions and rashly join in hand-to-hand fighting. Under these conditions the fire-power of the Cossack muskets began to tell, and the line of battle surged back to the crest of the abatis. Kuchum's native allies, the Voguls and Ostiaks, wavered, broke, and fled; and Mehmetkol himself was hit and wounded. He was rushed to safety across the Irtysh in a small boat so that he did not fall into the hands of the Cossacks, but his departure was a signal for the Tatar cavalry to turn and gallop away.

On the mountainside Kuchum, realizing that the battle was lost, turned and rode back to Sibir with his personal escort to rescue his valuables. A

*Yermak's river flotilla, led by a
holy banner, attacked by the
combined Siberian and Tatar
forces*

few days later Yermak at the head of his battered little brigade marched into
a deserted Sibir. One hundred and seven Cossacks had lost their lives in the
battle for its capture and when the new Russian city of Tobolsk was built
on a site some twelve miles away, it became a tradition for the names of these
107 Cossack heroes to be read out from a roll of honour in the cathedral on
the anniversary of their sacrifice.

Though the victor, Yermak now found himself sorely pinched. He had
routed his adversary but not killed him, and while Kuchum hid in the
forests and recruited men for a counter-attack, the Cossacks were dangerously
exposed. They were sadly depleted by battle losses, war weary, and running
short of munitions. Sibir made a poor winter camp, for it had already been

stripped of supplies by Kuchum and it was a modest little place, scarcely larger than the houses of the khan's own retinue, defended on two sides by a wooden palisade while its other flanks were lapped by the Irtysh and a small tributary brook. Yet Yermak knew that retreat was out of the question. Winter would catch the Cossack's expedition on the move; Kuchum's men would take heart if they heard that the Cossacks were in retreat; and the Siberian natives were likely to rise up and cut the stragglers to pieces. Moreover there was nowhere for the Cossacks to go – they were already outlaws in Russia, and the Stroganoffs would not be kindly disposed towards a Cossack brigade stumbling out of Siberia in distress. So Yermak decided to cling to Sibir and gamble on a direct appeal to Tsar Ivan for help. He set about strengthening the defences of the settlement, sent scouts to gather winter supplies from the natives and demand the inevitable *yasak*, and dispatched *ataman* Ivan Kol'tso on an extraordinary winter march across country. Travelling on snow-shoes and with long narrow sledges pulled by dogs or reindeer, Kol'tso and his escort took Yermak's bold, almost impudent message that he was placing the conquered territories under the rule of the tsar, and with it a magnificent tribute of fur – 2400 sable, twenty black fox skins, and fifty beaver pelts, as proof of Siberia's value.

The Kol'tso mission to Moscow was Yermak's master-stroke. It raised him from a mere brigand chief to the ranks of successful courtiers by achieving an instant reversal in Russian policy. When Kol'tso and his men first arrived in Moscow, their reputation could scarcely have been lower. In the last year of his life and increasingly vindictive, Tsar Ivan was furious with Yermak's Cossacks. He regarded the Siberian affair as an irresponsible and mutinous adventure, and he was enraged that Yermak's Cossack brigade should have gone marching away across the Urals leaving the Russian frontier defenceless. In their absence the Voguls and Ostiaks had taken to raiding Russian territory, and the tsar had been writing fiery dispatches to the Stroganoffs accusing them of damaging his interests by allowing the Cossacks to leave. He threatened to punish the Stroganoffs severely, and he promised that unless the Cossacks were recalled immediately, he would order Yermak and his *atamans* to be hanged.

This outburst was at its height when Kol'tso arrived with his gift of Siberian furs in Moscow, and stunned the tsar and his advisers. The Cossacks, they now saw, had turned out to be loyal Russian empire-builders, and the Moscovites so hastily reversed their earlier decision that the church bells of Moscow were rung in celebration; special prayers of thanksgiving were offered up in the churches; and at the prospect of so much new wealth the tsar even ordered the distribution of extra alms to Moscow's beggars. The Cossack messengers were given money and lodged at the tsar's expense, and to Yermak himself the tsar drafted a special message, praising his successes and granting him and all his followers a full and complete pardon. To seal his bond, Ivan promised to send a force of Russian *streltsy* under a *voevoda* or military governor to relieve the hard-pressed Cossacks; and for Yermak himself Ivan sent a silver cup, two suits of body armour and, from his own shoulders, a fur coat.

Meanwhile Yermak and his men, now reduced to fewer than four hundred, had been trying to hold on to their position in the strange and unreal world

*The legend that grew from
Yermak's power struggle with
Kuchum: the small black dog
nightly vanquishes the great
white wolf*

of aboriginal Siberia. It was a disconcerting situation, as they were so cut
off from outside help that they might as well have been marooned. The
Cossack scribes were like men shut up in a darkened room, and their sense
of time began to slip out of joint as they lost sight of events and years. The
date of Sibir's fall became uncertain: all the accounts agree that it was in
October, but whether 1582 or 1583 nobody was precise. Instead the march of
seasons became the all-important factor; that and the constant skirmishes
against the Tatars and the struggle to find food for survival. Yermak
strained every sinew to establish a degree of supremacy over the indigenous
Siberian tribes. But it was exasperating work. The Cossacks were dealing
with strange and unpredictable peoples, and all too often treated them
callously and with unnecessary cruelty. If the natives refused to hand over

their food caches or *yasak*, the Cossack scouts beat them up or shot to maim. The Cossack reputation for ferocity built to such a pitch that in most villages it was enough to give a demonstration with their muskets, knocking down targets set up in the village centre, and to practise a little simple psychology by dressing themselves in bright clothes to receive the *yasak* in a ceremony that impressed itself upon the natives.

On the whole the Siberian tribes were timid simple folk, and they offered little resistance to a change of masters. They lived by clans, widely scattered across the countryside in small hamlets of usually no more than half a dozen lean-to shelters covered in skins to keep out the rain and cold. They lacked fire-arms and, in some cases, had not yet entered the Iron Age but still used needles of fish bone and spears of hardened wood. They belonged

One of Yermak's strokes of genius was to offer Siberia to Ivan the Terrible and send a present of magnificent furs as an indication of its wealth

53

to several different tribes and groups, but essentially they shared a northern forest culture broadly similar to the Lapps in the west. In summer they fished the lakes and rivers, set snares for wild animals, and collected fruit and berries; and in the long dark winter days they hunted the fur-bearing creatures with bow and arrow and traps. Fur was their real wealth and even that counted for nothing in the struggle to acquire sufficient food stocks to last them through the harsh winters. In place of chiefs they were ruled by the strongest man in each group and they put their trust in shamans and medicine-men who dreamed prophetic dreams and fell into trances to the hypnotic rattle of drums and bells so that they could commune with their gods living among the rocks and trees, and in the sky. They were, the Cossacks found, utter and complete heathens. They burned fat and reindeer horns before crude little stone fetishes set up in forest clearings, and a Cossack captain, Bogdan Briaja, sweeping north among the tribes in summer, found one band who swore fealty to their new masters by solemnly kissing a bloody sword, and another tribe whose holiest veneration was to pour water over a stone statue and then lick up the drops. The Finnic groups believed that every man had a shadow of his own spirit living in an icy underworld beyond the mouth of the Ob, and that as he grew older, the shadow dwindled gradually until it was no larger than a black beetle which – upon his death – vanished for ever, never to return. A natural world of animals, weather, and landscape dominated the lives of these ancient peoples. None of them practised agriculture, and most kept herds of reindeer, some tame enough to ride, so that they travelled the forests like strange jockeys on antlered mounts or went to war on reindeer-back. Like their cavemen ancestors, a few also followed the ancient cult of bear worship and killed the sleepy beast as he emerged at the end of hibernation, then adored the pelt with mystic ceremonies to honour the creature as their messenger to the spirit world.

Streaked viciously through this strange native fabric was the constant threat of Tatar raids on isolated Cossack groups. Yermak soon learned that to have captured Kuchum's capital meant little. The enemy were nomads by nature, and the loss of their capital did not cut the heart out of their resistance. Kuchum and Mehmetkol kept up a constant pressure, circling Sibir and waiting for a chance to hamstring their opponents. A party of some twenty Cossacks who went to Lake Abalak to catch supplies of fish, were careless about keeping a lookout and Mehmetkol caught them unawares. His Tatars killed all but one man, and the sole survivor brought the news of the disaster to Sibir.

Once again Yermak showed how quickly he learned his lesson. He saw instantly that the struggle for Siberia would not be won by pitched battles but in raid and counter-raid with victory going to the sharpest reaction. So, informed of Mehmetkol's whereabouts by friendly natives, he sent a Cossack flying column of sixty men on forced marches through the snow to repay Mehmetkol with his own tactics. They located the Tatar camp without themselves being observed, and in a devastating night attack utterly defeated their enemy, taking Mehmetkol prisoner. And then for a second time Yermak acted with much more restraint than a mere cut-throat brigand. Hoping to use Mehmetkol as a pawn in negotiating with Kuchum, he treated

the Tatar prince handsomely instead of executing him, and when Kuchum refused to negotiate, Yermak sent Mehmetkol in chains to Moscow to meet the tsar. Later the Siberian prince lent his considerable military talents to his conquerors, swore allegiance to the tsar, and was to be found serving as an officer in the Russian army fighting the Swedes and in the Crimea.

A shaman of the Tungu clans

When the tsar's promised reinforcements finally did arrive in Sibir in the autumn of 1584, Yermak's Cossacks had subjugated most of the native clans but were far from pacifying the Tatars of the Ob basin. Cossacks on patrol were still being lost to Kuchum's raiders; *ataman* Kol'tso had been killed by a treacherous and unusually warlike Siberian tribe, and there was a chronic shortage of food in Sibir. Ironically the arrival of Russian reinforcements produced the worst winter of all. Without enough food to feed the extra men, scurvy broke out in the stockade. The Russian *voevoda* was one of the many men who perished of disease and starvation, and the survivors took to cannibalism, eating the flesh of their dead comrades in order to last through until the spring. As a final scourge, Kuchum's troops grew bold enough to lay siege to Sibir until they were driven off by a series of desperate sorties.

Finally, in the summer of 1585 Yermak's meteoric career blazed out as suddenly as it had begun. He decided to sweep south to consolidate his domains, and with fifty Cossacks was probing along the Irtysh to locate new tribes and collect more *yasak*. He also hoped to rendezvous with a caravan rumoured to be on its way up to Sibir from Bukhara, a development which promised him an entirely new supply route to the south. But the Bukharans never appeared, and instead he stumbled unawares into Kuchum, still lurking near the Irtysh. Yermak did not realize that Kuchum's scouts had found him and, quite oblivious of any danger, made camp for the night of 6 August on a small island near the mouth of the Vagay river where it runs into the Irtysh. The weather was said to have been atrocious, with drenching rain and heavy cloud, so that Kuchum's warriors were able to approach the camp completely undetected and with any noise covered by the storm. Legend has it, too, that Tatar scouts managed to wriggle unobserved through

Tatar victory over the sleeping Cossacks

the Cossack lines and steal three muskets and cartridge-cases from their sleeping owners, taking them back to Kuchum as proof of Yermak's unpreparedness.

The Tatar attack was a massacre. Most of the Cossacks were cut down before they were really awake and Yermak himself was forced to run the gauntlet. Clad in his coat of chain mail given him by the tsar, he tried to batter his way through the Tatar ring and succeeded in bursting the circle. Then, according to Cossack legend, he ran for the safety of the Cossack boats moored in the river. But coming to the river bank he leaped out to try to reach a boat and fell short, plunging into the water where he was dragged down by the weight of his armour and drowned in the fast-running current.

In the confusion of battle and the darkness the Tatars were not sure whether thay had killed their chief enemy, and so it was not until several days later that Yermak's corpse was found. With it came the beginnings of a macabre tomb cult. According to tradition, a Tatar boy was fishing in the river when he caught sight of a strange object in the water. It turned out to be a man's foot, with the body hanging head down in the water. Drawing the corpse to the bank, the Tatar recognized the body of Yermak and immediately summoned the village elders. To their amazement as they loosened the heavy armour, so the tale went, fresh blood began to flow from Yermak's mouth and nose, though the body itself was long since dead. Kuchum and his *murzas* arrived to see the miracle, and when they set up the corpse as a target and fired arrows at it, the same phenomenon happened as fresh blood gushed from the arrow wounds. Awed, they took down the body, noticing that the carrion birds refused to touch it, and began treating it as the Siberian natives treated a dead bear. They held a great feast to celebrate the passing of the hero's soul, and then they buried Yermak's corpse at the foot of a crooked pine tree on the banks of the river Ob. The grave was declared a sacred place, and a ghostly blue light was said to flicker over the spot at night. The Tatars took to scraping earth from the grave which they hung round their necks in small pouches as talismen, or they gave it, diluted in water, to invalids to drink as medicine. But most of them were too superstitious to go near the grave, and over the years the spot was shunned until Yermak's last resting-place was lost to memory.

So, with a mysteriousness to match his arrival, Yermak who had marched into history apparently from nowhere, vanished quietly into the same elusive void, leaving only his legend behind him. Quite how serious his loss was to the Cossacks can be judged from the fact that on hearing of Yermak's death, they began pulling out of Sibir and started on the long retreat to the Urals, taking their spoils with them. Fortunately, they had not crossed back over the mountains before they met a second Russian army sent to relieve them, and together the Russians and Cossacks slowly re-established control over Yermak's old domain.

But this was an altogether different campaign, a reconquest of Siberia, because Kuchum's resistance lay in ruins, the Cossacks knew the terrain, and already there was the heroic image of Yermak to encourage them forward. Like the Cid, the dead man still seemed to ride at the head of his troops, and all manner of semi-miraculous details began to cling to him. Cossack ballads and stories were woven around his exploits, giving Yermak a flesh-and-blood appearance which no eyewitness had previously supplied. He became a man of colossal strength, broad shouldered and compact, with a flat face, twinkling brown eyes, and black curly hair. Besides his victories in battle, there came stories of his piety and devotion, of how he ordered his Cossacks to fast forty days before giving battle against the Muslim Tatars, and how, when his brigade first came upon the future site of Tobolsk, they saw an unearthly city rising through the ground before their eyes like a mirage, with fine houses and a multitude of church steeples, and even heard the sound of ghostly church bells ringing in muffled joy.

The living Kuchum, on the other hand, was eroded inexorably from the scene. As soon as Yermak beat him in open battle, the khan's *murzas* began to fall away. Some openly changed sides and pledged allegiance to the

Russians; others tried to set up as independent princelings and were promptly gobbled up by the conquerors. One naïve band of Tatar nobles foolishly accepted an invitation to a banquet at Tobolsk and were surprised when their Russian hosts broke faith, seized their weapons, and shipped the ringleaders off to Moscow while they hanged the rank and file. Only Kuchum, like the gaunt white wolf of the legend, managed to stay free. Surrounded by a few loyal followers, he withdrew to the borderlands and waged a bitter campaign of harassment until in 1599 he was finally tracked down to his lair by a special strike force of Cossacks and Lithuanians led by renegade Tatars. They located Kuchum in the marshes and after a fearful battle virtually exterminated his group, killing two of his sons, six Mongol princes, ten *murzas*, and 150 of his last 500 men. Another 100 were drowned as they tried to escape, fifty more were taken prisoner, and eight of Kuchum's wives and five surviving sons were captured alive and sent to Moscow where they made a grand entry draped in furs and scarlet cloaks, pulled on gorgeous sledges so that the population turned out to cheer and stare at the once-invincible Tatars. Not long afterwards there was public rejoicing when one of Kuchum's grandsons renounced his religion to become Christian and changed his name from Abulkair to Andrew.

Kuchum himself was spared a similar indignity, for he died like a true Tatar. He escaped from the massacre in the marshes and fled with his bodyguard, first stealing horses from the neighbouring Kalmucks, and then riding south to join the Nogai Horde. But the Nogai remembered their dynastic feud and put to death the last independent Khan of Siberia.

In Russia, too, Yermak's legend had far-reaching effects. His Siberian success brought on a raging attack of fur-fever. From the day that Kol'tso arrived in Moscow laden with Yermak's fur tribute for the tsar, rumour spread that there were fabulous riches to be won in the east. Russian adventurers of every stripe began to pour across the Urals, either to join the Cossacks or set up as *promyshlenniks*, private fur-trappers and traders. The latter were as important as the Cossacks or the tsar's regular troops in occupying the newly opened spaces of Siberia. They spread across the continent as if by osmosis, soaked up from one river basin to the next, and snatching at the flimsy prize of Siberia's fur hoard. Their system was remarkably simple. Many *promyshlenniks* trapped the fur-bearing animals for themselves, but in the early days it was far easier with Cossack help to terrify the Siberian natives into handing over furs as their *yasak*. It took only twenty Cossacks to subdue the main tribe of the Yakut people, and the rewards were often immense. The natives of the Yenisei proved to be so fur-rich that they lined their snow-shoes with sable skins, and farther east there were tribes who thought it a great bargain to buy a copper cauldron by filling it with as many fine sables as could be crammed into the pot. Behind the *promyshlenniks* came Russian Government agents to build *ostrogs*, the vital garrison posts which commanded the waterways and tied Siberia firmly to Russian control. These *ostrogs* were incredibly lonely places, sometimes a month's journey from their nearest neighbour, and every one was like a thumb poised over the river artery, ready to block off circulation. Protected by a thirty foot high wall of logs with a parapet for sentries and corner towers for cannon, here lived the local commander, his detachment of troops, and the usual assortment of visiting pedlars, trappers, and Cossacks. Here, too, lived the Government tax-collector, watching over his fur monopoly, neatly packaged in bundles between two boards, sable skins sewn together and counted in lots of forty, fox pelts in tens, and the smaller skins of squirrel and mink tied in packets of sixty to a hundred, and every packet sealed with the Government stamp.

Soldier, Cossack, and *promyshlennik* all earned their livelihood in the face of appalling physical difficulties. They marched through the gloomy and disheartening forests of the great coniferous belt, picked their way across the interconnecting quagmires of marsh and swamp, and on the outer fringes penetrated the northern tundra and the steppe country of the east. When spared the mosquito swarms of summer they had to face the floods and mire of spring or the sudden frosts and gales of autumn. The savagery of

Yermak's death turned into a living legend when the Tatars found fresh blood flowing from the wounds on his corpse

winter almost surpassed belief. In late November came the notorious blizzards which forced even the reindeer-driving aborigine to lie down beside his animals, head-to-wind for as long as two or three days on end. From November to early May all the rivers froze solid, huge icicles congealed from river-bed to surface, and in the *ostrogs* fresh milk, when it could be obtained, was sold by the chunk. In January and February the cold reached an intensity found nowhere else on earth as the frontiersmen reached the world's Pole of Cold where the average winter temperature was minus fifty-nine degrees, and on very bad days fell to ninety degrees below zero Fahrenheit, close to the absolute minimum for human survival.

Yet in the face of these obstacles the width of Siberia was opened up within eighty years of Yermak's arrival. The Cossacks and *promyshlenniks* met and subjugated the reindeer-riding Chukchi, the pagan Tatars who worshipped the storm spirits of Lake Baikal, and the Tunguses whose habit was to sew their dead in a bag of reindeer skin and, because the ground never thawed, hang the corpse in a tree like a satchel, mournfully clanking against the dead man's armour and a cooking-pot with a symbolic hole punched in its base. Only when the Cossacks ran headlong into the Chinese empire in the very farthest east did their advance come to a stop. And even then a handful of die-hards contested the matter by building an *ostrog* with every intention of claiming the entire basin of the Amur river from China until they were thrown back by an overwhelming Chinese army.

It had been a stunning display of European territorial adventure, and in a sense the conquerors of Siberia had improved upon Cortez and Pizarro. In time and method the Cossacks stood midway between the Spanish conquistadors and the French *coureurs-de-bois* in Canada, and like these, they represented a triumph of fire-arms over the bow and arrow and, more important, the success of a handful of audacious and self-confident men over entire native populations. But where the Cossacks differed was that in Yermak they had created a unique symbol into which these qualities were distilled. From a tsarist outlaw they created for themselves a hero of Russian imperial destiny, a common man who became a great general, and from a river pirate they made an apostle of Christianity to the heathen. It was an extraordinary transition from villain to hero, and its effect lingered for generations among Siberians of all classes. Long after Yermak's death when the Nogai Horde were planning war against the Kazaks, their *murzas* wrote to the tsar to ask the loan of Yermak's armour which, they said, would still lead to victory; and a hundred years after that, parties of Russians would be mounting expeditions to scour the Urals for the cave of Yermak's legendary treasure where, like another Blackbeard, he was supposed to have cached his pirate's booty before he marched to conquer Siberia.

PRAISE IMPERIAL FOR DOCTRINE CELESTIAL

EVERY ASSUMPTION DAY WHEN PORTUGAL was at the crest of her imperial glory in the second half of the sixteenth century, a contradictory procession could be seen pacing down the streets of Lisbon to the Tagus Docks. Its contradiction was that while enthusiastic crowds lined the road to wave and cheer in festival mood, the procession itself had all the appearance of a funeral. At its head walked at solemn pace a group of sober-faced students, all of them dressed in black. Next, equally sombre and looking as if the cares of the world rested on their black-clad shoulders, marched a conclave of their professors, and behind them another group of sedate marchers in black gowns. A file of a dozen or so men formed the core of the procession, each escorted by two companions and each displaying on his chest a large crucifix, which the happy spectators saw as a Crusader's cross but to a less optimistic eye might have seemed as much like the San Benitos worn by victims of the Inquisition as they were led to an *auto-da-fé*.

The black-clad procession was, in fact, just as much an act of faith. Assumption Day was the traditional departure date for the Royal Indies Fleet, and the file of crucifix-wearers was the annual draft of missionaries which the Society of Jesus was sending to the East. Many of them would never see Europe again, and statistically their greatest danger lay just ahead. Shipwrecked by foul weather off the Cape of Storms, cast ashore through the incompetence of amateur sea-captains, or drowned in ships so rotten that they simply gave up the struggle and sank in the Indian Ocean, half the Jesuit draft in an unlucky year failed to reach their destination. There, at the port of Goa on the Indian coast, the sickly survivors would be rushed ashore from the pest-ridden fleet and deposited in the Jesuit hospital, while the healthy were led up the beach in a procession which mirrored their send-off from Lisbon, a column of Jesuit students, their professors, and lay-brothers from the Goa College escorting the new arrivals to fall on their faces in the collegiate church and give thanks for their safe journey. Then they would be led to the tailor's shop to be stripped of their fetid shipboard clothing and soak off the grime and vermin of their voyage in huge tubs of hot, scented water. By evening the transformation was complete, and they emerged dressed in new looser clothing; their beards shaved and tonsured in Indian fashion; and every man equipped with a parasol to ward off the sun. Thenceforth, in appearance as well as vocation, they would be regarded as Oriental Jesuits.

It was typical of the Society that no other religious Order took the Oriental Adventure quite so seriously or so professionally as the Jesuits, though they shared their mission with Franciscans, Augustinians, Silesians, and many other Orders. In its prime the Jesuits' Eastern Mission extended a vast

Ioan: Miele delin.

network from Ethiopia and Persia, through Goa and the Malabar Mission of the Indian peninsula, on via the Malacca Strait to Peking, and all the way to Japan. Across this interconnecting web Jesuit missionaries moved along the fine strands of the Society's mission houses, hostels, and residences, greeted by colleagues in the Jesuit international tongues of Portuguese or Latin, perhaps calling at the Goa hospital which specialized in difficult tropical diseases, or registering with the College of St Peter in Macao in order to train for the Japanese crusade, and all of them coming to rest sooner or later wherever their superiors had ordered them to preach, study, and to serve the wishes of the Society in the East.

The Jesuits saw themselves as 'the light horse of the Church', and the *élan* with which they flung themselves into the battle for Christianity in the Orient produced some of the most remarkable personalities in Europe's involvement with Asia, including the first European to become a Brahmin *sannjasi* or sage, and another Jesuit whose princely Oriental benefactor decided to elevate him to the status of a minister, gave him an escort of mounted troopers, and insisted that he should be carried everywhere in a palanquin. Jesuit missionaries also managed to compile an intellectual record which none of their rivals could match for style or brilliance. The initial Jesuit endeavour in Asia lasted from the mid-sixteenth century to the mid-eighteenth, and it helped to bring about a revolution in Western knowledge about the Orient. Each priest had orders to take notes of all the places he visited; and this data was passed back to the Society to be collated and disseminated as maps, tracts, and the famous overseas Letters or Annals of the mission, which the Society regarded as integral to its world-wide effort. These Letters and the other Jesuit reports were to alter profoundly Europe's view of Asia; and in Asia itself the Jesuit experience was invaluable, because it gave a rare chance to compare the great Asian kingdoms with one another in the light of the Jesuits' experience. To put it another way, the Oriental Jesuits were a common touchstone with which to test the different cultures they encountered, and the Jesuits not only epitomized the religious aspect of the Oriental Adventure but gave the religious experience overall unity.

Opposite *An allegorical picture of the Jesuits' mission in the East, from a history of their Oriental achievement*

Fittingly, the brand-new Jesuits at Goa were taken from their thanksgiving in church to visit the grave of the man they had chosen to imitate: St Francis Xavier, the 'Apostle of the Indies' who had set the style and scope of the Jesuit Eastern Mission for all time. 'Good – I will go' had been his terse reaction when told that the Portuguese Crown needed missionaries in India, and forthwith he had begun his grand reconnaissance of Asia, shuttling incessantly about the continent until dying of neglect and pleurisy on the obscure offshore island of Santchan, waiting patiently before the 'closed door' of China. With just the same mixture of hope and patience, his successors were asked to greet their tasks joyfully and labour resolutely for as long as their health could stand the strain or until they were recalled by higher echelons. From Goa they could be sent almost anywhere – to work among the peasants of the immediate hinterland, to convert the pariah castes of the Carnatic, to catechize the pearl-fishers of Malabar, or sail onwards with the monsoon to China and Japan. Yet the most immediate road from Goa and the one which the early Jesuit missionaries believed

64

promised the greatest apostolic reward, lay directly inland to the kingdom of Mogor, the land of the Great Mogul, and it was here in 1580 that, only a month's journey from Goa, the Jesuits encountered the quintessence of Oriental despotism.

Rather to their surprise, the Jesuits did not have to batter down the gates of Mogor. On the contrary they were invited there in a flourish of regal good manners. Emperor Akbar, the Great Mogul himself, wrote formally and very politely to the Jesuit fathers in Goa to say that he had heard of their merits and would reward handsomely any two of their priests who would visit him, bringing their holy books in order to explain their religion. Akbar's invitation was completely serious. He was a free-thinker, secure on his throne and boldly experimenting with all manner of novelties in government, ethics, and religion in the hopes of finding a durable and satisfactory system for his empire. In his fantastic new palace of carved sandstone at Fatehpur Sikri he had even built a special courtroom for the purpose, the Ibadat-Khana or 'house of worship', where teams of learned holy men, whether Zoroastrians, Brahmins, Jains, Shiah or Sunni Muslims were invited to debate their cases against one another in a verbal game of Royal Tennis. Akbar himself liked to sit cross-legged on his imperial cushion in the centre of the court, and act as the royal umpire, noting successful points and keeping score with a bag of gold coins to throw money to the winners. But for the Portuguese colonial officials, peering into the little-known interior of India, the Mogul's invitation had a different ring. Akbar's reputation was as a drink- and opium-sodden despot, the 'Terror of India', whose barbarous splendour was based on treachery and ruthlessness. So worried was the Portuguese viceroy at Goa by the Mogul's invitation that he warned the Jesuits not to send anyone to Akbar, because their emissaries would certainly be seized and used as hostages.

Opposite *Akbar inspecting the building of Fatehpur Sikri, near Agra, which was completed in 1584*

The three Jesuits who asked to be sent on the Mogor Mission were timid creatures to deliver to such a lion. One was a Persian-born convert from Islam who agreed to serve as the mission's interpreter; the second, Anthony Monserrate, was a scholar-priest who by inclination preferred dictionary and exegesis to preaching before a live audience; and the last, Rudolf Aquaviva, who was to lead the little band, was not thirty years old and so humiliatingly shy that he could never speak without blushing. Aquaviva was also absent-minded to the point that he was constantly forgetting where he had left his books or his spectacles or his hat, and on several occasions had been known to go to bed having forgotten to get undressed. Even at first encounter he was a disconcerting figure. Usually dressed in a tattered and threadbare gown, he had a quirk of humming under his breath little songs of his own invention in praise of the Virgin Mary, whom he regarded as his personal patron.

The impact of this trio on Akbar's Ibadat-Khana was a good example of the profound change which the Jesuits' unflinching sense of mission could have on the Society's meeker members. Forgetting their natural reticence, the three priests appeared in the Ibadat-Khana and lambasted their opponents with exceptional vigour. Initially the fathers were cool enough and argued calmly, but when the opposing mullahs insisted on referring to 'Jesus the Prophet' instead of 'Jesus the Son of God', the Jesuits so far forgot

themselves as to shout out 'Son of God, Son of God', until the mullahs clapped their hands over their ears or cried 'God forbid', and Akbar was hugely amused. The mullahs neither knew Christian doctrine properly nor were permitted by Islamic law to read it up but the Jesuits had the considerable advantage that they came with a Portuguese translation of the Koran, its key passages already marked and prepared. In one wrangle they drove their advantage so hard that Akbar had to take them aside and warn them in the interests of fair play not to press the mullahs too closely. And on another occasion, when apparently half drunk, he slyly suggested that perhaps the Christians and mullahs should settle their quarrel once and for all with a contest. He proposed having a pit dug and filled with a great fire, so that a mullah holding the Koran and a Jesuit with a Bible in his hand should each have the chance to fling themselves into the flames to see who should survive. Both sides blamed the other for retreating from the ordeal.

Of course it was Akbar himself who was the real target of the Jesuits' campaign. They felt that if only they could convert the Great Mogul in person, the rest of his subjects would follow suit in a landslide of missionary success. It was the principle of conversion from the throne downwards which was to be such a distinct hallmark of the Jesuit effort in the East, and with Akbar and his successor Jahangir, the Jesuit mission in Mogor laboured unceasingly, because nowhere else was access to the monarch so easy nor the stakes so high. At his first meeting with the emperor, Aquaviva presented Akbar with a sumptuously bound version of the Gospels in Portuguese, Latin, Hebrew, and Chaldee, and was thrilled when the Mogul took the volumes reverently, kissed them, and raised them to his head in a gesture of respect. Mogul and missionary got on very well, and it was not unusual for Aquaviva to be invited to stroll through the palace gardens with the emperor, discussing religious topics with the Mogul's arm affectionately round the priest's shoulders. Akbar was always scrupulously polite and friendly towards every Jesuit who came to his court. He paid their expenses, listened patiently to their lectures, and when they complained of poor lodgings, moved them to rooms in his own palace and ordered that food should be served to them from the royal kitchens. But on the supreme question of religion Akbar was exasperatingly elusive. He pleaded he had too little time to examine the new religion properly; and when the fathers boldly suggested that he might try studying at night, he promised to do so, but never did. Also he was an atrocious listener, constantly hurrying the argument by asking a new question before he had heard the answer to the last one, 'like a man trying to swallow his food at a single gulp', as Monserrate glumly put it. And he had the disconcerting habit of being able to divide his attention several ways at once, so that the priests occasionally found themselves preaching to him while the Mogul simultaneously listened to his secretary reading out army lists, leafed through books, or perhaps watched trained camels fighting to the death outside the palace windows. Then, too, Akbar could suddenly pose awkward and acute questions. He pointed out that many of Jesus's miracles could have been due to his medical skill. And on the subject of marriage he felt that Christianity was utterly illogical. It was absurd, he explained to the priests, to expect an Indian emperor to give up his plurality of wives because this was an essential means of enlarging his

Opposite *The martyrdom of Rudolf Aquaviva and four comrades in 1583*

67

Opposite *Father Ferdinand
Verbiest dressed as a Chinese
astrologer; a Japanese view
illustrating the widespread
impression the Jesuits made
in the East*

league of allied states and enhancing his own prestige. Also he thought that ordinary Christian marriage was quite out of balance, for it raised the woman to a position of great and unique respect, and yet anticipated nothing in return. Would it not be more reasonable, Akbar asked, at the very least to expect that in return for such honour the wife should commit *suttee* upon the death of her benefactor, as the Hindus did?

So the Jesuits laboured on, never quite sure whether Akbar was really on the point of becoming a Christian and never grasping the fact that for political reasons neither he nor his successor Jahangir could ever embrace Christianity, as to do so would have resulted in a Muslim revolution in their kingdom. The hot-house atmosphere of the Mogul court seemed to stupefy the Mogor Jesuits into forgetting just how artificial their situation really was – they were no more than exotic and puny shrubs specially imported by the Mogul himself, and they were only one element in the entourage of holy men to whom the emperor had access. Yet Aquaviva and his successors never thought of giving up. Jesuit reinforcements came and went. Aquaviva himself was transferred nearer Goa where, ironically, he was martyred by a common mob far more dangerous than the Terror of India, and his replacement, Jeremy Xavier, the grand-nephew of St Francis, also survived the posting, only to die in his bed in a Goa fire. Jesuit churches sprang up in the various Mogul centres at Lahore, Agra, and Delhi, and always the priests watched the throne itself for the slightest flicker of Christianity. There was rejoicing when Akbar took to wearing round his neck a reliquary showing on one side the Virgin Mary and on the other the Lamb of God; and equally happy speculation when he asked to be given more religious paintings. The Jesuits had completely overlooked that Akbar was an art connoisseur in his own right and was keenly building up an art collection. With Jahangir's accession, the same optimism persisted. It fastened on the rumour that Jahangir secretly wore an enamel cross hidden beneath his robe, and once he was seen to be so intrigued by the Crucifixion story that he spent hours standing in his palace with arms outstretched to test how long he could bear the crucifix position. Report had it, too, that the gold forceps used for sealing the imperial letters carried Christian marks engraved on the faces of the two square-cut emeralds which impressed the seal.

In the imperial household the mission seemed more on the verge of success. Akbar turned over one of his sons, Prince Murad, to be taught Portuguese by the priests and they successfully tacked religious rubrics on to his essays. Then a great triumph was scored when three of Jahangir's nephews were officially received into the Church with royal agreement. A jubilant procession was organized to celebrate their baptism. The three lads were dressed up in Portuguese clothes and golden crosses and were paraded triumphantly through the streets of Agra on elephants. A cavalcade of all the Christians in the city, mainly the foreign diplomats, carried flags and banners to accompany them to the baptism; and the Jesuits rang the church bell so vigorously that it shattered. Philip III of Spain had written to say that he would act as godfather and so the three Indian princes were duly renamed after Iberian royalty. But the conversions were premature, and after a short interval the three lapsed from Christianity, while Prince Murad, of whom so much had been expected, proved keener on hunting and hawking

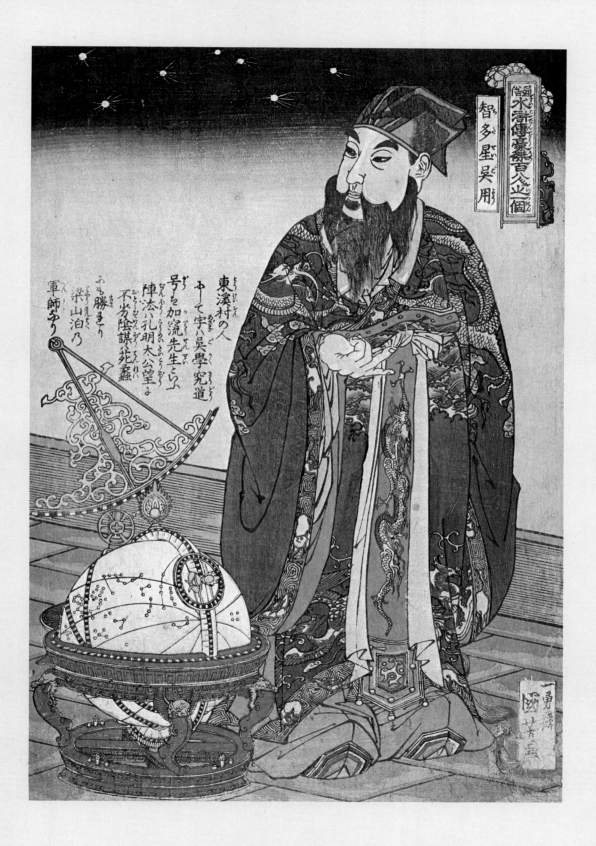

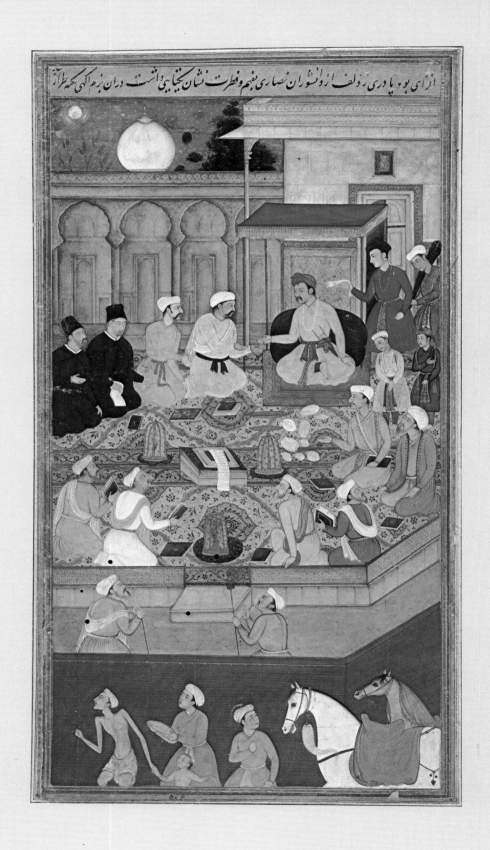

than on religious reform, and died of drink while his father, Akbar, was still alive.

All the same, it was not a bad life for the Jesuits at the Mogul court. They found the money to buy and equip comfortable residences conveniently near to the palaces, and indeed the Lahore residence was so close to the palace that the fathers were not allowed to sleep on its flat roof in the heat of the summer because it overlooked the forbidden territory of the *zenana* where the Mogul kept his women. As compensation the Mogul ordered a barge to be moored for them in the river by royal order where the priests could cool off at night. Akbar himself often visited their residences, respectfully removing his turban in the chapel; and Jahangir enjoyed being wined and dined by the fathers, much to the disgust of his orthodox courtiers who strongly disapproved of their emperor's drinking and complained that the Jesuits deliberately served him pork. In exchange for the Mogul's interest and protection, the Jesuits offered up prayers for his well-being, acted as interpreters and go-betweens for European visitors and embassies; while Monserrate, as a sort of peripatetic priest-adviser, spent one extremely uncomfortable season actually campaigning in the field with the Mogul army, leaving with a very low opinion of Mogul military efficiency. The huge force, according to his report, behaved more like a herd of wild animals, shambling across the hot Indian plains in disorder, kicking up clouds of dust, and fouling all the streams and water-tanks as it passed. To a humble footman like Monserrate it was all very disagreeable. He found it impossible to obtain clean water to drink, had to carry his tent all day long, and at the end of the day was obliged to stay up late at night in case the emperor needed to consult him.

The same chaos characterized everyday life in the Mogul cities. No restrictions were placed on the Jesuits as to where they might preach and seek their converts, but the all-pervading sense of disarray and muddle worked against them. The streets of Agra and Lahore were filled with a babble of conflicting religions and prophets crying their wares to the common people. In this huckstering turmoil the fathers found themselves reduced to using the same methods and enticements as their rivals. They tolled their bells, hired drummers to announce services by banging tom-toms outside the churches, and lined up processions of their converts to walk through the streets demonstrating their belief to the crowd. At times a note of hysteria crept in. A funeral service was more likely to be seen as the chance to go tramping spectacularly down the streets with lighted tapers in hand than as a Christian duty of burial, and even the Indian spectators, hardened to most religious excesses, were taken aback by the sight of Christian penitents publicly lashing themselves so that the blood flowed down their backs. More restrained methods seemed to have a greater appeal. So the fathers took to rehearsing large powerfully voiced choirs, and asked that church organs and trained flute-players be sent up from Goa.

Their greatest success was the annual Nativity display which came to be a great feature of every Indian city where there was a Jesuit church. These displays had begun as little more than simple Nativity cribs set out in front of the churches for passers-by to see, but quickly they developed into major spectacles when it was realized how much attention they earned. The

PRAISE IMPERIAL FOR DOCTRINE CELESTIAL

Opposite *Father Rudolf Aquaviva and Father Francis Henriquez taking part in a debate with Muslim divines before Akbar in the Ibadat-Khana*

71

Indians were fascinated. They stopped to examine the cribs, asked questions, and often came into the church to look around, and were seen carrying away straws as souvenirs. Those Jesuits who could speak the vernacular stationed themselves beside the crib to explain to the crowds the meaning of the Christmas story until they had shouted themselves hoarse. And as year succeeded year the displays grew more and more elaborate. Professional Indian carpenters were hired to produce more intricate constructions; and more money was spent on design and materials. The model figures in the crib were increased to include those prophets who had foretold the birth, and soon there was an entire cast of wooden mannequins in every display, a whole galaxy of saints, each with a placard propped against its feet to explain its identity to the onlookers. By the end the whole affair had got out of hand, and special water-driven models were being imported from Europe to give the scene a contrived and slightly ludicrous air as miniature fountains played near the manger, and real tears rolled down the cheeks of the Magi.

This over-popularization of the Nativity was symptomatic of the desperation of the Mogor missionaries to increase their number of conversions at all costs. In practice their record had been rather poor. Very few Indians were converted to Christianity, and many of those who were, had worldly motives. Some were members of the lower castes; others were servants at the residences, and there was the inevitable leaven of opportunists seeking to gain advantage with the Portuguese. It was not surprising, therefore, that the Jesuits began to suffer from a mixture of irritation and disappointment. 'A well sharpened sword', was one Jesuit suggestion for the only effective way of winning souls in Mogor. And as Jesuit morale sank, so the strain of their position began to show. Several priests were withdrawn; one committed suicide very effectively by trying to remove his own appendix, apparently while the balance of his mind was disturbed; and those who stayed on began to grow accustomed to increasing disappointment and persecution. There had always been bad moments; when, for example, Akbar had faced a pro-Muslim revolt in Bengal and for political reasons reverted to a semblance of orthodox Islam; or when reports reached the capital that in Goa the Koran had been hung round a pig which the Christians had then chased through the city. In retaliation the Muslims wanted to tie a Bible round a donkey's neck and beat the animal through the city. But it was Jahangir's death and the succession of his son, Shah Jehan, which really signalled the end of the Jesuits' enjoyment of royal patronage. Shah Jehan was an aggressively orthodox Muslim, so much so that he set about destroying the great Hindu monuments including one of the most important temples at the holy city of Benares. Towards the Jesuits he adopted a policy of deliberate indifference, and when he moved his capital to Shahjehanabad in 1648, they were in such low esteem that they were not included in his entourage but left stranded in Agra. Under the influence of his beloved wife Mumtaz Mahal, 'The Chosen One of the Palace' for whose tomb he built the Taj Mahal, the Mogul became more violently anti-Christian. The fathers found their churches being ransacked by the imperial police; they were taunted by mobs in the streets as 'black devils'; and they suffered the ignominy of seeing their church bell hauled away round the neck of an

P.MATTHEVS RICCIVS MACERATENSIS QVI PRIMVS E SOCIETAE
IESV EVANGELIVM IN SINAS INVEXIT OBIIT ANNO SALVTIS
1610 ÆTATIS 60

elephant because its tolling had kept awake one of the emperor's invalid friends. More subtly, the Jesuits were also squeezed by the landlords and money-lenders who sensed their fall from imperial grace and wanted to repossess the land on which the Jesuit residences stood. Nor were personal attacks unknown. Several priests were unaccountably and violently sick, so that poison was suspected; and one Jesuit became so accustomed to having stones thrown at him in the street, that when he was caught by a hailstorm one summer night as he lay asleep on the residence roof, he woke up shouting at whoever it was to stop stoning him.

So, in increasingly ragged style, the Mogor Mission limped on. The ascetic and wily Aurangzeb, Shah Jehan's successor, was no more favourable to the Society, and though he allowed Jesuits to remain in the Mogul's dominions, they found themselves ministering more and more to the spiritual needs of the European community rather than seeking conversions among the Indians. Some of the Jesuits found jobs with other potentates. The Viceroy of Bengal, who was very pro-European, kept a favourite Jesuit adviser, and the Rajah of Jaipur hired an entire team of Jesuits to design him an astronomical observatory, for which he had an eccentric craze. One resolute priest, as much scientist as missionary, quietly went off to make a map of the Ganges, producing a beautifully detailed chart of the river, over eight feet long which must have taken years of survey work with sounding rod and line, and was the first of its kind. Yet the core of the mission, the reason for its foundation, was gone as soon as the Society lost the attention of the Great Mogul himself. And as the Mogul empire began to crumble, so the Mogor Mission collapsed with it, at just the moment when their brothers in the Society, after years of frustration, were at last making some headway with an even more powerful emperor in China.

Draped in their Indian garb, Jesuit recruits assigned to the China Mission

Above, left A portrait of Jahangir to gladden the Jesuits' hearts; his interest in Christianity, however, was curiosity, not conversion. **Above, right** *Matteo Ricci, master-builder of the China Mission*

73

The formal equipage of a
Chinese viceroy, from a
Jesuit's geography of China

Iome II.page 5o.

shipped onward from Goa in May. Their destination was to be the 'town of the Blessed Name of God' as Macao was clumsily called, and to get there they had to pass through the Strait of Malacca in time to catch the southwest monsoon which blew the fleet up to the China coast. All being well, after sixty to ninety days' passage the newcomers arrived at the College of St Joseph and began at once their studies for the Chinese service. It was an exacting curriculum. The Portuguese enclave at Macao stood to the China Mission as Goa stood to Mogor – a well-flexed springboard – but there the similarity ended. In Macao the novice was tutored for a ministry that was far more demanding, less popular in its style and manner, and balanced on a knife-edge. The college staff knew that a single blundering Jesuit in China might bring about the expulsion of the entire Order from the country, and so they trained their new recruits with extreme severity. An excursion to Xavier's death-place on Santchan to recite Mass and sing a Te Deum made a suitably intense introduction, and there was nothing frivolous about the difficult courses in Chinese language, history, and custom which every recruit was expected to master. And before he left for the mainland, the new missionary for China was advised to put off his Indian dress, because the Chinese considered Indian holy men to be lightweights or charlatans. Instead, the Jesuit in China wore at formal occasions the garb the Society had approved for him: a long and stately silk gown of Chinese cut, and on his head a special hat modelled on the traditional Chinese headpiece which denoted the rank of a serious scholar.

Hero to the China Mission was Matteo Ricci, the man who in all its essentials created the mission's structure and method. Brilliant of intellect, patience, and faith, Ricci was the first of the three great pillars on which the China Mission stood, and it was an instructive contrast with India that whereas the Mogor Mission had depended upon native emperors for survival, in China the mission depended very largely on its own outstanding captains.

Ricci was the son of an Italian pharmacist, born a few months after Xavier's death in 1552, and he had entered the Society against his father's wishes. Going to Rome he studied under Clavius, the 'Prince of Mathematicians' and friend of Kepler and Galileo, and in 1578 he turned up in Goa with the annual Jesuit draft. There he spent four years as a professor of rhetoric before being transferred to Macao, at the particular request of the official Visitor of the Society, with special instructions to prepare himself for China. Just how important was his selection can be judged from the fact that his collegiate superiors in Macao were told that Ricci was to be assigned to no other tasks which might interfere with his Chinese studies.

There was good reason to be so determined. At that time there was not a single permanent Christian settlement in China despite nearly thirty years of persistent effort. The Chinese authorities flatly discouraged missionaries, regardless of Order and pretensions. Jesuits, Dominicans, and Augustinians had all tried to enter China and failed, though not for want of ingenuity. The first Jesuit had simply been asked to leave China because he had not been invited; and the second was fobbed off with the advice that he should first learn to speak Chinese. The third, who boldly had himself put ashore from a small boat, was deported so brusquely that for the sake of their future hopes the Society quietly shipped him back to Europe. When Ricci started his studies in Macao, the only Jesuit to have any real contact with the Chinese authorities was a fellow Italian, Michele Ruggieri, who had taught himself enough Chinese to practise a mild deceit on the mandarins. Claiming to represent the Bishop of Macao in negotiations with the city authorities of Canton, Ruggieri had got to know the city governor and applied for a licence to reside on the mainland. But so far this permission had not been granted.

Ricci's first task, as ordered by the Visitor, was to research and write a description of China, partly to make himself familiar with its culture and partly to leave a record for those who might follow him. There was very little information to go on, but the key to the situation seemed to lie in the structure of China's civil government. Ostensibly at least, China was ruled by a professional civil service of mandarins, each selected by examination and promoted on merit. From the magnificent viceroys who controlled entire provinces, right down to local magistrates at district level, a vast inter-locking bureaucracy ran China, fuelled and recorded by masses of paper-work, scrutinized by travelling inspectors, motivated by neo-Confucian philosophy, and taking its orders from the relevant head offices or depart-mental boards in Peking. It was to this permanent Chinese civil service that Ricci chose to address his efforts, and it is unlikely that the parallel between the mandarins and his own Society escaped his notice. Both systems dedicated their members to service through example and obedience after a rigorous training; both were directed by a formal system of ethics; and both were prepared to advance their cause through intellectual argument and practical expertise. In short, the Society of Jesus could scarcely have been a more sympathetic shoot ready to be grafted on the main stem of Chinese society.

Overleaf *Ricci's World Map*

The success of the graft was Ricci's doing. By a typical mix-up of bureau-cratic paperwork he and Ruggieri received permission to establish them-selves at the town of Chaoching in Kwangtung province. This permission had actually been granted by a previous viceroy but countermanded by the Canton authorities. The latter, however, omitted to file their reasons for their objection, and so when a new viceroy took over and consulted his predecessor's records, as far as he was concerned the permission was still valid. Losing no time, Ricci and Ruggieri promptly moved to Chaoching where they acquired a construction site next to a new victory pagoda and began to erect a house in European style, hanging near the front entrance the viceregal edict granting them immunity from harassment.

Their house was a most unorthodox mission station. Originally designed as a two-storey building, money ran out before completion of the upper floor so that it remained a truncated bungalow with only a central hall which served as a chapel, and a single room on each side. Over the chapel door was fixed a plaque by Chinese order describing it rather quaintly as 'the House of the Saints of the Flower', and next to the entrance to the reception-room was another legend in Chinese which read 'a Holy People from the Occident'. Here, besides the usual chapel furniture, the two Jesuits laid out a European museum. On display were European-made prisms of glass which split light into colours, large and small chiming clocks, solar quadrants and spheres, oil-paintings, and a small collection of European books with diagrams and

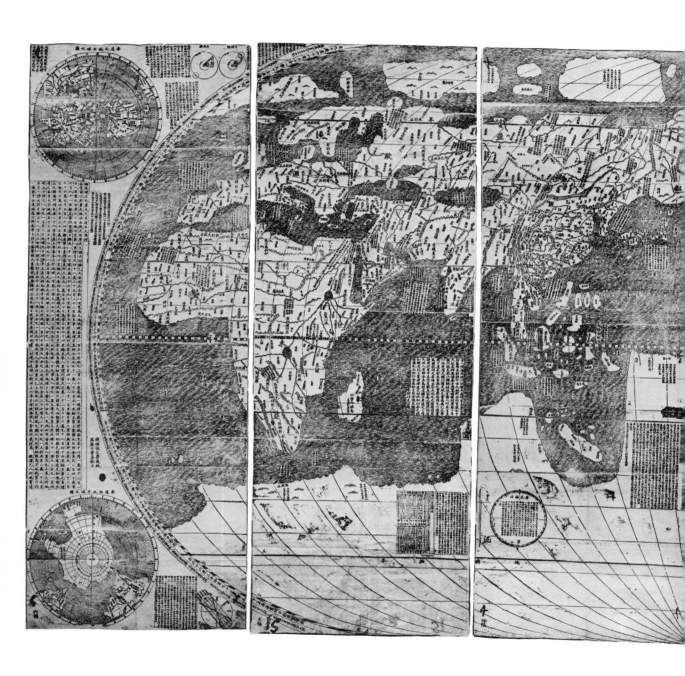

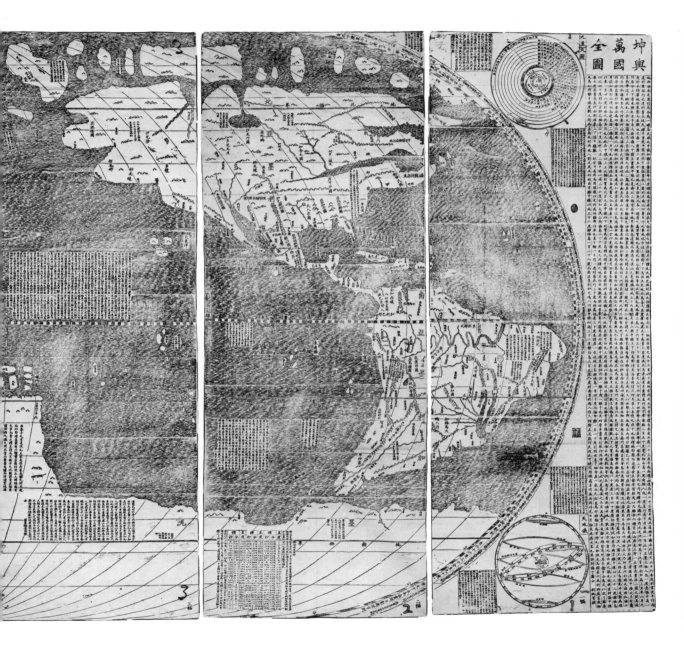

坤輿萬國全圖

79

maps and views of European towns and architectural drawings of European buildings. All these were new to the Chinese, and Ricci himself (Ruggieri was recalled to Europe in 1588) demonstrated on request the technique of painting in perspective, an art previously unknown to his audience.

As with Aquaviva's debates before Akbar, the European museum of Chaoching was nothing but a bait for the hook of Christianity, but it was a measure of Ricci's genius that he did more than merely set his lure. During the twenty-eight years he lived in China, he succeeded in getting inside the mandarin mentality and projecting his religious crusade in a *tour de force* of cultural sympathy which has seldom been equalled. First Ricci taught himself the official language of the mandarins until he knew it so well that he could deploy its most elegant and sophisticated subtleties as a fine cutting tool of the intellect. Almost casually and as a by-product of his language studies he compiled the first Mandarin-Portuguese dictionary and helped devise a system of Romanization of Chinese sounds and symbols. Next, he started to read the Chinese classics to discover any points of contact with Christian doctrine. Finally, he brought together his literary, calligraphic, and philosophical skills to write a series of *chuan*, the elegant Chinese theses on scrolls which circulated among the mandarins like the correspondence of an academic community with its latest monographs for criticism and review. Into this circulation Ricci's *chuan* slid under Chinese-sounding titles like 'Twenty-five sentences on Christian Moral Doctrine' and 'Ten truths contrary to common opinion'. His most famous *chuan* was so well regarded that it eventually became a recognized Chinese standard work, and was picked by the Chinese professors as an example which Chinese students should study for style and content. Simultaneously Ricci was also producing translations of Euclid and Clavius, books on hydraulics and geography, and one treatise entitled 'Western Memory Techniques' which explained how he, who was gifted with a phenomenal memory, could memorize at a single reading a list of four hundred different Chinese written characters and then recite them on demand, either forwards or backwards.

His greatest contribution, though, was to Chinese geography, for he was the first man to show the Chinese their country in relation to the rest of the world, and the first to inform the Chinese of the existence of the new continent called America. An oval-shaped map of the world, probably by Ortelius, was hung on the wall of his original museum at Chaoching, and it so startled the mandarins, who were accustomed to a traditional Chinese view of the Middle Kingdom surrounded by insignificant slivers of barbarian territory, that at their request Ricci turned cartographer and worked up a special Chinese version. Tactfully he redrew the boundaries of the map so that China appeared in its centre, and used a projection which made the country look larger than it really was. His map was so successful and so many woodcut copies were requested by the mandarins that Ricci with his usual versatility decided to produce an entirely new map of the world, larger and based on all the most recent information and discoveries, including much new data from Chinese sources. In its revised version Ricci's world map was a landmark of cartography. It stood six feet by twelve, was printed on six strips of fine paper or silk, and was annotated across its surface like a vast gazetteer with geographical information. One hand-painted copy

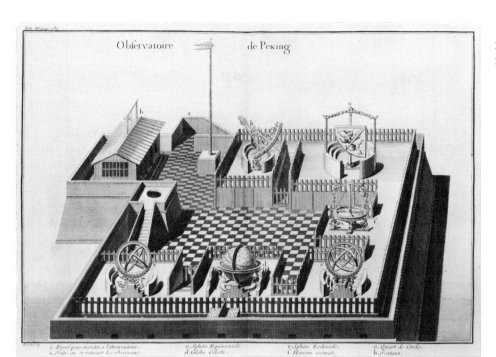

Obſervatoire ✦ de Peking

a. Deſſé pour monter a l'obſervatoire.
b. Salle ou ſe retirent les obſervans.
c. Sphere Equinoxiale.
d. Globe Celeſte.
e. Sphere Zodiacale.
f. Horizon azimut.
g. Quart de Cercle.
h. Sextant.

reached the emperor himself and its existence was recorded in the annals of the Ming Dynasty by the royal historians. Several copies were taken westward to bring Chinese geographical knowledge to Europe, so that Ricci found himself in the rare position of a geographical intermediary, introducing the outside world to the Chinese just as he was discovering China for himself and for the Europeans.

It was small wonder that such a prodigy of a man should have impressed his hosts. Ricci was taken up by influential mandarins. He was commissioned by them as a private tutor and consulted as a technical expert on matters ranging from clock manufacture to hydraulics. He was also, in 1601, accorded the singular honour of being summoned to Peking by order of the Emperor Wan Li, and allowed to spend the last nine years of his life in the Chinese capital. There Ricci continued to behave with the utmost tact. With what can best be described as truly Oriental patience, he advocated to his Society an excruciatingly slow growth of the China Mission, and advised that handpicked Jesuits should follow very carefully in his footsteps, conducting their ministry in Chinese dress and language, and observing Chinese custom.

By a fortunate coincidence the fame of his world map and a second Chinese bureaucratic blunder in 1610, the year of Ricci's death, combined to open wider this gap through which the Jesuits were infiltrating deeper into the fabric of Chinese society. In December of that year the imperial astrologers at the Peking Mathematical College wrongly predicted an eclipse. What might have been a trivial error in most countries was, in China, a most serious matter. The astrologers' calculations were the basis for the official calendar published each year by the Government, and this calendar was a vital document by which the entire machinery of Chinese government was

The Jesuits in China found themselves imparting heavenly knowledge of a rather different nature than intended

81

PEKING

*A seventeenth-century view
of Peking*

painstakingly regulated according to Confucian principles, taking into
account the movements of the sun, moon, stars, and their various conjunc-
tions. These calculations had to be absolutely precise, and after the Chinese
astrologers made their error, it was suggested that the learned Western
foreigners might perhaps be called in to reform the calendar, since they were
obviously skilled in astronomy and possessed accurate instruments for
measuring the stars. So radical a suggestion took a long time in being
accepted, but in the end it brought about the creation of a special review
board, the Calendrical Bureau, charged with overseeing the preparation of
the annual calendar. Initially only assisted by the Jesuit priests, the Calendrical Bureau was eventually dominated by them and for a century and a
half this intimate part of China's government was directly controlled by
Christian priests, to whom in 1638 the Son of Heaven awarded the highest
mark of imperial favour, the right to display a *pai-paen* or ideogram based on
four characters chosen by the emperor. With splendid ambiguity the Jesuit
pai-paen read 'Praise imperial for doctrine celestial', without clarifying
whether it referred to the foreigners' religion or to their astronomy.

This vantage point of the Calendrical Bureau brought to prominence
Ricci's two outstanding Jesuit heirs – Adam Schall and Ferdinand Verbiest,
who followed one another as leaders of the China Mission and shared
Ricci's dazzling variety of skills. Both were first-class linguists, Schall
speaking five languages to perfection in addition to faultless Mandarin, and
both were imaginative engineers who turned their hands to any of the
succession of bizarre tasks which their Chinese hosts suggested. Schall
advised on city fortifications and made plans for a sailing-boat for the emperor.
Verbiest invented a new gun-carriage for the Chinese army, directed the
construction of an aqueduct, and made a boat and a land carriage driven by
steam. His most enduring project was to design a massive new observatory
for the Imperial Palace containing, among other items, an azimuth compass

and two ancillary spheres each six feet in diameter, and a gargantuan sextant eight feet across. These instruments were mounted on a special observation tower in the palace grounds, and each of them was so beautifully made in white brass that it could be manipulated with ease. The priests' skill as metallurgists also brought them the unlikely role as gun-founders for the imperial artillery. The Chinese army was chronically short of cannon, and at the emperor's command Verbiest produced an arsenal of 132 guns, which he blithely named and baptized after saints; while Adam Schall read prayers over the casting of his initial batch of twenty guns. A demonstration of his new weapons so delighted the emperor that an order was placed forthwith for another five hundred of them.

The ease of their relationship with the reigning emperor was another essential part of the style which Schall and Verbiest shared. Schall in Peking saw the collapse of the Ming Dynasty, its last emperor hanging himself in a garden shed as rebels advanced on the capital, and during the city's sack he had to stand guard like a priestly berserker in the entrance of his residence, sporting a beard and waving a huge Japanese sword to frighten off the mob. Fortunately the revolution brought a six-year-old Manchu boy to the throne as a minor, and Schall was selected to tutor him in mathematics and astronomy. The friendship between the future emperor and his teacher blossomed so well that when the boy took over as Emperor Shun Chih, it was not unusual to find the supreme ruler of China stretched out in Schall's rooms reading a book or chatting with his former tutor. In a similar, though lesser, role, Verbiest was appointed as royal instructor for four or five months to Emperor Kang Hsi and could be seen regularly arriving at the palace at dawn with his textbooks under his arm, to stay until three or four in the afternoon discussing principles of geometry or mathematics with his highly intelligent pupil who was sufficiently enthusiastic to make his own translation of Euclid.

Life for a Jesuit in China in these years, as in India earlier, was a confusing mixture of extraordinary privilege with intervals of severe and sometimes terrifying oppression. Ricci had insisted that the Society should maintain a low profile in China, adapt itself to Chinese custom, and make every effort to avoid friction. The half dozen Jesuit mission houses scattered round the country were staffed by only two or three European priests and about the same number of Chinese lay-brothers. No bells were rung; Chinese converts were advised to come to Mass in small groups no larger than five men at a time; and, as Ricci remarked, it was only a pity that he was unable to change the shape of his nose and the slant of his eyes in order to adjust more sympathetically into his Chinese environment. But even this chameleon policy was not enough to deflect persecution by hostile Chinese politicians. During Prince Oboi's xenophobic regency, Schall and Verbiest were arrested, loaded with chains, and kept in prison for six months under almost daily interrogation by an inquisition of mandarins. Condemned to death by strangulation, Schall was saved by a tremendous fire and an earthquake which ravaged Peking, two omens which caused his captors to change their minds.

Such times of persecution were even more harrowing for the Jesuits working in the provinces. In the periodic waves of nationalistic hysteria which swept the country, they were abominably treated. Once there was a

*Hazards encountered by
Benito de Goes, a Jesuit
traveller in the East:* **right** *an
attack on his caravan by
bandits;* **opposite** *a poison
attempt on his life by
companions*

scare that the Jesuits were a fifth column preparing for a Japanese invasion of China. They were said to be trained soldiers, keeping weapons stored in their churches, and that they concealed their passwords in the liturgy. Another time they were described by a senior mandarin as 'contemptible rats' who were polluting China's soil, and two Jesuits were bastinadoed and carried out of the country like common criminals, locked in tiger cages with placards hung round their necks denouncing their activities. Their Chinese lay-brothers were even less fortunate. Regarded as turncoats, some were executed, others imprisoned, and at least one was sent to work as a forced labourer on the Great Wall.

The truth of the matter was that the Jesuits, having entered China in the guise of Occidental technicians, were steadily being caught in a trap of their own invention. More and more they came to depend on their scientific skills to retain the good will of their hosts, and they found themselves having to justify their presence in China by the steady performance of scientific feats. On one famous occasion Verbiest was called to the palace to face a competition against the Chinese astrologers. A rod, a couple of feet in length, had been stuck in the ground, and the contestants were called upon to predict the precise length of its shadow at noon. Verbiest's answer was not only more accurate than the opposition's, but the Jesuit then used his chance to lecture the smarting Chinese astrologers on the deficiencies of their calculations. But these small victories detracted from the essential fact that science having come to the aid of the mission, was tending to choke it.

Nowhere was this more true than with the 'Mathematicians to the King', a batch of French Jesuit astronomers sent by Louis XIV of France to assist the mission. With that extraordinary continuity which characterized the

mission, these savants entered Peking after a three-year voyage from
Europe just twelve days following the death of Verbiest, and they proceeded
at once to assume the mantle of his scientific reputation. The task they picked
was the mapping of China, and it left them very little time for anything else.
It was a stupendous project because the only available maps of the country
had to be recast entirely to a European format, and there was a multitude
of towns and villages to be located, named, and marked. Some idea of the
immensity of the task can be gained from the fact that a preliminary survey
round Peking, begun in 1701, revealed that there were some seventeen
thousand villages to be plotted, and that until the Jesuits took to the field
with their surveying cords and sextants, there was no precise guide to the
length or direction of the Great Wall itself. In fact the Jesuits chose the Wall
as the baseline for their grand survey, and to produce the key map, a scroll
fifteen feet long, took a year's intensive field-work. Despite an unremitting
pace, the Jesuits required another nine years to plot the rest of China, carefully calculating latitudes and longitudes by star and sun sights and then
cross-checking the figures by triangulation; and it was not until 1717, after
a map-making endeavour which equalled anything previously attempted in
Europe, that the 'Jesuit Map' finally came off the press. In many ways it
was a culmination of the Society's geographical campaign in the Orient. A
remarkably accurate representation of more than a million square miles of
country, it took up 120 sheets of paper, and included data from as far afield
as Formosa and Turkestan where adventurous Jesuit surveyors had penetrated hundreds of miles beyond the boundaries of China proper, even including a corner of Tibet where two specially trained Chinese Buddhists had been
sent. What Ricci had started in Chaoching with his novel world map, the

French Jesuits had crowned with their imperial map which was to remain in useful service until late into the nineteenth century.

The question of what country might lie sandwiched between the great empires of India and China was one which naturally attracted such indefatigable geographer-priests. Besides the obvious advantage of opening a land route between their two missions, there was the evergreen puzzle whether China and the country of Cathay, as Marco Polo had written of it, were in fact the same place. One theory, much under discussion, was that Cathay was merely a name for China's western frontier town. This neat blend of intellectual challenge with the tantalizing possibility of finding an entirely new country for missionary work could only be solved by someone repeating Marco Polo's trail, and so in 1602, the year after Ricci had moved to Peking, a Jesuit blithely set out from the Mogor Mission to put the theory to the test by trying to reach Peking overland. The traveller was Benito de Goes, a tough ex-soldier from the Azores. Disguised as an Armenian, he set out under the pseudonym of Banda Abdullah, 'Servant of the Lord', and carried his prayer-book hidden in his turban. The route he chose was a horrifyingly difficult one through Afghanistan, over the Pamirs, and then down to join the Silk Road across the Western Desert to the frontiers of China. Totally worn out, he eventually staggered into the Chinese frontier town of Suchow, where he died of exhaustion, though not before he had heard about Ricci in Peking, and by an extraordinary coincidence had actually seen a Portuguese letter which had been carried to Suchow as an example of the strange Western style of calligraphy.

De Goes's journey, proving that China and Cathay were indeed the same place, also emphasized that a large and unexplored area must lie between the empires of the Great Mogul and the Son of Heaven. North of Mogor, within the curve of de Goes's route, rumour reported a country ruled by priests who worshipped an invisible God, prayed with their hands folded, and wore tall caps and long gowns. Wondering whether perhaps they might not discover a colony of long-lost Eastern Christians, Jesuits from India promptly set out for the Himalayas and thus stumbled into Tibet, partly to their chagrin and partly to their delight. The physical obstacles were as bad as anything they had ever experienced. The first Jesuit to enter Tibet, once again in disguise, had to join a party of Hindu pilgrims visiting the holy sources of the Ganges and walked with them up the headstreams as they chanted the sacred Hindu rubrics, and shuffled perilously over natural bridges of melting snow which spanned torrents foaming eighty or ninety feet below them. Higher still and far beyond the pilgrim trail, he found the passes still closed and, abandoned by his guides, tried to swim through the snow by lying face downward and moving his arms and legs to make progress. He gave up the attempt and returned to India only when the cold became so intense that he failed to notice he had knocked a piece off his finger until he saw the spurt of blood.

But when the Society did finally establish its first mission station at Tsarapang in Tibet, the harvest of souls was disappointing. The religious quarrels of the lamas between the red hat and yellow hat sects, complicated by dynastic quarrels, dismayed the Jesuits. The robed priests of rumour turned out to stink abominably, blew mournfully on trumpets made of

human leg and arm bones, and wore beads carved from dead men's skulls. Two Jesuits, who came overland from China by the reverse route into Tibet in the 1660s, were thunderstruck by the lamas' callous ceremony of turning a half-crazed young man loose for the day in the streets of Lhasa, armed with a sword, quiver and arrows with which he slew any living creature he met because it was believed that his victims would find eternal happiness. The Jesuit travellers were depressed to discover that the famous cure-all pills distributed by the priests were compounded from the faeces of the nineteen-year-old Dalai Lama, and this sense of frustration and hopelessness so disheartened Ippolito Desideri, the last of the Jesuits to spend any length of time in the Tibetan capital that he himself retreated to a lamasery, ostensibly to study Lamaism the better to refute it, but emerging from this seclusion after reading the 115 volumes of the classic *Kaanghuir* only to abandon the country before putting his new-found knowledge into print.

Opposite *Shah Jehan holding a turban jewel*

Desideri's account of Lhasa was to be shelved in the Vatican and not rediscovered for 150 years, but the Jesuit maps of the Great China Survey, the torn scraps of de Goes's notebook from Suchow faithfully preserved by his travelling companion, the official provincial letters, and the other Jesuit accounts from China were steadily accumulated in the archives of the Society until there was almost too much material for it to be digested properly. For want of space some of the data had to be deliberately omitted; several items got lost in the sheer volume of paperwork; and doubtful matter was deliberately suppressed. Yet the bulk of it was published, some of it gloriously, as in Kircher's *China Monumentis Illustrata* or Du Halde's great *Encyclopaedia of the Chinese Empire*, enormous leather-bound descriptions lavish with woodcuts; and some of it over-optimistically, like a panegyric on China written by Father Longobardo, one of Ricci's over-enthusiastic assistants, when the way seemed open to complete Chinese conversion. Longobardo praised China so highly that for generations afterwards those who read him thought that the Chinese were paragons of virtue, spotlessly polite and peaceable, charitable, godly, and blameless. Some of the Jesuit information quickly reached a wide readership. The leading map-makers like Blaeu put coloured vignettes of the newly described natives round the fringes of their maps, and the French cartographer, d'Anville, mass-produced copies of the famous China map. But other items were so esoteric that they defeated even the experts. Father Tieffenthaler, the surveyor of the Ganges, had a habit of sending unsolicited parcels of his Indian notes, of great scholarly value but usually without explanation or covering letters, to total strangers in European museums who could neither read nor comment on his efforts which were then put on one side until they fell by chance into the hands of some delighted Orientalist, perhaps generations later.

This outpouring of new and valuable information, gleaned piece by piece from the remotest parts of Asia, ultimately confirmed the quality of the Jesuit contribution to the Oriental Adventure. The depth and variety of their scholarship were astonishing. Father Thomas Stevens, the first Englishman to go to live in India other than for trade, laboriously compiled a ten-thousand-line Biblical epic in Kankani, a local Madras dialect; Father Martini set himself to decipher some sixty thousand Chinese documents for his history of China; Father Roth, a German with the Goa Mission, became

Two engravings from China
Monumentis Illustrata *by
Athanasius Kircher:* **right**
*the Grand Lama's residence
in Bietala (Potala);* **opposite**
a Chinese scholar writing

the leading authority of his day on Hinduism, providing Kircher with his illustrations of the Sanscrit alphabet complete with Latin equivalents and the Lord's Prayer and Ave Maria written out in Sanscrit as an exercise for beginners. At times, it is true, the scholastic effort was overdone – the Jesuit priest who translated the Missal, Breviary, and Book of Ritual into Chinese took twenty-four years to do so – but this pedantry was balanced by some delightfully elegant touches. Castiglione, one of the last Jesuits of the Chinese court, delighted Emperor Ch'ien Lung with his cheerful watercolour portraits, and his companion Benoist, a brilliant mathematician, turned his hand to devising ingenious water-driven clocks and automatons, just as Ricci had formerly taken time out from his studies to teach four of the palace eunuchs to play a spinet which had been presented to their master.

Sadly, though, the depth of Jesuit scholarship and the Society's eagerness to adapt to native cultures became a weapon which was used to destroy them. Their enemies at home accused them of spending more time studying the natives and copying their ways than in spreading the true Gospel. Certainly some of the Jesuit behaviour in India had become distinctly unorthodox. The Society banned Europeans from some villages which it controlled, and it raised money by entering into business, particularly the jewel trade. Tavernier, the travelling French jeweller of whom more will be heard, once met two native-born Jesuit lay brothers who were gem-smuggling from the kingdom of Golconda. They had disguised themselves as fakirs and were travelling about dressed in tiger-skin clothes, hats of lamb skin with the four legs dangling over their foreheads, large crystal rings in pierced ears, sandals on bare feet, and they carried fans of peacock feathers.

Such unorthodoxy was brought to a head by the notorious Rites Question. Complicated by years of argument, the essence of the Question was whether

Overleaf *Reception of a
European ambassador at the
Chinese court. Frequently,
resident Jesuit priests were
called in to act as interpreters
on such occasions*

or not the Jesuits had compromised their faith by attempting to conform too
closely to Oriental tastes. It was asked whether in China it was right to have
painted shoes on the pictures of the crucified Christ because the Chinese
were offended by the sight of naked feet, to have hung a picture of the
emperor in the chapel itself, to have conducted Mass in the Chinese language,
and to have permitted Chinese Christians to continue to revere their
ancestors. The Rites Question was all the more damaging because it was also
double edged. In China Emperor Kang Hsi who began by allowing the
Question to be debated freely, eventually lost patience with the new Christian
puritanism which forced Chinese Christians to abandon native ways, and
told his mandarins to reduce the number of Jesuits permitted in his kingdom.
Simultaneously the Rites squabble corroded the Jesuits' reputation at home,
making it easier for their arch-enemy, the Portuguese minister Pombal, to
move against them. Determined to break the power of the Society, he banned
the Jesuits in Lisbon and, in 1762, the civil authorities in Macao were
ordered to enter the College of St Joseph and arrest its entire staff. The
removal of Portuguese support for the Jesuit mission was a disaster. For far
too long the Society had clung to its old mechanism, and it still relied on the
annual departure from Lisbon of the Royal Indies Fleet and the dispersal
points at Goa and Macao. Now, with Pombal's persecution they were robbed
of their base at the same moment that their Oriental patrons turned against
them.

In China the French Jesuits, being independently sponsored, managed to
struggle on for a time. They tried to keep the China Mission alive in the face
of increasing Chinese hostility, hopefully growing pigtails and straggly
beards and going ashore dressed as Chinamen. One optimist climbed into a

W. Hollar f.

1 Palace where the Emperours Throone is. 2 The two Ambassadors, 3 Ambassador from the G

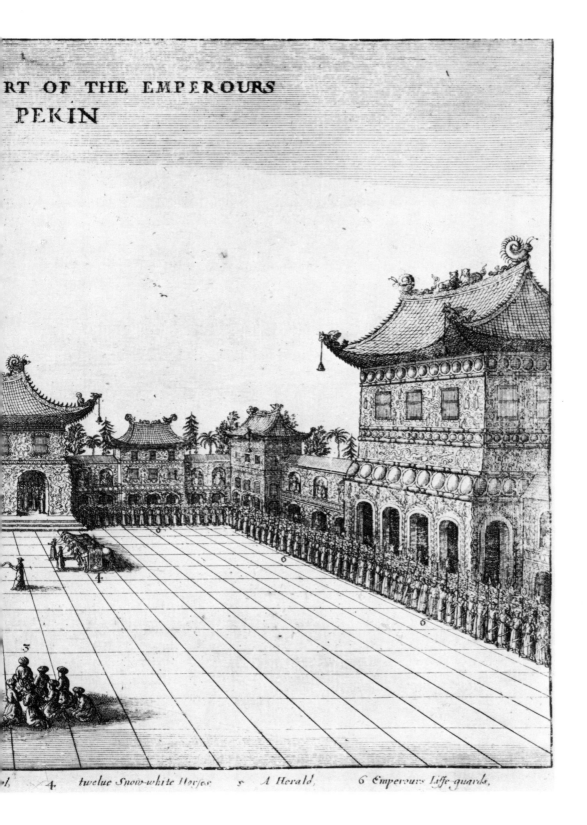

4. twelue Snow-white Horfes   5 A Herald,   6 Emperours liffe guards,

travelling coffin to escape detection. But it was of little use. For a brief space they ministered to the Christian Chinese, but as they made almost no new converts and were themselves gradually evicted, the movement petered out. In Tibet the Jesuits were formally withdrawn by Rome and their mission handed over to the Capuchins; while in Mogor the last of the Jesuit missionaries had already begun their retreat back to the bridgehead at Goa.

In the last analysis and despite all the years of effort, none of the three missions could have been counted an overwhelming success. In Mogor most of the Christians were foreigners; in Tibet they had seldom won more than ten converts a year; and although in China it was estimated that there were once as many as 160,000 converts, it was an insignificant proportion of the country's vast population. St Francis Xavier had foreseen precisely this difficulty long before, when he recommended that the Society should avoid contesting the established religions of Asia and concentrate instead on converting pagan tribes. But if they had not attempted the wider mission, the Jesuits would never have achieved so much as scientists, travellers, philosophers, and humanists in all the Eastern countries they had visited. The knowledge they gathered of the East was a superb bequest to Europe. As one Chinese mandarin put it when soothing Jesuits' doubts about casting cannon, it was a question of the needle and thread. The tailor used his needle as a means to an end, to draw the thread through the cloth; and once the work was done, the garment remained and the needle was put aside. But for the Jesuits in the Orient, the garment of Christianity they had sought to create was never completed. It was the bright sharp needle of their intellectual and personal achievement which remained.

THE FAKIRS AND PEDLARS

IN 1615 THERE WALKED INTO INDIA with the baggage-train of a large Persian caravan an English eccentric whose behaviour matched any performance of the native fakirs. He was Thomas Coryat, and he had publicly set out to travel on foot from his home in Somerset to the river Ganges. Starting with a capital of just £3, he had already visited Constantinople, spent several days sightseeing in Jerusalem, and his wrists were tattooed with Crusaders' crosses as a memento of the Holy Land. Robbed in Turkey by a soldier and swindled in Armenia by a merchant, he still boasted that his travelling costs had not exceeded twopence a day, and in a letter to his friends in London he announced that like Ulysses he intended spending a full seven years on his travels before returning home. As for his physical condition, he assured them, 'I do enjoy at this time as pancratical and athletical health as ever I did in my life; and so have done ever since I came out of England, saving for three days in Constantinople where I had an ague.' His legs in particular, he reported, were in fine working trim.

Thomas Coryat was an important as well as an entertaining wanderer. He was a friend of Ben Jonson and a fellow member of the Mermaid Club, whose tavern wits and poetasters met regularly to discuss affairs of the day. Among them Coryat with his Winchester and Oxford education was inclined to quote the classics at the slightest opportunity and had such a reputation for bombast that he became a butt for the club's jokes. Their ridicule, though, was mixed with affection, for when Coryat came back from a preliminary walking tour round Europe and wrote a book about it under the characteristically vaunting title of *Coryat's Crudities, hastily gobbled up in five months' travels*, his Mermaid friends banded together to contribute humorous introductory verses to help the sales. Always impossible to subdue, Coryat bounced back happily, dubbed himself 'the Gallo-Belgic Legstretcher' and made a special pilgrimage to his father's church at Odcombe in Somerset where he hung up his walking shoes for all to see and gave a public speech claiming that he had worn the single pair for the entire two thousand miles of his European hike. Now, two years later and bursting with curiosity, he was all set to stride down the Imperial Highway from Lahore to Delhi in order to satisfy three whimsical ambitions: he wanted to stand on the banks of the Ganges; to see the Great Mogul in person; and to ride upon an elephant.

Such self-confessed curiosity was another reason why Tom Coryat was important to the Oriental Adventure. In his own bizarre way he represented a new phase – the beginnings of a genuine tourist interest in the East. Of course there had been travellers before him who had wanted to see the Orient for its own sake, but behind Coryat would come a troop of tourists which eventually reached such impressive proportions that it affected the

West's entire view of the East. Partly these tourists began to arrive because
the overland route via Persia was now easier and safer than it had been for
centuries since the days of Marco Polo; and partly, too, because a new
spirit of inquiry was encouraging Europeans to learn from experience of
the East. Coryat was a herald of the new advance. He was not only pioneering
the way on his twopence-a-day budget, but he was writing a book about it
for others to enjoy and follow. His single most important item of luggage
was a large sheaf of notes, and he had already left substantial wads of his
travel diary at Aleppo and Isfahan, enough writing, as Sir Thomas Roe, the
English Ambassador to the Mogul, unkindly put it, 'to make any stationer an
alderman that shall but serve the printer with paper'. Finally, and possibly
even more important, Coryat was showing his contempories that it was now
conceivable for an individual to visit the Orient on his own initiative. No
longer was it necessary to go there as a member of some official embassy,
with a trade venture, or attached to a military expedition. In short, the day
of the private tourist to the Orient had arrived.

The main attraction was, of course, the Great Mogul himself, Emperor
Jahangir. In an age when Europe was becoming obsessed with the personal
magnificence of its own kings, the Great Mogul made their own monarchs
look very humdrum. Rumours circulated about the Mogul's extravagant
wealth, his habit of being weighed every year in bullion, his stupendous
hoard of gems, and his exotic harem. An indefatigable sightseer like Coryat
was so determined to see this resplendent figure that on his way to India he
had been memorizing a speech in Persian which he intended to deliver in
person to the Mogul at the earliest opportunity. Finding Emperor Jahangir
at his capital of Ajmer, Coryat learned that the Mogul regularly held public
audience from a balcony in the palace. So the bumptious English tourist
slipped down to the palace in disguise, mingled with the petitioners, and
judging his moment, suddenly stepped forward and launched into his carefully prepared eulogy, beginning with the words, 'Lord Protector of the World,
all hail to you. I am a poor traveller and world seer which am come hither
from a far country, namely England, which ancient historians have thought
to have situated in the farthest bounds of the west, and is Queen of all the
islands in the world.' To his delight, Jahangir not only heard him out but
afterwards chatted affably with the Englishman and threw down a hundred
rupees as a tip which fell into a sheet specially hung beneath the Mogul's
balcony. Scooping up the cash gleefully, Coryat estimated that it would
keep him on his peregrinations for several more months.

Coryat was a tourist of the restless variety, unable to relax in any one
place for any length of time, 'a sort of perpetual motion', as Ambassador
Roe's parson put it. Coryat preferred his own title of a 'propatetic' or 'walker-
forward', arguing that this was his true occupation as opposed to one who
was merely a peripatetic or 'a walker-about'. In Ajmer he was constantly
scurrying from one tourist sight to another. He watched the emperor weighed
in gold, and he went to gape at the animals in the Mogul's zoo, particularly
the rhinoceros which Coryat misunderstood to be a unicorn. And twice a
week he faithfully attended the royal elephant fights when the maddened
animals battered away at one another in the lists 'like two little mountains',
as he reported to his Mermaid correspondents, 'and were they not parted in

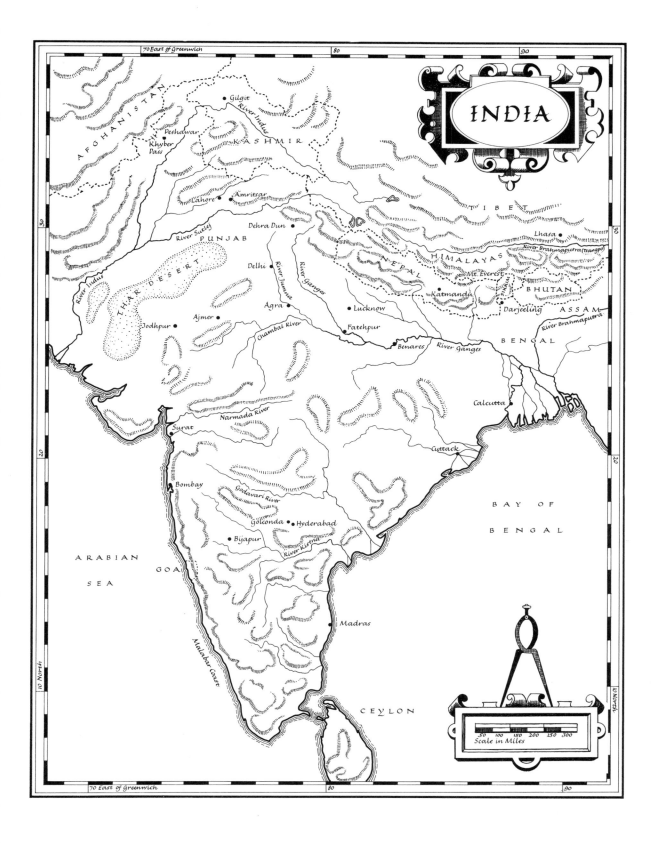

98

the midst of their fighting by certain fireworks, they would exceedingly gore and cruentate one another by their murdering teeth'. He even turned out in the muggy warmth of the mid-August rains to stand in the street and watch the state arrival of an embassy from the King of Bijapur with its string of thirty-one splendid elephants all hung about with gold chains, gold ornaments on their foreheads, and 'furniture for their buttocks in pure gold'. From Ajmer he went on to Agra, again by foot, to visit the tomb of Akbar, and trudged forward to his final goal, the Ganges. There at the holy city of Hardwar he fulfilled his ambition of standing on the banks of the river, and witnessed the extraordinary spectacle of hundreds of thousands of pilgrims immersing themselves in its sacred waters during a religious festival.

But Coryat was not just a passive sightseer. He was a celebrity in his own right. Within India the European community of merchants, diplomats, and traders scattered across the continent heard about him and exchanged gossip about this 'painful gentleman', as one of them aptly called him. Ambassador Roe offered him hospitality and enjoyed chatting with him about his experiences, and gave him money to cover his expenses. In his own unique way Coryat repaid the gift by silencing a native washerwoman who had been plaguing Roe's household with her constant scolding and railing from sunrise to sunset. Coryat had learned enough colloquial Hindi to be able to outshout her gabble by eight o'clock in a single morning's attack. Nor was Coryat forgotten in England where King James I had asked after him, and when told that the eccentric walker had last been reported heading east, His Royal Highness snorted derisively, 'What! Is that fool still living?', a royal gibe which was not so wide of the mark, as Coryat's long walk was almost ended.

Opposite An elephant contest. In the foreground is the attendant armed with a torch to separate the enraged animals after each bout

Coryat's constitution was plainly unable to withstand the prolonged punishment he was giving it, and despite his boasts of perfect health he was beginning to show signs of exhaustion. In Ajmer he suffered from recurrent fevers and dizziness, and once nearly fainted in the presence of Ambassador Roe, and had to cling to a tent-pole to stop himself falling down. When he obstinately set off to walk down to the Indian coast, intending to find a ship to take him on to Africa for a tramp to meet Prester John, the Negus of Ethiopia, he was in gloomy spirits and had a foreboding of his own death. The last Europeans to see him alive were some merchants residing in Surat, into whose home he burst boisterously shouting, 'Sack, sack! Is there such a thing as sack? I pray give me some sack!' These were his last reported words, and a few days later he was found dead of dysentery. The Europeans of Surat arranged for him to be buried a short distance outside the city gates with two simple gravestones right beside the Indian highway which had been the last road the Legstretcher had walked. And in England, where the last five letters of his Indian travels were published for all to read, a kind-hearted editor generously embellished the text with a picture of a jubilant Coryat riding, as he had always wished, on an elephant.

Of course, tourists in Mogul India were not necessarily obliged to travel as rough as Coryat with his slender purse, though only a few would have claimed that the local travel facilities were luxurious. The Moguls tried hard to improve communications within their domains and to make the roads safe, but Indian travel never achieved the ease or facility of such journeys

made, say, in China at the same time. On the whole the Indian roads were
fairly good, and the Imperial Highway between Lahore and Agra was first
class. Coryat reported glowingly on its smoothness, its chain of water-tanks
conveniently placed for thirsty travellers, and the shade trees planted to
give protection to the passers-by. But elsewhere the condition and safety of
the highway depended very much on the enthusiasm and efficiency of the
local governor or noble who held his land grant direct from the Mogul. The
more energetic ones hunted down local brigands, and displayed their severed
heads in niches in roadside cairns like grisly beehives. But in rough country
it was difficult to suppress the swarms of highwaymen who worked in large
gangs and frequently with women accomplices. Their well-rehearsed trick
was to station a woman on the roadway with her clothes torn and her face
scratched and bleeding, to intercept gullible travellers with the story that
she and her family had just been robbed by footpads and that her children
lay injured in the bushes. Rushing to her help, the travellers would fall into
a genuine ambush. Even perfectly legitimate encounters could prove to be
costly or dangerous. The boatmen who manned the river ferries were
notorious cheats, who deliberately hid their boats when a traveller was seen
approaching, and then demanded exorbitant fees for going to the trouble of
finding their vessels and ferrying him across the stream. To salt the wound,
they then insisted on testing every single coin of their payment by throwing
it into a fire to see if it was counterfeit metal. In theory there was no counterfeit coinage in the Mogul's domain because the law demanded that any man
given a bad coin should hand it back to the donor. He in turn was to hand it
back to the man from whom he had originally received it, and so on back
down the line until it reached the counterfeiter himself who would be
arrested by the police, and a finger or hand chopped off by the public
executioner.

Itinerant dervishes were another peculiarly Indian travel hazard. They
could be found almost anywhere, wandering along the roads with their local
saint or master, and as often as not were a ferocious-looking band of men
armed with long steel swords and with war quoits in their hair. They took
offence very readily, particularly when they imagined any insult to their
master, and were liable to attack without warning, hacking about with their
great swords in half-crazed fervour and oblivious either to apology or to the
risk of injury to themselves. Less dangerous but more frustrating were the
immense convoys of the *banjaras* or hauliers, whose columns of slow-
moving bullock-carts could block the entire width of the highway for two or
three days at a time as they dawdled past with their creaking, overloaded
high-wheeled wagons. The *banjaras* were the official carriers of the empire,
licensed by the Mogul himself, and divided into specific clans, each responsible for the transport of a particular commodity, whether corn or rice
or salt. Their convoys were gigantic assemblages, more like mobile town-
ships, with as many as ten thousand bullocks pulling carts, and every over-
burdened vehicle was escorted by its squad of 'soldiers', whose task was to
hang on to the tail-ropes which prevented the loads from toppling over as the
carts bumped across the ruts. In charge of every convoy was its *banjara*
headman, often a man of considerable wealth who could be recognized by
the double chain of pearls hanging round his neck; while the *banjara* women

Loe heere the wooden Image of our wits;
Borne, in first trauaile, on the backs of Nits;
But now on Elephants, &c:
O, what will he ride, when his yeares expire?
The world must ride him; or he all will tire.

101

II.ᵉ Partie fol. 376

103

'Modes of Transporting
Women in India', a drawing
from the journal of a
seventeenth-century
traveller in Asia, Peter Mundy

were magnificent, naked from the waist up, and their skins beautifully tattooed with the juices of roots so that they looked like living coloured and flowered fabric. When two *banjara* convoys met head on, an ugly confrontation usually developed. Each headman would refuse to pull aside and relinquish the road, and so violent fights broke out between the 'soldiers', lasting until one or other party had been physically forced into the ditch.

By sundown a wise traveller made sure that he had reached one of the large caravanserais which the Mogul provided at intervals along the main roads. These caravanserais were sizeable compounds with enough space in them for the visitor to tether his beasts, a cluster of victuallers' shops and eating-places to supply him, and rooms for rent. But they were far from restful. 'In these serais', observed one European visitor wearily, 'travellers are pestered by dealers who offer for sale different kinds of cloth, not only white but coloured, also by musicians, dancing boys, women dancers, barbers, tailors, washerwomen, farriers with horse shoes, endless cheating physicians, and many sellers of grass and straw for the horses.' The compound gates were closed at dusk and no one was allowed to enter or leave. But organized gangs of thieves operated inside the caravanserais, and the only precaution taken against them was that before the gates were opened in the morning, the keeper of the caravanserai called upon every traveller to take an inventory of his possessions. If anything was missing, the gates stayed shut – at least in theory – until the missing items had been found and the thief caught, the punishment being a summary hanging opposite the main gate. In practice, however, the thieves threw their booty over the wall at night to their accomplices waiting on the other side.

The best precaution a prudent tourist might take before travelling to India was to read a book by Jean-Baptiste Tavernier describing no less than five trips which the author had made successfully between Europe and the kingdom of the Mogul. Moreover Tavernier was someone who had every reason to look after his purse and his safety, for he was a gem dealer and habitually carried with him a stock of pearls and precious stones, sometimes valued at more than £30,000. It was instructive that Tavernier never lost any large sum to the Indians, but suffered his worst setback when he was swindled by Dutch East India merchants who reneged on some bills of credit.

Like Coryat before him, Tavernier was smitten by a straightforward love of travel. 'I am able to say that I came into the world with a desire to travel', was how he bluntly put it, and his wanderlust led him into the ambitious venture of carrying gems into Asia to sell to Oriental princes. The first journey took him only as far as Persia, where he did business with the shah and brought back turquoise at such a handsome profit that he was able to invest in gems of good quality and set out again on his second journey, this time to see the Great Mogul himself. This trip and those which followed were so regular and so successful that Tavernier quickly built up a constant clientele of Indian grandees whom he contacted on every visit, offering them jewels which he had collected on his travels and sometimes acting as their agent and buying *objets d'art* for them when he was in Europe. When he finally retired from business in his sixties, Tavernier had earned such a name for himself as an Oriental wanderer that Louis XIV summoned him to court and raised him to the lesser nobility. Characteristically Tavernier took the opportunity to sell the Sun King a collection of diamonds and turned his social elevation into a handsome cash profit.

Inevitably, Tavernier did much to confirm the opulent image of India which men like Coryat had already established. Voltaire complained that Tavernier wrote of merchandise in place of philosophy; but in fact the royal jeweller had a straightforward and easy-going approach which won him a large readership and turned his book into English, German, and Italian translations. He wrote about exactly those sort of details which interested the ordinary reader, and was not too aloof to marvel at the tricks of the Indian jugglers and tumblers, the peculiar behaviour of Indian ascetics on their beds of nails, or claim that the capital of Golconda had twenty thousand prostitutes, each of them with a lighted candle at her door when she was ready for business. And it was left to Gibbon to praise Tavernier as 'that wandering jeweller, who had read nothing, but had seen so much and so well'.

Above all, it was Tavernier's trade in precious stones which influenced his description of India and in turn coloured his readers' impression of the Great Mogul and his court. Tavernier loved gems. He was not just interested in buying and selling them; he was a genuine connoisseur. Sometimes, if he could not buy a particular jewel which interested him, he would have a model of it made in lead so that he could enjoy its shape and technical quality; and whenever he was allowed, he made sketches and plans of the more remarkable jewels which he saw during his travels. As a gem dealer of international repute, Tavernier was permitted insights into a side of Mogul India which very few natives, let alone foreigners, had ever been privileged to witness. He was, for example, specially invited to be a guest at the ceremony of weighing Emperor Aurangzeb on his birthday. Two months had been spent in preparing for the ceremony, and on the occasion the Mogul received more than £2,000,000 worth of presents in jewels, elephants, horses, carpets, and brocades from his nobility. The several courtyards of the great palace had been covered with huge marquees of velvet, held up by poles as thick as ships' masts, thirty-five to forty feet high and all plated in gold. Teams of nautch-girls danced and sang on special stages; thirty of the emperor's horses stood in line with jewelled bridles and large gems dangling from their necks; and the emperor's son was on parade, solemnly mounted on an exquisite little pony to match his size. Seven of the finest imperial war elephants were led in to Aurangzeb's presence, and one by one bowed down to the Mogul and trumpeted their congratulations.

Amid all this splendour Tavernier only had eyes for the Mogul's throne, set out in public view in the main reception-room. It was a truly fantastic sight. More a bed than a throne, it blazed with the gems which encrusted every surface. At a guess Tavernier estimated that it measured about six feet by four, and every bar of its frame was studded with diamonds, rubies, and emeralds. From where he stood, Tavernier counted no less than 108 balas rubies, all of them cabuchons, and the smallest one not less than a hundred carats. The four posts which held the throne's canopy over the Mogul's head were looped round with string upon string of pearls; and the inside of the canopy itself was sewn with a brilliant spangle of diamonds and pearls. Above it all spread the famous jewelled peacock, its tail made of sapphires, and for its breast a single enormous ruby from which dangled a fifty carat pearl. It was a throne which represented generations of looting, buying, and gem-collecting by the Mogul and his forebears, every one of them with a passion for precious stones which matched Tavernier's professional enthusiasm.

The Frenchman's greatest privilege, though, was a more private affair. Three or four days before the grand celebration of the Mogul's birthday a message reached Tavernier from the palace inviting him to inspect Aurangzeb's personal collection of gems, most of which were not seen by outsiders as they were normally worn by the women in the privacy of the *zenana*. Arriving at the palace, Tavernier was taken to a small chamber leading off the main reception-hall, and there he found the keeper of the crown jewels waiting for him. At a signal four eunuchs carried in two large gold-laquered wooden trays, each covered by a sheet of brocaded velvet. These covers were removed, and three clerks each counted and made separate inventories of all the jewels on the trays, before Tavernier was allowed to handle them. Spread before him was a dazzling assortment of individual diamonds, all of the finest water, and a vast pile of pearls, emeralds, and rubies, each of them pierced so that they could be worn casually as necklaces by the Mogul, his wives, and mistresses. But dominating the display Tavernier saw the Koh-i-noor diamond itself, the 'Mountain of Light' which as a professional dealer he had heard about ever since he had come to India. When discovered, the Koh-i-noor had weighed an incredible 793 carats in its uncut state, though by the time Tavernier was allowed to pick it up and admire it, it had already been reduced to 279 carats due to bad cutting by an itinerant Venetian diamond-cutter, whom the Mogul had fined ten thousand rupees for his incompetence. Even so, as Tavernier indicated, it was a jewel fit for an emperor.

It would have been extremely difficult for Tavernier under the circumstances to have avoided giving a lopsided view of Mogul India. The rich nobles he visited, the palaces they lived in, and the social and political structure of contemporary India presented a magnificent façade. The Mogul and his emirs stood at the top of a pyramid devoted almost exclusively to their personal luxury. In theory the entire wealth of Hindustan belonged to

Tavernier in old age, a portrait celebrating his Oriental Adventure

the Great Mogul in person, and he parcelled it out to his emirs as he saw fit, and then only for their lifetimes. In return they were expected to pay an astonishing quantity of rent and tribute. Tavernier once met a convoy of bullock-carts plodding up from the province of Bengal, bringing the stunning total of four and a half million rupees of tribute from its governor. Most of this revenue was spent on warfare or ostentation. Between his first and last visits to India, Tavernier saw the Taj Mahal begun and ended, a twenty-two-year construction project which occupied a labour force of twenty thousand men and, because there was not enough wood, the builders made their scaffolding from a stupendous quantity of bricks, an extravagance which it was estimated finally doubled the cost of the work.

In his privileged position as a court jeweller, Tavernier also had permission from the Mogul to enter or leave the palace whenever he wished, even when the Grand Council was in session and the palace was officially closed. So he saw for himself the constant outflow of money on all the trappings of imperial splendour – the coming and going of nobles riding through the main gate on their elephants and escorted by soldiers in silk uniforms; the exquisite complex of ornamental watercourses and gardens which graced the palace courtyards; the grand audience-hall with its thirty-two marble columns, musicians' gallery, and a diamond-covered couch for the emperor to recline on as he listened to his ministers; the huge imperial stables with their remarkable stud of horses, each animal hand-fed on balls of flour and butter by grooms, protected by mosquito screens of bamboo and flowered silk, and standing by day on priceless carpets spread on the floor of each stall. The opulence of the Great Mogul seemed to have no limit unless it was physical impossibility. Shah Jehan dreamed up the fantastic notion of decorating one complete gallery of his palace with a trellis of artificial vines made of precious stones. His extravagant idea was that the grapes on the vines should imitate nature, with emeralds used for those grapes which were not yet ripe, and rubies for those ready to be plucked. He drew the sketch for this project, and one or two wreaths were actually completed before he was obliged to admit that there were not enough gems available in all the world to complete this preposterous design. In such surroundings and with such patrons, it was difficult for Tavernier to pay much heed to the squalor and poverty of the ordinary Indian populace whose efforts supported this peak of extravagance.

Yet this enthusiasm for gem-hunting also took Tavernier into rural India. Like Coryat's ambition to see the Ganges, Tavernier's interest in precious stones made him a genuine tourist as well as a merchant, and led him into corners scarcely visited before by Europeans. Diamonds, above all else, fascinated him, and as India was the world's major producer of diamonds, he was determined to visit all the main areas of diamond production. 'The diamond', he wrote,

is the most precious of all stones, and it is the article of trade to which I am most devoted. In order to acquire knowledge of it, I resolved to visit all the mines, and one of the two rivers where diamonds were found; and as the fear of dangers has never restrained me in any of my journeys; the terrible picture that was drawn of these mines, situated in barbarous

The Indian jewel trade involved a lively mixture of skill, artistry, luck, hard bargaining and deceit

countries to which one could not travel except by the most dangerous routes, served neither to terrify me nor to turn me from my intention.

In the end his quest took him all the way from Chota Nagpur on the borders of Bengal right down into peninsular India and the diamond-mines of Golconda. Usually he found that the diggings were no more than two hundred paces in circumference, and within this small area as many as fifty to a hundred hired miners clad only in breech cloths scrabbled eagerly in the soil with iron hooks, watched by suspicious overseers to see if anyone was hiding the stones in his clothing. Any diamonds which were found, had to be handed over to the merchant who leased the diggings, and he in turn paid a miserly reward of cloth to the finder. Then the rough stones were passed to the Indian diamond-cutters, men whose skill in Tavernier's opinion was so extraordinary that it was useless for a European cutter to hope to improve on their performance. Using simple steel cutting wheels, on which a small boy steadily poured a mixture of oil and diamond-dust, the Indian cutters made the best of any stone and knew all the ruses of their profession. They hid bad flaws behind a confusing myriad of facets, and heated up stones with disfiguring red spots until the blemishes turned black. The diamond-cutters and the diamond-buyers worked together as a cartel, with even their children involved. Under the largest tree in the town square Tavernier would often find a circle of diamond-dealers' children aged between ten and sixteen, all patiently waiting to conduct business. Their fathers had equipped them with

sets of diamond scales and a small amount of cash; and their daily task was to buy small loose stones so that their parents could assemble and match larger parcels of diamonds. Each evening the children would return to their homes where they would sell their stones at a profit to their parents, and so combine their professional education with the earning of their own pocket-money. Against such dedicated merchants Tavernier admitted there was little chance of successful trading unless circumstances were unusual. Just once, in a diamond village, his commercial interest was aroused when a half-naked and destitute-looking Indian shyly came up to him with some small, poor-quality ruby rings for sale. Sensing that the man's appearance was deliberately misleading, Tavernier treated him civilly and purchased one of the rings for more than it was worth. His intuition was rewarded: when his Muslim companions were called away to their prayers, the Indian slipped back into Tavernier's hut and unwinding his hair, pulled out a superb ruby which Tavernier was able to purchase direct, bypassing the local cartel.

Making a profit in the Orient as a foreigner, Tavernier advised his readers, was largely a matter of knowing the market and understanding the tricks of the trade and not being caught out by them. He himself made enough money in the jewel business – mostly by concentrating on pearls for which the Indian princes had an almost insatiable appetite – to splash out, on his retirement, forty-three thousand écus to buy a Swiss castle and the title of baron which went with it. But he warned his reader that it had not been an

Opposite *An Indian view of a
European visitor in the
seventeenth century*

easy road. The first obstacle was always the cunning of the Indian *shroffs*, the money changers. They were to be found in every village, conducting all manner of business and 'all the jews who occupy themselves with money and exchange in the empire of the Grand Seigneur [Turkey] pass for being very sharp; but in India they would scarcely be apprentice to these changers'. The Indian *shroffs* could keep in their heads all the multiplying and varying combinations of exchange rates between the different currencies circulating in India. Day to day they knew the fluctuating values of mohurs, rupees, Persian abbasis, German rix dollars, Spanish and Mexican reals, copper coins, cowrie shells, and even the tiny bitter almonds which in some areas were used as small change. The Mogul's mint rupees were the only officially recognized coinage of the empire, but their value varied from one issue to the next, and there was so much smuggling – European traders resorted to the trick of carrying gold coins hidden under their wigs – that all manner of foreign currencies could be met with. As an illustration of the *shroffs'* thrift Tavernier explained how they tested every single coin with a touchstone before they would accept it, and after every test rubbed their touchstone on a ball of wax to pick off the tiniest filings. After several years of such work they would then melt the wax ball and retrieve the gold for themselves.

Having changed his money, the hopeful merchant from Europe still had to be on constant guard. If buying musk, he had to be sure that he was not cheated with artificial musk sacs made of animal gut filled with treated blood. Buying cloth, he should carefully examine every bale because the clothiers slipped short or poor-quality piece-goods into their larger consignments. And in the indigo trade it was a common trick to weight the balls of indigo with sand or let them sit out on wet ground so that they absorbed the moisture and became heavier. Nor were princely clients any more likely to be honest towards the foreigner. Tavernier's sales technique was merely to offer to every prince he visited his entire stock of gems, reserving only those jewels which had been specially ordered by another customer. The understanding was that the prince would make an offer to buy those gems which took his fancy, and the price was based partly on a cash sum and partly on a complicated system of 'presents' between the jeweller and his customer, which left Tavernier his profit. But even his most loyal customers sometimes tried to cheat him. The governor of Bengal, the aptly named Shaista Khan, whom Tavernier considered 'the cleverest man in the kingdom', and his best regular client, was very pro-European, yet always gave him the most trouble. On one large sale the khan tried to pay Tavernier in a debased issue of Mogul rupees, and when Tavernier protested, he was amused that Shaista Khan feigned astonishment and blamed his treasurer for the mistake, promising to have the man flogged for such carelessness. After much haggling the price was finally adjusted when Shaista Khan agreed to buy an additional pearl which he and Tavernier both knew was overvalued by two thousand rupees. Yet even then, the prince could not resist trying to trim the Frenchman. He gave him as a parting gift an official *khilat* or presentation dress of gold brocade with a fire-coloured turban to match, a basket containing six apples brought all the way from Kashmir, a melon from Persia, and a horse. The *khilat* Tavernier accepted gratefully, and the fruit he gave to the wife of a Dutch mercenary captain with whom he had

been staying; but the look of the horse warned him off. So he asked a young man to try it out. The horse promptly kicked off its rider, nearly killing him, and leaped clear over a small hut or hovel in the exercise-yard. Straightfaced, Tavernier returned the animal to the khan and requested something less exciting which would be more suitable to a man of his age. Unabashed, Shaista Khan gave him a twenty-eight-year-old nag, which he had inherited from his own father.

As far as travelling in India was concerned, Tavernier showed that a well-lined purse could eliminate most of the hardships encountered by the masochistic Legstretcher. While Coryat had represented the most humble level of foreign traveller, Tavernier journeyed not so much as a merchant, but as a grand gentleman. He like to ride either in a palanquin carried by two relays of half a dozen bearers and with an attendant holding a parasol over his head; or in a light travelling cart, curtained and cushioned, and drawn by high-paced trotting bullocks which went at a surprisingly fast turn of speed. Generally he hired an escort of eight or ten watchmen, whom he armed with muskets he brought with him, and he always sent advance notice of his arrival to his princely clients. Nor did he travel empty-handed. He discovered that local officials could usually be sweetened with gifts of wine or spirits, and for his most important customers he always brought special presents. To the Mogul he gave an extravagantly decorated shield, fancifully worked with pictures of classical heroes, and a battle-mace made with solid crystal. And it was the final compliment to his great tact and large store of patience that when he finally retired from trade, both the Mogul and Shaista Khan were complaining that Tavernier's prices had risen almost beyond their means, but they still kept buying from him.

Opposite *European artillery experts and mercenaries help Shah Jehan's forces capture the Portuguese-held fort of Hugli in 1632: European technician v. European technician*

Tavernier was not the only jeweller who had realized that the Indian potentates made a well-stocked covert in which to hunt for custom. And he was by no means the only European jewel dealer to try his luck in India. Besides the Venetian cutter who split the Koh-i-noor so badly, several other European gem dealers were circulating within the Indian empire. One of them was hired to decorate the Mogul's palace with silver leaf but was poisoned by his rivals before the project got under way; and another, Jean Chardin, combined Tavernier's techniques in Persia and India so successfully that he finished up as court jeweller to Charles II in England and merited a tomb in Westminster Abbey.

But the Mogul and his wealthy emirs were not merely lavish spenders, they were also open-handed patrons and generous employers, and many of the shoal of enterprising foreigners who came to India arrived not on sales trips but intent on entering Indian service and passing their lives attending upon this luxury. Some spent as many as thirty or forty years as full-time employees of native princes, acquiring a deeper knowledge about the country than casual visitors like Tavernier or Coryat, and although most of them only enjoyed their Eastern experience for its own sake, a handful reported back to Europe about their Oriental experiences. And once again, their reports helped to reinforce the already highly coloured picture painted by the earlier travellers.

This enthusiasm was due to the fact that usually it was only the successful adventurers who reported back; but partly, too, it was because life for a skilled European selling his labour in India was very comfortable. The over-whelming majority of Europeans resident in India were employed as technical experts, a large number being mercenary soldiers who specialized in artillery. By the time of Emperor Jahangir virtually the whole of the Mogul's artillery force was being run by European gunners, and they held a very privileged position. They were not expected to arrange the transport of their guns, nor even to maintain them, nor even to load, elevate, or aim them. Their sole responsibility was actually to fire the guns in battle, and for this brief moment of action the foreign gunners were paid excellent wages, given officer's rank, and treated with special consideration by the Mogul himself. Even Emperor Aurangzeb, a strictly orthodox Muslim, gave orders that in teetotal Delhi a special park should be set aside where his European soldiers could make and buy liquor and get drunk. What was true of the imperial army was even more noticeable among the armies raised by pro-vincial governors and by lesser Indian princes. Their artillery-trains were almost invariably commanded by European mercenaries; European gunners garrisoned their key fortresses; and when it came to paying his troops, a native commander took care that the first share went to his foreign mercenaries to keep them loyal before a rival hired them. In return the mercenaries were quite prepared to serve the highest bidder and showed far more interest in enjoying India's delights than in military zeal. 'Without slandering anyone', wrote one observer sourly, 'I can say with truth that the Christians who serve in the artillery of the Moguls, retained of Christianity nothing but the mere name, were worse than the Mahomedans and the Hindus, were devoid of fear of God, had ten or twelve wives, were continually drunk, had no occupation but gambling, and were eager to cheat whomsoever they could.'

The man who penned those bitter words was a well-qualified judge, for he had himself been a mercenary. A Venetian adventurer named Niccolao Manucci, he had first-hand experience of fifty-four years in India in the service of royalty with much of the time in the artillery, and his life was so packed with fantastic escapades that his contemporaries sometimes found it hard to believe that his story was true.

Originally Manucci had gone to India by accident. At the age of fourteen he had run away from his home in Venice and hidden aboard a ship bound for Smyrna. Feeling seasick, he was obliged to appear on deck and was taken to see the captain. By an extraordinary stroke of luck there was also on board another fugitive: the romantic, one-armed Lord Bellemont, a Royalist who was acting as Charles II's secret envoy to the Mogul and was in fear of arrest or assassination by Cromwellian agents. Bellemont was kind to Manucci and hired the boy as his servant, taking him right across Persia and into India. But on the way from Agra to meet the Mogul at Delhi, Bellemont was struck down by fever and dysentery, and died suddenly. He actually expired while Manucci was going to fetch a cup of water he had asked for. Within seven hours his corpse was so blistered and stinking that it had to be buried in the bank of a reservoir, and very soon after that all the ambassador's other servants ran away, leaving Manucci stranded. To make matters worse, two English gunners, hearing about the ambassador's death, falsely claimed to be Bellemont's relatives in order to get their hands on the dead man's possessions. These two rogues bundled Manucci out of the way and carried off their spoils to Delhi.

Left to his own devices, Manucci also went to Delhi where he found his way into a public audience given by Prince Dara, the eldest son of the reigning Mogul, Shah Jehan. Like Coryat, Manucci had chosen to dress up in Eastern finery, and was wearing a red velvet turban and a gold flowered cummerbund. This costume and his knowledge of the correct way of making a salaam attracted Dara's attention, and Manucci was interviewed, told his tale, and taken to meet Shah Jehan himself. He made such a good impression that the Mogul ordered the arrest of the two English gunners and the return of all Manucci's belongings. Prince Dara gave him a job as an artilleryman in his forces at a salary of eighty rupees a month plus the gift of a horse and a suit of clothes.

Manucci, however, was a cut above his fellow gunners, both in intelligence and ambition. One of his first schemes was to set up an illicit still in the house of a friend, where he illegally brewed liquor to sell to the Indians. Among his customers was one of Shah Jehan's daughters, who was so alcoholic that she had to hide her daily drink in a concoction of rosewater and aromatic herbs, and frequently finished the evening in such a stupor that she had to be carried off to bed by her handmaidens.

Unfortunately the Venetian's flourishing business was ruined by the violent war of succession which broke out soon afterwards between Shah Jehan's sons, when it became evident that their father was ailing. The Mogul's sons mobilized their private armies, and Manucci marched out with Dara's artillery in time to find himself an eyewitness at the decisive battle of Samugarh. It was his education in the unglamorous reality of Oriental warfare. The two massive armies sparred unenthusiastically with one another, while their generals got down to the serious matter of bribing the opposition. The night before the battle Manucci rode out to a near-by hillside and saw a steady trickle of deserters slipping away from Dara's camp to cross over and join the enemy forces. The following day the leviathan armies closed with one another but they were so huge and cumbersome that they took hours to manoeuvre, and even then only their front ranks actually encountered, while the hordes of followers-on milled around in the back ranks, waving their swords and shouting bloodthirsty slogans at the tops of their voices, taking care to come nowhere near the fight. The confusion was made worse when Dara's hangers-on began plundering their own baggage-train while the battle was still in progress; and the prince's vaunted gunners soon proved useless. They banged off their cannon while the enemy was still out of range, and found it impossible to re-site the artillery properly as the guns had been chained together to form a solid battle-line. The moment Dara's defeat looked inevitable, Manucci decided to save his own skin and galloped back to his house in Delhi, his horse falling dead at his doorstep, only to find the city virtually deserted by its panic-stricken citizens. Trying to get clear, he was turned back by one of Aurangzeb's cavalry patrols who were already sealing off the capital, and had to disguise himself as a native beggar and slip out of the city in the train of a Mogul army setting out to pursue Dara. Pushing on ahead of the troops, Manucci learned another disastrous effect of any collapse in imperial authority. Bandits and mutinous

soldiers were pillaging the countryside, and he was lucky to escape with his life. The driver of his ox-cart was delayed in the bushes by a bad attack of diarrhoea, and Manucci was separated from his travelling companions. A few miles down the road he found their mutilated bodies, butchered by one of the many bands of cut-throats who were taking advantage of the chaos.

When he at last caught up with Dara again, Manucci was promoted to captain in his artillery and given a bounty of five hundred rupees for his supposed loyalty. But the prince's cause was hopeless and the Venetian spent most of his time trying to evade Aurangzeb's troops who were remorselessly hunting down Dara and his supporters. For a time he looked after the cannon in a fortress covering Dara's retreat, and when that strongpoint fell to the enemy, he was again on the run. He escaped one dragnet by charging at his pursuers waving his sword and bursting through their line, and on another occasion fled from Aurangzeb's police clad only in his underdrawers. Chased, robbed, and dispirited, it was to his credit that even after Dara was captured, Manucci refused to enter Aurangzeb's service like the rest of his companions who happily switched to the new Mogul's army at four rupees a day.

Instead, Manucci preferred to change his profession. A runaway Dutch doctor, who had killed a man in Goa, arrived in Agra where Manucci, who now spoke fluent Hindi as well as Persian, served as his interpreter for a time and helped him establish a medical practice among the city's rich inhabitants. Quickly picking up enough medical knowledge to set up as a doctor on his own, Manucci chose for his first patient the wife of a senior court minister. His experimental treatment was to mix a ferocious enema of wild endives and olive oil, and administer it through a tube taken from a hookah, using a cow's udder for a funnel. To his amazed relief the treatment was a success, and no less a grandee than the viceroy offered to hire him as his physician. Knowing the viceroy's stinginess, Manucci wisely turned down the offer and decided instead to continue in private practice. Yet even this choice had its dangers, and when he offended the newly appointed governor of Kabul by refusing to go to Afghanistan with him, he was obliged to slink about Lahore in disguise until the hue and cry had died down. Nor did his rapid success with well-to-do patients make him popular with the other European doctors in the city. He claimed that thieves were sent to steal his medical books; there was an attempt to have him assassinated; and ugly rumours were spread that he practised black magic. His liquor bottle, which he found very useful in administering to patients, was said to contain an evil genie, and it was alleged that he collected human fat from the corpses of condemned criminals so that he could give it to his patients to eat. But Manucci was a plausible and successful enough charlatan to keep his patients content. He relied on good sense rather than medical tradition for his remedies and as many of his rich patients were hypochondriacs he prospered with them. His technique, he later boasted, was to charge them handsomely and subject them to long courses of emetic, tricks, bullying, cautery, and evil-smelling fumigants until they pronounced themselves cured; and he never lacked for trade.

But his ill luck did not desert him. After saving enough money to retire early, Manucci went to live in a village near Bombay but soon afterwards

Opposite *Murad Bakhsh,
one of Shah Jehan's sons,
fighting on an armoured
elephant, a drawing
commissioned by Manucci*

lost all his capital in a bad investment. Obliged to return to Mogul service, he scratched along in a variety of trades, sometimes as a doctor, sometimes as an interpreter, and once or twice as a go-between when the Mogul was negotiating with the European coastal colonies. Eventually, when he felt that he had again saved up enough money, he deserted his employers by galloping off into the King of Golconda's territory on a stolen horse and with his saddle-bags filled with gold. But as usual he had picked the losing side, and when Golconda fell to the Moguls, Manucci had to hurry on to Madras where he found and wooed an English widow, and finally settled down as a citizen of that colonial enclave, finding time to write his racy memoirs.

Thus in his own way Manucci provided the counterpoint to Coryat, for while the Englishman heralded the private tourist in the Oriental Adventure, the Venetian was a prime example of the voluntary expatriate, the sort of man who went eastward with scarcely any thought of returning, and decided to spend his life there permanently. Manucci himself was good material for such a radical change. He lacked any real ties with his native Venice which he had left at an early age; he adapted exceptionally well and quickly to the foreign customs; and he had no difficulty in picking up foreign languages. Indeed his eventual account of India was dashed off in a strange mixture of French, Italian, and Portuguese, as the mood took him. Like Coryat and Tavernier he also had a genuine love of travel or 'an inborn inclination to visit foreign nations', as he put it; and like them too, he was attracted by the power and pomp of the Great Mogul in a way that was to make the Mogul's glamorous reputation self-sustaining. Traveller after traveller was reading about India and its emperor in these terms, and then went out to see India for himself and report back on his impressions. It became a process which fixed the vision of the dazzling prince ever more firmly in people's minds, and it was all the more effective because it was done by men who personally reflected popular tastes. Gullible or poorly educated, travellers like Tavernier and Manucci often reported wrongly or exaggerated what they saw. Yet what they did say was precisely the sort of material their audience remembered from their reading, and so their impact was all the more profound until stories of the magnificent Mogul blotted out all else. When Francis Bernier, a well-known philosopher who had himself visited Delhi in 1659 and travelled along the Ganges with Tavernier, went to call on a geographer friend on his deathbed in Paris, the dying man's first question was: 'Well! What news have you of the Great Mogul?' It was a fitting epitaph to the way the West saw and enjoyed the Orient at its moment of greatest splendour, and it was a tribute to the wandering instinct of the ordinary men who had shared in the Oriental Adventure and brought back their experiences.

CHAPTER SIX

EMBASSY EXTRAORDINARY

AT FIFTY-FIVE, GEORGE, LORD MACARTNEY, Baron of Lissanoure, had the comfortably plump face and shrewd eyes of a man who had made a considerable success of life. His career had been a dazzling series of precocious feats, from the age of thirteen when he had been accepted into Trinity College, Dublin, as a Fellow Commoner, to the astonishingly early appointment at twenty-seven as Envoy Extraordinary to the court of Russia with a knighthood to go with it. Son of an Irish country gentleman, he had become in his youth a friend of Voltaire and in his middle age a crony of Dr Johnson. Macartney's talent had a great deal to do with his success. He was intelligent, observant, and very accommodating. He made few enemies and he had an easy gracious manner which people found hard to resist. He was also intensely ambitious and knew to a hair's breadth exactly how to obtain and manipulate patronage.

Fresh from Dublin and on his European tour he had met Lord Holland's ne'er-do-well son, Stephen Fox, and helped the young man out of a scrape. In gratitude Lord Holland invited Macartney to visit him in London, and the young Irishman swiftly became a member of the politically influential Holland House set. It was Lord Holland who suggested him for the diplomatic post in Russia, and it was Holland who arranged for Macartney on his return to England to take a rotten borough seat in Parliament. Since then Macartney had also held the appointments of Chief Secretary to Ireland, the governorship of Grenada in the West Indies, and finally the office of President of Madras, a post which had taken him to India for five years. In short, he was the very model of a highly successful eighteenth-century career politician, and few of his acquaintances would have complained that he had not deserved his advancement.

Indeed Macartney had seen more than his share of bad luck. As Governor of Grenada, his island had been captured by the French, and Macartney was arrested. His house had been looted; his books, plate, and furniture all auctioned off in public to the French soldiers; and Macartney himself was hustled off ignominiously to France as a hostage with, according to gossip, only the coat on his back in which to attend official Parisian functions. Nor had his official patronage at Holland House been scot-free. Lady Holland had arranged a politically advantageous marriage for him to the ugly and prim Lady Jane Stewart, daughter of the retired prime minister. Lady Jane was an exceptionally dull person, and had the curious feature of a right eye which was blue and a left eye which was brown. She also suffered from increasing deafness so that it was scarcely surprising that her husband preferred to leave her at home when he went off to Madras. There he fell out with his senior army general, and it was proof of Macartney's personal

bravery that when the general challenged him to a duel, Macartney accepted, though he was a civilian and so short-sighted that it was doubtful if he could even aim his pistol accurately. As the duel turned out, Macartney missed, his adversary's pistol-ball hit him in the right shoulder, and their seconds broke up the affair before any more damage was done. Now, in 1792, he was finishing his convalescence in London and Northern Ireland when he was delighted to be offered the post of ambassador from the King of Great Britain to the Emperor of China.

It was a unique opportunity. There had never before been a successful ambassadorial visit from Britain to Peking, and so it would be making British diplomatic history. Fully as appealing to a man of Macartney's character was the chance of seeing at first hand the Chinese empire which so fascinated his contemporaries. Dr Johnson himself had declared that the grandson of any man who actually saw the Great Wall would be entitled to boast about it; and because China remained a closed region, barred to all but a handful of travellers, it was a curious anomaly that after Captain Cook's recent voyages more was known in London about the people of Tahiti and the tiny coral atolls of the Pacific, than about the oldest continuous civilization on earth. The inquiring minds of the Enlightenment had to make do with reading about China from the writings of the Jesuits or accepting the notions passed on by the East India Company merchants at Canton, like the ex-supercargo Sir William Chambers who designed the pagoda tower at Kew in imitation of the famous porcelain tower of Nanking.

Now Macartney was being offered the chance to make the trip in style, and in terms of the Oriental Adventure something equally untoward was

Lord Macartney and Sir George Staunton pictured together several years before their trip to China

121

about to occur: for the first time in Europe's involvement with the East, a major expedition, properly equipped and thoroughly prepared, was about to subject China to a rigorous examination. Large enough in men and material not to be over-awed by the foreign environment, the first British embassy to China would also have the self-confidence and unabashed curiosity to attempt to form an objective assessment of the Orient's senior empire. In short, Macartney's embassy was the first time that a fully confident Europe, in official guise, saw China on a level footing.

It was the East India Company who put in hand the new embassy by the simple but extremely effective device of offering to pay for it. The company's representatives at Canton were complaining bitterly about the restrictions placed upon them by the Chinese authorities. Bled relentlessly by the notorious Chinese overseer of customs, the *hoppo*, they were forbidden to buy land or to establish themselves permanently at the port. The Cantonese were banned under penalty of Chinese law from teaching them the language; and all trade had to be channelled through the Co-Hong, the local cartel of Chinese merchants. All this, moreover, was at a time when England's trade with China was seen to be on the point of enormous growth. In the past few years China's annual exports to England had risen from scarcely £100,000 to nearly £1,500,000 sterling, chiefly in tea. In the opposite direction, English trade to China was worth about £1,000,000 sterling, plus half as much again in illegally landed opium which was an extremely profitable company monopoly in India and then smuggled into China. All in all, the powerful East India interests in London felt that it was high time to redress these grievances and regularize their China trade, and they did not find it difficult to persuade Prime Minister Pitt, who was anticipating a substantial tax revenue from the increase in tea sales, to organize an official embassy to Peking.

By contrast, on the other side of the world, the rulers of the Celestial Empire were by no means sure that they wanted to play hosts to an embassy from Britain. China was at one of the periodic peaks of her power. On the throne sat Emperor Ch'ien Lung, whose long reign had been an almost unbroken run of successes. His armies had conquered south into the border states and westward into Tibet. Seen from its hub at Peking, his kingdom was stable, prosperous, and thoroughly set in its ways, and there was no good reason why it should pay any attention to the British whom the Chinese considered to be uncouth red-haired barbarians from the Western Ocean, pugnacious, excitable, and sly. The Government of China felt that there was nothing it wanted from the British, least of all an increased trade in opium which up till now had been a useful medicine rather than a harmful drug.

And yet, too, there was something flattering about the notion of a British embassy. In Chinese eyes it had the character of a compliment paid to the emperor in the same way that for centuries the barbarian tribes on the outer fringes had been sending tribute-bearing envoys to kowtow before the emperor and acknowledge his supremacy. Their homage served to reinforce the pre-eminence of China and, by extension, imposed upon the emperor a duty to receive these deputations graciously. And so, when Peking heard from the East India Company's agents that the King of Great Britain was proposing to send an embassy, the emperor gave permission for it to proceed. Quite what he and his Cabinet expected to encounter, it is hard to say. Despite a Portuguese embassy some forty years before and several Dutch envoys, Chinese knowledge of Europe was at a low ebb even among senior mandarins, while the common people had the most extravagant misapprehensions. It was said that the Western barbarians were roaring bullies who dabbled in black arts and, if given the chance, would seize and eat a Chinaman raw. Macartney was to find that one Chinese servant refused to sleep under the same roof as an Englishman, for fear of being devoured in the night. Those Chinese who knew of the embassy's impending arrival anticipated it with a mixture of curiosity, scepticism, and mild repugnance. And with several centuries of bureaucratic caution behind them, the Imperial Cabinet prudently began drafting a letter of rejection to Macartney's requests, even before the British lord had stepped ashore.

William Alexander (1767–1816), a self-portrait done on the voyage out to China by the man who recorded the everyday scenes of the first British embassy to the court of Peking

Macartney was officially appointed Ambassador to the Emperor of China on 3 May 1792, and raised to the suitable rank of viscount soon afterwards. The only condition he made before accepting the post was that he could take along as his second-in-command, his old friend and ally, Sir George Staunton, whom he had known for sixteen years, in Grenada, the United Kingdom, and as his secretary in Madras. The two men hit it off perfectly. Staunton was the archetypal aide-de-camp, meticulous, something of a plodder, and intensely loyal. It was typical that he should spend his Chinese tour compiling a massive two-volume history of the embassy, a monument of pedantic accuracy which utterly wore him out so that he died soon after it came off the press. All the other appointments to the embassy, Macartney announced, would be entirely upon merit, and so the post of comptroller went to the unlikely figure of a former mathematics teacher, John Barrow, who had been tutor to Staunton's twelve-year-old son. Barrow was to head the scientific side of the embassy which included one doctor advertised as its 'Physician and Philosopher' and another who was plain 'Surgeon and Physician'. They were supported by the flamboyant figure of Dr James Dinwiddie, a well-known scientific demonstrator who liked to be described as the embassy's 'Conductor of Mathematical and Astronomical Presents'. In fact Dinwiddie was as much a showman as he was a scientist. He specialized in giving public demonstrations of recent inventions and had gone on lecture tours in England and Ireland, remarkable for their vivid displays of fireworks. He had also constructed an air balloon which he now proposed taking out to China to show the Chinese how it was assembled and filled, before taking off in a flight himself. He proposed shipping out a portable diving bell, too, so that he could demonstrate a journey in the opposite direction.

The rest of the embassy's civil list was a similar mixture of the normal with the unlikely. There were Macartney's two secretaries and an under-secretary to look after the mountains of paperwork for which the Chinese Government was already notorious; a man called Baring to look after the East India Company interests; and an out-of-work portrait-painter named Hickey who had recently done Macartney's picture and was now instructed to catch in watercolours the major scenes of the embassy. In the event Hickey turned out to be uncommonly idle, and the vast majority of the Chinese pictures were done by the embassy's intelligent and industrious 'draughtsman',

William Alexander, who provided a unique record of the visit. In keeping with his elevated station Macartney also engaged a personal retinue of a steward, an under-steward, two valets, a cook, two couriers, and a footman. There was also a band of six German musicians who, it was intended, should add dignity to the embassy with their battery of two violins, two basset-horns, viola, cello, hautbois and bassoon, clarinet, flute and fife. In their idle hours the band was also expected to entertain the Chinese crowds with concerts of European music. This prospect and the annual salary of £60, however, were not enough to deter one of the musicians from deserting at Portsmouth so that the band eventually sailed as a five-piece ensemble. Other 'useful civilians' with the embassy included a carpenter and joiner, a saddler, and two gardener-botanists to look out for valuable and interesting Chinese plants, particularly any new varieties of tea bush on whose careful transportation they had been advised by the great Sir Joseph Banks who had recently done the same for Captain Bligh's breadfruit on the *Bounty*. There was also a tailor, a watchmaker, and a maker of mathematical instruments. These last two were needed to repair and maintain some of the embassy's more intricate clockwork presents to the emperor, because it was believed that the Chinese were mad on mechanical gadgets. Finally there was Staunton's own pair of manservants – he was also paying for one of the gardeners – and a valet to accompany Lieutenant John Crewe.

Lieutenant Crewe was the most obvious exception to Macartney's announced rule against favouritism. Crewe had no qualifications whatsoever to be on the embassy except that he was a cheerful young rakehell, and the son of the renowned Mrs Crewe, a leading beauty of her day and patroness of the Whig Party. Her boy was an inveterate but likeable gambler who was continually getting himself deep into debt. So at Mrs Crewe's pleading Macartney personally agreed to take him on the embassy, provided young Crewe swore solemnly not to touch cards or dice on the trip. Of course he failed to keep his promise and lost several thousand pounds on board ship, as Barrow commented grumpily, 'not any part of which he could pay . . . it was also said he had compounded the debt for an annuity of as many hundred pounds as he had lost thousands. My cabin on the passage home was on the lower deck, and scarcely a night passed in which I was not disturbed by the rattling of dice or by Mr Crewe on the bass-viol.'

A job for Crewe was found with the ambassador's military escort, a show-piece detachment led by a Colonel Benson, comprising ten men from the Eleventh Light Dragoons to give it a dashing appearance, twenty draftees from various infantry regiments, and the same number of gunners from the Royal Artillery who had been drilled in rapid fire to seven rounds a minute with the latest model of lightweight brass cannon. Six of these guns were taken along with the notion that they would impress the Chinese with the technical mastery and deadliness of English weapons, as well as a scale model of the pride of the Royal Navy, the *Royal Sovereign*. More subtly, the artillery's lieutenant was a trained surveyor, and he was instructed to draw plans of Chinese military defences including the Great Wall itself.

The post of interpreter to the embassy gave the most difficulty. It was an indication of British ignorance about China that there was not a single person either in Britain or her overseas possessions, the Indian territories

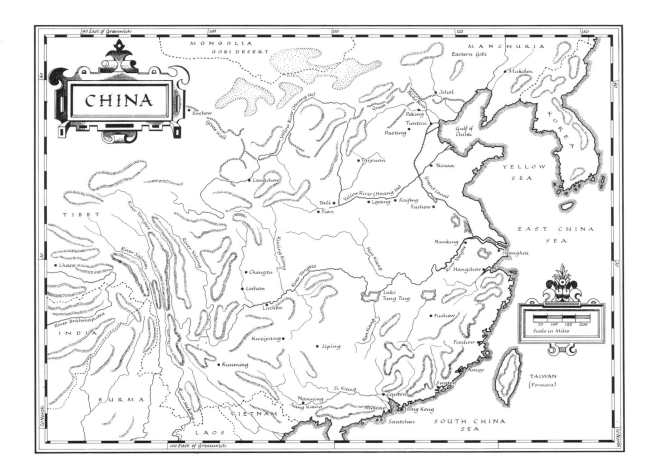

The mass of China

included, who could be recommended as a suitable Chinese interpreter. No educated Briton was available who knew enough of the language, and it was feared that the Chinese interpreters used by the traders in Canton would have only a limited knowledge of simple business English. Staunton, therefore, was sent to ransack Europe for a suitable interpreter, and luckily found in Rome the perfect man – Jacobus Li, a Chinaman who was just completing his training for the priesthood and was about to be sent back home as a Christian missionary. Mr Plumb, as the British called Li from the translation of his Chinese name, proved a most popular choice. Loyal and capable, he stood up to the considerable pressures brought against him by the mandarins in his home country and became universally admired by his companions on the embassy, though his colleague, another Chinese priest from Rome, was to prove far less staunch.

To everyone's surprise, the interpreter shortage was also solved by the most junior member of the embassy, Staunton's twelve-year-old son, also called George, who joined the embassy at his father's request as Macartney's page. Staunton senior was a devotee of the idea that his son should learn by the constant example of his elders, and he boasted that the lad had never been exposed to childish influences. He even discouraged him from ever having toys, and had begun him on Latin just after his fourth birthday so that young George Staunton already spoke Latin, Greek, French, and English. During the embassy this intellectual rigour was to bear fruit, and on the voyage out to China the lad learned enough Chinese from the two priests to begin as an interpreter on his own account. With practice he soon improved so rapidly that he became the embassy's second interpreter, and to the admiration of the Chinese officials, he also learned to write Chinese script, so that he was employed in copying all the embassy's written Chinese dispatches. Simultaneously, and again quite by luck, his tutor, Dr Huttner, taken along to keep up the boy's academic curriculum, proved another valuable asset because he was a classical scholar and could rapidly convert into English the translations from Chinese made by interpreter Li who spoke Latin and Italian but no English.

In all some ninety-five people sailed from Portsmouth on 16 September 1792 with the embassy. They went on the sixty-four-gun warship *Lion* and a large East Indiaman loaded with presents for the Chinese emperor, together with a small brig to serve as a scout. Their voyage was a fairly leisurely one via Madeira, the Cape Verde Islands, Rio de Janeiro, Batavia, and Cochin China before the squadron finally raised the mainland of China on Wednesday, 19 June 1793, and next day came to anchor off Macao.

The plan was to skirt northward along the Chinese coast until the squadron reached the mouth of the Pei-ho river in the Gulf of Chihli. This was the nearest convenient point to Peking, and here the embassy would disembark and proceed by river under Chinese escort to the capital. Yet already, some two thousand miles from the throne, the awe and power of the Chinese emperor was felt. At Macao the second priest-interpreter took fright at the mere notion that his association with the embassy might be disapproved of by the Chinese authorities. So he jumped ship, refusing to serve. Next, as the squadron worked north along the coast, a group of Chinamen who came on board to inspect the great foreign ship, were seen to catch sight of a portrait of Emperor Ch'ien Lung hanging in Macartney's cabin. Immediately every one of them fell flat on their faces and kissed the deck several times with great devotion.

By Thursday, 25 July, the mouth of the Pei-ho had been reached, and Dr Huttner, interpreter Li, and one of the naval lieutenants went ashore to make contact with the Chinese officials. They were taken at once to meet the two senior mandarins who had been sent by Peking to greet the embassy. To Huttner's surprise, the mandarins immediately bombarded him with an enormous list of precise and highly detailed questions about the embassy. How many persons did it have? How old were they? And what were their ranks? How many presents had they brought for the emperor? What precisely was the value and size and nature of these gifts? How large were the *Lion* and her consorts? How many guns did they carry? The answers to these and several dozen more questions were carefully written down by a secretary-in-waiting, and then the Europeans were courteously dismissed with polite assurances that everything would be made ready.

In fact Macartney and his colleagues were about to be embraced by the massive but supremely efficient mechanism of Chinese imperial government, an experience in ponderous hospitality not to be equalled anywhere else on

Opposite *A Dutchman's
impression of an
entertainment at the Mogul
court. The girls in the centre,
front, are mimicking
elephants.*
Overleaf *Ping-tze-Muen,
one of the western gates of
Peking*

earth. Nothing was hurried or bungled by the Chinese. For five days the embassy was made to wait patiently on their ships, until at noon on 31 July, the lookouts saw seven junks making straight for the anchored fleet. They came alongside, and from their holds poured dozens of Chinese coolies to unload a prodigious heap of supplies on to the visiting ships – 20 bullocks, 130 sheep, 120 hogs, 100 each of fowls and ducks, boxes and bags of tea, bread, flour, three different types of rice, fruit (both fresh and candied), and even three baskets of china in case the embassy did not have sufficient crockery. All this, Macartney was assured by the mandarins, was provided at the emperor's expense, so that the visitors should be well fed. Any deficiencies were to be made known so that they could be remedied immediately.

The two senior mandarins charged with looking after the embassy were now introduced formally. The quieter of the two was called Chou, a civil service mandarin who had recently been governor of Tientsin and was a renowned legal expert. He and Macartney got along famously, and indeed the two men were very alike in their background and manner, for they shared a calm, rather cerebral approach to affairs and had both done well in their administrative careers to finish up as highly polished Government officers. The other mandarin, Wang, was to become the favourite of the lesser members of the embassy. Wang was a professional soldier, a war mandarin, whom Macartney's valet, Aeneas Anderson, described as 'about five feet nine inches in height, stout, well made, and of a dark complexion, but of a remarkably pleasing and open countenance'. It was almost certainly Wang who cast aside his dignity and openly showed his glee as he was hoisted aboard *Lion* dangling giddily in an accommodation chair at the end of a block and tackle. He and Chou attended a ship's dinner and though at first they had trouble in handling knives and forks, they soon got over the difficulty and made a most enjoyable meal, constantly plying Macartney with questions, sampling the Europeans' wines and spirits of which cherry brandy was voted their favourite, until they were finally escorted back to their junk by the Marine Guard and to the tunes of the German band.

The disembarkation of the embassy was another *tour de force* of Chinese efficiency. On the following day a number of junks warped alongside the European ships, and a cadre of smart junior mandarins directed the transfer of the embassy's entire cargo into the junks. At breakneck pace several hundred packages containing presents for the emperor were whisked out of the holds and into the junks while the mandarins busily made notes of every item and directed the efforts of a horde of Chinese sailors who, Macartney observed approvingly,

> are very strong and work well, singing and roaring all the while, but very orderly and well regulated, intelligent and ingenious in contrivance and resource, each of them seeming to understand and exercise his proper share of the business . . . all the Chinese whom we have seen from the highest to the lowest, have their heads close shaved, except on the crown where the hair is left untouched by the razor for about a couple of inches in diameter and is suffered to grow to a great length, being considered as a very becoming ornament. It is always black and as strong and as coarse as horse hair, which it much resembles.

W.Alexander. f. 179?

By Sunday the unloading was complete, and next day the British crews lined the rigging to give Macartney three hearty cheers as he and his companions left the larger ships and proceeded across the sand-bar which guarded the mouth of the Pei-ho, where they were to meet the fleet of river vessels which the mandarins had provided to take them up river. It was, Macartney observed, high time he closed all the reference books about China and saw for himself the country he had come to visit.

The first curiosity to catch the embassy's attention after they had passed the low-lying countryside of the mouth of the Pei-ho and the drab dun-coloured sprawl of mud houses which formed its port, was the fleet of river junks which lay waiting for them. To a European eye they were extraordinary vessels, more like floating wooden castles or fanciful galleons in an Oriental masque than real ships. Built up with great boxy superstructures they were as much as one hundred feet long, but with flat bottoms and made of such light materials that they could carry substantial cargoes without drawing more than eighteen inches of water. Ideal for navigating the shallows, the top-heavy river junks were propelled either by large cane-matting sails, rowed with two enormous sweeps, or punted along difficult stretches by their crews using long bamboo poles. The Chinese authorities considered river junks to be the safest and most civilized way of travel, and the British had nothing but praise for the comfort of their accommodation. On his own 'yacht', as Macartney disarmingly called it, the interior of the hull was given over to a comfortable residential suite consisting of an ante-chamber, a saloon, a closet, and a sleeping-cabinet. The main saloon contained a massive ceremonial sofa on which the ambassador could hold court in mandarin fashion, while the floors of the cabins were divided into hatches, each with its brass ring, and by pulling these up one reached the cargo space below deck where the Chinese officials had already stowed the luggage.

Opposite Macartney's embassy mostly approved of Chinese justice as severely efficient and necessary for running a vast kingdom

The cabin windows were covered with glazed transparent paper – on Macartney's vessel the windows had glass panes in deference to his rank – and these could be removed to admit the breeze on a hot day; while on the outside of the vessel and running its whole length was an ingenious sunshade, which could be unfurled to shut out the glare. In winter or during stormy weather, the windows were fitted with protective shutters, and so that the crew might work the vessel at all times without disturbing the passengers, there was a very sensible arrangement of a wooden catwalk, extending two feet beyond the gunwale and running right round the hull, which allowed the crew to pass freely to any point of the boat. The crew, however, were by no means so well looked after. On some of the river junks the Chinese captain had his own cabin at the stern of the vessel, but in nearly every case the sailors slept on the top deck in a series of tiny hutches which Barrow thought were no better than dog-kennels.

Before the embassy could set off upstream, protocol dictated that Macartney should meet the local provincial governor who had come specially to greet him. So on the morning of 6 August, Macartney, Staunton, his son, and interpreter Li went ashore by a temporary wooden bridge, its rails hung with scarlet silk, which had been erected between the ambassador's junk and the river bank. At the foot of the bridge they found palanquins, carried by four chair-bearers, and an escort of Chinese cavalry waiting for

133

them. Stepping into their palanquins, they were carried about a mile at a brisk pace and set down in front of a temple which the governor had converted for the ceremony. Going in past a guard of Chinese soldiers, Macartney was gratified to see that the temple with its buildings arranged round a central court was exactly as he had expected from reading Chinese books of drawings, though he was astounded that the ornaments which he had imagined to be made of painted and varnished wood, were in fact made of intricately designed porcelain. Taking tea with the viceroy, who proved to be a benign seventy-eight-year-old wisp of a man with sparkling eyes, a long silver beard, and an air of great calm and dignity, Macartney was struck by 'the apparent kindness and condescension with which the people of rank here speak to and treat their inferiors and lowest domestics', an attitude which he had not expected in a land renowned for its strict adherence to law and order.

Returning to his junk, Macartney began making preparations for the inevitable return visit by the viceroy, only to be told very tactfully by Wang that the viceroy's great age and unsteadiness would make it hard for him to climb down the steep river bank in order to cross the bridge to the junk; and so, taking the hint, Macartney gravely asked for Wang's advice. He was told that Chinese etiquette would be satisfied if the viceroy merely sent his visiting card; and accordingly, at ten o'clock precisely on 7 August, a great stir of people announced the arrival of the viceroy behind a large parade of mandarins, guards, and officials. The viceroy descended from his palanquin; his entire retinue knelt down to pay homage; and the old man sent to Macartney by hand of a Chinese officer a large square of paper, folded several times and painted in red with the governor's name and titles. The ceremony then being considered over, the viceroy re-entered his palanquin with the same obeisance as before and was trotted away ceremonially to his quarters.

Chinese protocol, as Macartney was discovering, was made much easier for the foreigner by an Imperial Regulation obliging all members of the mandarin class to wear in their hats a large button denoting their exact status within the bureaucratic order. Thus a first-class mandarin could be identified immediately by his button of smooth red coral; a second-class mandarin by a similar button, but carved; a third-class mandarin by his light transparent blue button, and so on via opaque blue, clear crystal, opaque white, and smooth brass gilt, down to the lowest rank of an eighth-grade official with an engraved gilt button in his cap. Only the emperor's family and persons extremely close to his household were granted the privilege of wearing a special button of amethyst or ruby and the ceremonial jacket of yellow silk. Mandarins in high favour, like Wang himself, were also permitted to wear a peacock feather dangling from their bonnet to denote some particular service, while, conversely, those mandarins who were in special disgrace, were sometimes seen wearing a placard hanging round their neck which announced the reason for their demotion. To help the foreign observer still further, Chinese court dress also stipulated that the mandarins should wear on the backs and fronts of their gowns special embroidered patches about twelve inches square marked with the insignia of their grade. These cloth patches distinguished between the civil and war grades of mandarins so that, for instance, the civilian hierarchy descended

A portrait of Wang, a military mandarin, which clearly shows his grade button and embroidered insignia

from the white crane of the first rank through the golden pheasant of the second rank down to the eighth-grade quail. Reading these patches was scarcely more difficult than reading a pack of court cards though, as with cards, it was also important which suit represented the trumps. Thus while it was clear at first glance that mandarin Wang with a red button in his cap outranked Chou who was a blue button mandarin, the latter was in fact a civilian mandarin and so his voice carried more authority in the day-to-day running of the embassy which was considered to be a civil matter.

The deafening uproar of dozens of large copper gongs, vigorously beaten on shore and aboard the junks, was the signal for the river fleet to weigh anchor at noon on Friday, 9 August, and in less than an hour the whole concourse of thirty-seven junks and store-ships was being swept upstream by the rising tide at a good four knots. The fleet made a splendid spectacle. Every vessel was gaily hung with banners and bunting of coloured silk; the leading junks of the two high mandarins flew special flags; small messenger boats shuttled back and forth between the larger vessels; and every now and then the brazen clash of a gong would be the signal for the fleet to execute some stately manœuvre. The fleet appeared like a moving diorama, rippling with flags as it glided along past the flat surrounding countryside, and the Chinese peasantry would put down their farm tools and come running to the bank to watch the procession pass. Those who could do so also read the flaunting signal hoisted on the leading Chinese junk which announced 'the English Ambassador bringing tribute to the Emperor of China'. Macartney, when informed of this motto, wisely risked no complaint lest he ruin his mission.

The British officers were enjoying themselves hugely. Everything seemed new and wonderful as they gazed at the peasants in their straw hats, blue cotton frocks and trousers, and thick clumsy shoes often made of straw. They noted how sharply the style of the poor citizens contrasted with the rich Chinese in their smart short jackets with wide silk sleeves, splendid petticoats and black satin boots with curved soles of thick paper. The visitors eagerly took observations on the height of the tide, the sextant angles for latitude and longitude, the crops in the fields, and when the fleet passed a gigantic park of sacks of salt neatly stored by the Chinese Government, Barrow made frantic sums and calculated that there was 600,000,000 pounds' weight of the stuff in stockpile. Relations with the escorting Chinese mandarins were excellent. Several of the embassy gentlemen gathered on the junk of one particularly amiable mandarin to drink his rice wine and listen while Lieutenant Crewe played English tunes on his viol and the mandarin happily tapped out the refrain with his fan on Chinese porcelain bowls. At night the junks all moored together near the bank. Gangways were put up to allow people to go ashore, and vast banquets of Chinese food were served on board. On land, immediately opposite the fleet, an honour guard of local Chinese militia would appear and set up their tents so that the lights of the soldiers' lanterns combined with the lamps of the motionless fleet and their reflections in the river to produce a magical effect as if a complete town lay glittering half on land and half on the water.

The British servants, on the other hand, were not nearly so happy with what they found. They grumbled about the Chinese food, complaining that

The embassy's barge trackers cooking their meagre provisions at a stove

it was all in little bits and pieces and too much fried, and when the Chinese chefs obligingly tried to imitate English cooking by boiling whole geese and great lumps of beef, they made a mess of it and irritated the British still further so that eventually they appointed their own cook. Nor was valet Anderson very taken with the common Chinese. He thought them scruffy and dirty, ridden with lice which he saw them pick and eat, and thievish. He pitied the wretched life of the junk deckhands who begged from the British their used tea-leaves, which they then carefully spread in the sun to dry and used and re-used several times; and he was disappointed in the constant stream of what he thought were trivial presents – pieces of silk, nankeen cloth, balls of green tea, and the like – which were given to the British at nearly every stop. And he was nearly driven to distraction by the constant banging of the gongs which he compared to the lids of stewpots, and being kept awake all night by the rattling clacks as Chinese sentries loudly struck the hours and guard changes with wooden mallets on sounding-boards.

Samuel Holmes, a private in the Light Dragoons of Macartney's body-guard, was also keeping his own notebook of the trip, and was not much more impressed by the Chinese soldiers. Several times each day the fleet passed honour guards of Chinese militia drawn up on the bank to salute the embassy, and Holmes was amazed to note that the soldiers often kept their pipes in their mouths or held fans in their hands even on parade. And some could be seen sitting down in the ranks. 'Their dress', Holmes remarked acidly,

put me in mind of a mountebank's fool's dress, though I dare say very serviceable in the time of action. It consists of a helmet of steel and made in such manner that it would shelter any cut. It comes down to the brow and neck; it is round and comes off tapered to the top, on which is fitted a kind of spear about a foot long ornamented with red horse hair, hanging down. Their jacket or what they wear instead, is really frightful at a distance; it is beset with thin pieces of iron or brass, which imitates an English brass nailed trunk; it is made to cover any part of the neck which the helmet leaves uncovered, and buttons to it on each side, and meets itself above the mouth so that no parts of the head or face are exposed, but just the eyes.

Peering tortoise-like from beneath his helmet, the ordinary Chinese militiaman was armed with a bow and arrow or a pike, and a curved sword which he wore on his left side with the hilt facing backwards, so that in order to draw it he had to reach behind his back with his right hand to grasp the hilt and unsheath the blade. Every third man on parade also had an odd little staff stuck in his collar behind his neck from which flew a small coloured pennant, and every twelfth man clutched a banner on a pike. Only a very few had fire-arms and these were ancient matchlocks, while the bombards with which they noisily saluted the embassy, were equally decrepit. Often they were merely tubes of bamboo rammed upright in the earth and filled with coarse gunpowder which gave a loud bang and a satisfying cloud of smoke as the junks glided past.

Macartney soon ran headlong into his first diplomatic hurdle – the notorious problem of the kowtow. By age-old tradition the Chinese authorities expected every foreign envoy to perform this ritual act of submission in front of the emperor. This meant kneeling on the ground three separate times in the imperial presence, and each time falling forward prostrate and knocking the head on the floor thrice while the chamberlain bawled out the necessary instructions. The Chinese attached enormous importance to the performance of the kowtow. To them it symbolized the supremacy of the emperor, the inferiority of the envoy, and the correct functioning of court procedure. But Macartney, who had been forewarned, had already made up his mind not to submit to the kowtow in order to show that he came as the ambassador of an independent monarch and not as a supplicant. He told the mandarins that he would kneel in front of the emperor in the European manner, but he absolutely refused to kowtow. This stubbornness rapidly brewed into a major scandal. The emperor's legate, a stupid and prickly high mandarin by the name of Cheng Jui, saw Macartney's reply as an insult. The imperial secretariat wrote to say that unless Macartney agreed to kowtow to the emperor, the embassy's supply of food would be cut down as a sign of imperial displeasure, and the escorting mandarins Wang and Chou, caught in the middle of the quarrel, were so worried that they called on Macartney to demonstrate exactly how the kowtow was performed, and they plaintively reassured him that if he feared he would be ungainly, no one would be offended if he took off his English knee-garters. Macartney, however, would not yield and the discussion was deferred.

On 11 August the British had their first sight of a major Chinese city when the fleet reached Tientsin. It was a rather stark place, mile upon mile of two-storey square houses with blank outer walls of lead-blue brick facing over the river. Its overwhelming impression was of a vast and teeming population. Every open space and alleyway was crammed with people, a multitude standing silently in rank upon rank to watch the arrival of the foreign barbarians as the junks drew up to the main town quay. This enor-

A Chinese soldier in full
uniform

mous crowd, ranged up the river bank as if in an amphitheatre, was uncannily
peaceable and well ordered. Despite the broiling sun every man had con-
siderately removed his straw hat so as not to block his neighbour's view,
and there was scarcely any jostling or clamour. For lack of space the front
ranks actually stood in the river itself, many of them up to their chests in
water, and the clusters of moored trade junks were black with spectators.
The only commotion was when the stern of one overloaded junk collapsed
beneath the weight of people, spilling into the river a score or so of spectators
who had to be rescued by their companions. According to Barrow, at least
thirty thousand of Tientsin's population actually lived on the water, a
permanent population of junkmen and their families.

Above Tientsin the fleet lost the help of the tide, and so Chinese trackers were employed to haul the vessels bodily against the current whenever the wind was against them. Two ropes were rigged, one from the top of the mast and the other from the prow, and led together to a long hawser which was pulled by the trackers on the shore. Smaller cords made into loops, were fastened near the end of the hawser, and each tracker placed a loop over his head and round his chest, often with a board to protect his chest, and thus yoked into position began pulling the vessel slowly along. It was desperately hard, dirty work, often lasting all day, and the trackers were perpetually round-shouldered, and frequently obliged to wade waist-deep through the mud and slime as they splashed across the tributaries flowing into the main river.

Twelve miles short of Peking, the junks finally reached the head of navigation at Tungchow, and here the embassy disembarked amid another burst of Chinese activity and efficiency. Within a few hours an army of coolies directed by junior mandarins had erected two warehouses, each over two hundred feet long, and roofed them with matting. Then the labourers began unloading the junks at a ferocious speed, carrying like ants the six hundred or so packages of official presents up to the warehouses where every item was carefully checked by a clerk, its measurements taken and noted, a ticket written out and pasted on, and then carried inside. By the end of the day the entire unloading operation had been done; Chinese guards were posted round the warehouses, and there were even notices displayed forbidding anyone to go near the buildings with fire. Only Lieutenant Parrish caused a serious loss of face. He took the chance to exercise his new brass cannon in rapid fire, and set up his battery pointing across the river. Seeing this, a number of the junior mandarins frantically rushed off, shouting at the crowds on the opposite bank to keep clear. But Parrish was only using blanks, and the mandarins felt very foolish when the lieutenant himself stood only ten to fifteen yards away from the muzzles of his guns.

In Tungchow itself the British made a great stir. They were followed everywhere by mobs of curious Chinese onlookers who were obviously fascinated by the tight clothing of the foreign barbarians and their strange habit of dressing their hair with flour paste and oil which, it was felt, was a very wasteful practice of edible material. Strolling through the town valet Anderson quickly learned that the Chinese were by no means as reticent as their reputation made out. He found they could scarcely conceal their giggles at his strange appearance, and such a swarm of onlookers trailed him that he had to dodge in and out of shops to get rid of them. In Tungchow, too, the Chinese were treated to the spectacle of a Christian funeral after the death of one of the humblest embassy employees. The man who had died, an elderly brass-founder named Eades, had begged to be allowed to go to China despite his ill health, pathetically believing that it would make his fortune. Now Macartney ordered a full ceremonial funeral for Eades, and the corpse was solemnly carried to a Chinese burial-ground on the outskirts of the town escorted by the entire junior staff of the embassy, the German band playing a funeral dirge, and an artillery detachment with reversed arms. At the graveside Anderson, for want of a chaplain, read out the funeral service, and the firing-party let off three volleys over the grave, watched intently by an immense concourse of Chinese spectators intrigued by these barbarian rites.

CHAPTER SEVEN

THE LAND OF SING-SONG

A WELL-PAVED ROAD CONNECTED TUNGCHOW with Peking, but for once the mandarinal organization broke down completely over the task of moving Macartney, his unwieldy entourage, and their mass of baggage into the city. Palanquins had been provided for the ambassador and his senior staff, and small covered carriages for the middle-grade officials, but the ordinary ranks were packed into unsprung country wagons which were disagreeably cramped and extremely uncomfortable, and the army of some three thousand porters needed to transport the baggage and presents was chaotic. Some were detailed off to trundle the embassy's smaller items in wheelbarrows; the larger gifts were hoisted bodily on to complicated latticeworks of bamboo held up by as many as thirty-two men; and to increase the confusion, Chinese victuallers with wheelbarrows full of food for the more important visitors were sent trotting on ahead so that whenever Macartney halted, he could be entertained to a picnic. As a result the whole cavalcade proceeded along in fits and starts with the porters jumbled among the dignitaries, his military escort separated from Macartney, and the whole conglomeration mixed up with the stream of ordinary Chinese travellers. It looked, Anderson sourly noted, more like a flock of paupers being returned to their parishes than a solemn British embassy entering a foreign city.

To everyone's disappointment the embassy did not stop in Peking itself but was led straight through the city and out to the old Summer Palace of Yuen Ming Yuen some eight miles distant in the country. The Chinese authorities intended Yuen Ming Yuen as the embassy's home until the emperor returned from his summer capital at Jehol, 140 miles away beyond the Great Wall, and in the meantime the presents for the emperor were to be set out in Yuen Ming Yuen to await his inspection. Only Macartney himself and a small entourage would be allowed to proceed to Jehol for a preliminary audience.

Macartney felt very insulted by the accommodation at the old Summer Palace. It was a run-down place, poorly maintained by a few surly eunuchs, and its buildings were in a dreadful state, dirty and unkempt. Furthermore it was surrounded by a high boundary wall on which Chinese guards were posted, and the British were ordered to stay inside this perimeter. Anyone who scrambled up even to peep over the wall was immediately shouted at by the Chinese guards, and Colonel Benson had a furious row with the Chinese sentries who refused to allow him to go outside the main gate. Equally galling was the fact that Yuen Ming Yuen was already a repository for cast-off presents given to the emperor by foreigners, and after looking through them Macartney and his staff were crestfallen to find a musical clock made in London's Leadenhall Street which played a dozen tunes from *The Beggar's Opera*.

Macartney lost no time in complaining about the shabbiness of his accommodation, and within a few days interpreter Li had arranged specially for the embassy to move back to Peking. There the Chinese officials offered them a large and elegant town house which, suitably enough, was the confiscated property of a disgraced *hoppo* of Canton who had been imprisoned for embezzlement. The joke circulating in Peking was that when asked by imperial officials if he would allow his house to be used by the British, the *hoppo* replied that as British merchants had indirectly paid for most of it, he saw no reason why Macartney should not now occupy it.

Barrow and the British technicians were left behind in Yuen Ming Yuen, where they got on with the task of assembling and setting out the imperial presents to their best advantage. In the Presence Chamber they hung up the two magnificent chandeliers specially designed for Ch'ien Lung, and on either side of the emperor's throne they placed a globe, one celestial and the other terrestrial. At the north end of the chamber they began the intricate task of assembling the principal gift from King George III, a massive working planetarium, and at the other end they displayed the items which London had calculated would arouse Chinese admiration for British craftsmanship: an orrery, several very ornate clocks in fine cases from the famous Vulliamy family, a barometer, and a whole range of Wedgwood products including ornamental vases of blue jasper, porcelain candelabra, a copy of the Portland vase, and a suitably bound volume of Wedgwood's factory catalogue.

The Chinese reaction to these presents was revealing. Mandarins and the imperial inspectors regularly arrived to see how the work was going, and adopted an air of casual indifference towards the clocks and planetarium; indeed it was clear that no one really knew how to use the latter. The military mandarins were equally bored with Lieutenant Parrish's brass cannon, much to the latter's annoyance, but they flocked round to test the latest sword-blades from Birmingham and were thrilled to be given them as presents. Wedgwood's porcelain was the real triumph of the exhibition. Nearly every Chinaman as he entered the reception chamber, made a direct line for the Staffordshire ware to look it over and admire it.

The greatest curiosity, however, was reserved for the three carriages which Macartney had brought in pieces from London and were now being assembled at Yuen Ming Yuen. They were exquisite products from the finest London coachmakers with velvet linings, glass windows, and shades which slid up and down. They were thickly decorated with gilt, and sported embroidered hammer-cloths. But they also caused the palace eunuchs great consternation. At first they thought that the carriages were intended as vehicles for Ch'ien Lung's harem, decently hidden behind the shutters, but when told the carriages were for Ch'ien Lung himself, they refused point-blank to believe that the emperor was expected to ride inside the coach. No one, they informed Barrow stiffly, could expect the Son of Heaven to allow any man, let alone a common coachman, to sit higher than himself on the coach-box and, worse yet, with his back turned towards the emperor. If the carriages were really intended for the emperor, then the British workmen would have to reassemble them so that the coachman's box was inside and lower down, while the emperor occupied the elevated and superior position.

Though irritated by their critics, Barrow and his technicians nevertheless

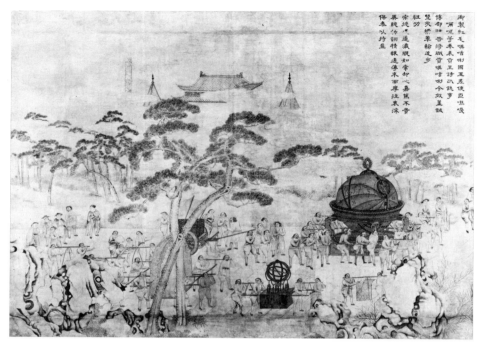

御製紅毛嘆咭唎國王差使臣貢物
喘咙等率來會呈詩訊敘事
傳郤咀普接職貢嘆唎今欵蓋誠
覽爾幙車輪近步
祖功
宗德久遠如當卻心嘉篤不肯
巽綏仿詞報遠來而厚注衷深
俯奉以持盈

Transporting presents for Emperor Ch'ien Lung: a Chinese view in silk of the British embassy which shows the visitors dressed totally anachronistically

respected the ingenuity of the native Chinese labourers who had been drafted in to help them. After much intricate work the British assembled the two chandeliers, only to learn that they were in the wrong position. Next morning, two ordinary Chinese workmen appeared, took down the chandeliers, disassembled them, packed and moved them, all in perfect order and without a single word of instruction or the slightest damage to a single crystal. On another occasion it was found that one of the glass panes of the planetarium was the wrong size and, try as they might, the British technicians were unable to trim it with a diamond glass-cutter. Informed of the difficulty, a Chinese workman took out the pane, heated up his iron tools, and casually shaved off the correct amount so that the glass fitted properly.

Meanwhile the main embassy had transformed its town house in Peking to give it a more ambassadorial air. In the largest room Macartney hung twin, full-length portraits by Reynolds of King George III and Queen Charlotte, and opposite them a splendid state canopy of red velvet overhanging two throne chairs on a red carpet, and at a lower level half a dozen smaller chairs. British soldiers were posted as ceremonial guards at the doors, and in preparation for Macartney's journey to see Ch'ien Lung at Jehol, four small Tatar horses were obtained to draw one of the famous carriages. Unfortunately Macartney had forgotten to bring a coachman with him, so one of the infantrymen, who was a former post-boy, was pressed into service for this role, and assisted by a volunteer dragoon who cut a splendid dash on the box, still wearing his helmet. The remainder of the servants were issued with green and gold livery from a chest of servants' clothing purchased in London. But when the chest was opened, there was a good deal of grumbling when it was discovered that the clothes were all secondhand and had been bought cheaply from the former French ambassador to London. Not only were they soiled, but most of them still had their former owners' names marked in them. Fortunately the constant stream of Chinese visitors to the residence did not seem to notice the difference, for they were too keenly interested in anything British and spent hours examining the foreigners' shaving tools, cutlery, and personal effects. One official Chinese inspector borrowed all the musical instruments from the band, laid them out on sheets of paper, and made meticulous tracings of them. Out in the streets of Peking amazed crowds followed Macartney's amateur coachman as he drove round the city, hurriedly trying to break his Tatar horses to coach harness before the embassy left for Jehol.

On 2 September all was ready, and Macartney, Staunton, his son, Li, Parrish, and about half the embassy went bowling off up the imperial road to the summer capital. Peering out of the windows of his post-chaise Macartney was flattered to see little detachments of Chinese troops come to attention to salute him as he passed, and hear them firing off their petards and banging enthusiastically on their military gongs as the embassy rattled by. At convenient intervals all along the road he found Government rest-houses where he could stay for the night, usually in the grounds of a chain of royal palaces where Macartney, like most of his peers in England a fine judge of landscaping, was delighted with the royal parklands. 'A Chinese gardener', he wrote approvingly in his journal,

> is a painter of nature, and though totally ignorant of perspective as a science, produces the happiest effects by the management of or rather pencilling of distances . . . by relieving or keeping down the features of the scene, by contrasting trees of a bright, with those of a dusky foliage, by bringing them forward, or throwing them back according to their bulk and their figure, and by introducing buildings of different dimensions, either heightened by strong colouring, or softened by simplicity and omissions of ornament.

An even more astounding example of imperial engineering was the emperor's personal roadway which ran parallel to the public road. This was the Imperial Road proper, used exclusively by the emperor himself when travelling between Jehol and Peking. It had its own bridges and causeways, its own shade trees, and there was a water-cistern every few hundred yards so that water could be sprinkled to lay the dust just before the emperor passed by. Though Ch'ien Lung himself was not expected to pass that way for weeks, Macartney saw work-gangs of Chinese soldiers, perhaps thirty thousand of them in all, already smoothing down the surface carefully, and preparing for the emperor's passage by laying soft matting on the bridges to reduce the noise.

The greatest known feat of Chinese labour greeted their eyes on 5 September when at last they came within sight of the Great Wall, and like eager tourists begged Wang and Chou to delay the journey while everybody from Macartney down to the humblest private in his escort scrambled about the foot of the wall, picking up wedges of brick to keep as souvenirs. Lieutenant Parrish quickly made an excellent set of strategic military drawings, and one of the embassy's doctors collected loose bricks in order to heat them in a crucible and see what gave them their bluish sheen.

The Wall marked an important division, both psychological and physical, within Ch'ien Lung's China. On the far side, the cultivated scenery of the Chinese farmlands changed swiftly to the wild rugged terrain of Tatary itself, and the travellers noticed very strongly that they were leaving one culture for another. This difference was brought home to them even more clearly when one of the embassy's native servants, a Tatar, was beaten with a bamboo for theft on the orders of the accompanying mandarins. Normally the incident would have passed off without note, bambooings being everyday occurrences. As Barrow remarked, the only difference was that the Tatars took their punishment in silence while the native Chinese cringed and wept piteously. Now, however, the moment the Tatar was released after his beating, he flew into a towering rage and spoke most insolently to the mandarins, insisting that no Chinese had the authority to whip a Tatar on the far side of the Wall. His impudence won him a second thrashing but Macartney shrewdly noted that there seemed some reason in his outrage because the farther north one travelled, the more the Tatars lorded it over the Chinese. As Marco Polo had observed five centuries earlier, there really seemed to be two Chinas, one composed of the ruling class from beyond the Wall, and the other of native Chinese. Indeed there were several coincidences between the visits of Marco Polo and Macartney: the reigning emperor Ch'ien Lung actually claimed descent from Kubilai Khan, and as he was the heir to the Manchu chiefs who had overrun north China, Ch'ien Lung depended on the outsiders he felt he could trust. His court was a Manchu court, dominated by Manchu nobles; his army was divided into well-paid, well-armed Manchu regiments and a utilitarian Chinese militia; and even in the civil service there was acute favouritism for Manchu officials so that every important post had to be shared between a Chinese and a Manchu appointee. One day near the Great Wall when Macartney was visited by a senior Manchu army officer, poor Wang, who was a native Chinaman, was in a dreadful state of nerves and would scarcely sit down in the Manchu's presence, even though Wang was of exactly the same rank and wore the same colour cap button.

On Sunday morning, 8 September, Jehol saw the formal entry of its first British ambassador. To the strains of 'God Save the King' rode one hundred mandarins on horseback followed by Colonel Benson at the head of his twelve Light Dragoons. Then marched Lieutenant Parrish with drummer and fife-player, eight artillerymen and their corporal, Crewe, ten servants and four musicians walking two by two, the embassy servants in their green and gold livery, the British gentlemen in scarlet uniforms embroidered in gold, and finally Lord Macartney and Staunton in their post-chaise which had a black servant in a turban standing behind. Macartney was delighted. It was, he wrote, 'a very splendid show', but Anderson, still rankling in his shabby livery, felt that apart from the soldiers and diplomats, 'the rest of the company exhibited a very awkward appearance; some wore round hats, some cocked hats, and others straw hats; some were in whole boots, some in half boots, and others in shoes with coloured stockings. In short, unless it was in secondhand coats and waistcoats which did not fit them, the inferior part of the suite did not enjoy even the pretence of shabby uniformity.'

Macartney was disappointed that the Imperial Grand Chamberlain was

not waiting to greet him, and instead he was conducted to his lodgings by junior officials. The cause of the snub, as he should have guessed, was the hoary question of the kowtow which was now in its final and most awkward stages. The Chinese continued to try all sorts of stratagems to make him agree to kowtow, but Macartney refused to budge, and so it was only after several days spent kicking his heels in Jehol that he received word that the emperor was prepared to meet him, and even then, it would only be informally, in an open-air gathering. For his imperial audience Macartney had brought along a special court suit of mulberry-spotted velvet which he now proposed to wear with his full regalia of the Order of the Bath, star, collar, mantle, and the ceremonial badge topped off with a hat and white plumes. Staunton, on the other hand, was thrown into a quandary. He wanted to look impressive but not ridiculous in Chinese eyes, and so on the principle that Chinese costume in general tended to conceal rather than reveal the human figure, he decided to deck himself out in a suit of velvet and over the top wrapped the scarlet silk cloak of an Oxford Doctor of Law with the appropriate velvet cap perched on his head. Thus strangely attired the two senior British delegates solemnly assembled with their escort for the procession to their audience early on the morning of 14 September.

The plan was for the escort to advance ahead of the ambassador's palanquin with the band playing a slow march. But unfortunately it was so early in the morning that in the darkness everyone got into a desperate muddle. The Chinese palanquin-bearers seized their load, and despite protests dashed up the road at such a smart pace that the band found itself playing slowly but marching rapidly. The footmen abandoned all pretence of keeping step and ran pell-mell to keep up with their master. To add to the bedlam the mounted escort were scared of falling off in the darkness, and a cohort of pigs, street dogs, and donkeys broke the ranks and threw everyone into turmoil. The only consolation, Anderson acidly pointed out, was that this wretched procession designed to make such a grand show, actually took place in the dark so that no one could see the débâcle.

Mandarins greeted the embassy in the small park where Ch'ien Lung had agreed to give the audience and there the visitors found a large crowd of Chinese courtiers already assembled outside a circular tent, one side of which was propped open. After about an hour's wait the sounds of drums and music heralded Ch'ien Lung's arrival in an open chair carried by sixteen bearers. Despite his eighty-three years, the emperor looked remarkably fit, and he was dressed in a very severe costume of plain dark silk with a velvet bonnet on his head, from which dangled the only jewel he was wearing, a single large pearl. The English accounts described him as being about five feet ten inches tall, very upright in bearing but slender, with a relatively fair complexion, regular features, and a somewhat aquiline nose. As he mounted his throne, he was attended by his principal household advisers who, whenever they spoke to him, fell on their knees. When Macartney's turn came, a master of ceremonies led the British ambassador forward, and Macartney marched firmly up the steps of the throne holding above his head a large gold box studded with diamonds which contained a letter from King George III. He dropped to one knee and offered the letter to the emperor, and in return received a carved jade sceptre as a token of friendship. After presenting the emperor with two enamelled watches which Ch'ien Lung casually handed on to one of his attendants, Macartney was allowed to present Staunton, still wrapped in his Oxford gown, who offered a further gift of two fine air-guns which were also put casually on one side. Only young George Staunton brought the affair to life, for he was serving as the page-boy to hold Macartney's train and when Ch'ien Lung asked his prime minister, Ho-Shen, if any of the British had learned to speak Chinese, he was told that the boy had made progress in the language. At once the emperor ordered young Staunton to step forward and asked him to say a few Chinese sentences. Seeming very pleased with what he heard, Ch'ien Lung took out a small yellow silk purse, used for holding areca nuts, and presented it to the boy as a token. Staunton's father thought the gift very paltry but he had to admit that the Chinese mandarins regarded it as an exceptional mark of imperial favour and effusively congratulated the boy on his good fortune. The audience with the emperor then concluded with an intricate banquet, served in almost total silence by a flock of trained waiters, during which Ch'ien Lung personally handed Macartney and Staunton their cups of warm wine, which Macartney said, 'we immediately drank in his presence and found it very pleasant and comfortable, the morning being cold and raw'.

The next few days were spent sightseeing in Jehol, and Macartney was considerably chastened by what he found. At immense labour the summer capital had been turned into a series of splendid parks dotted with exquisite lakes. A corps of gardeners and workmen kept everything in meticulous order so that scarcely a blade of grass was out of place. The prime minister, Ho-Shen, personally escorted Macartney by pleasure barge on a tour of the main lake where a series of artificial islands had been created and decorated in different tastes and styles. Some were planted with ornamental trees, some had been left to nature, others were decorated with fanciful rockeries. Here and there Macartney was invited to land, and he was thunderstruck to discover that the numerous pagodas were crammed with what the Canton traders called 'sing-songs', the intricate clocks, watches, and ornamental gadgets for which the Chinese had a curious passion, as well as a whole host of presents which previous petitioners had given the emperor, to the value in Macartney's calculation of over £2,000,000 sterling. By comparison, Macartney felt, his own gifts must 'hide their diminished heads'.

On another day he was taken to see displays by jugglers who kept plates spinning on sticks, a conjurer who produced a live rabbit out of a basin (much to Anderson's amazement who had never seen the trick before), and a most spectacular demonstration of fireworks which delighted even the sophisticated ambassador when out of a chest suspended in the air tumbled twenty or thirty streams of paper lanterns, each unfolding one after another and containing different coloured lights, some five hundred or so lanterns in all. Finally a pantomime was given in the emperor's honour, depicting an allegorical marriage of ocean and earth. Mobile models of dragons, elephants, trees, and rocks moved across the stage worked by cleverly concealed actors. They were joined by the figures of dolphins and porpoises, ships, sponges, and corals, and the grand spectacle was a huge whale which rolled forward and spouted from his mouth several tons of water which drained away through specially prepared holes in the stage floor.

Unfortunately the business side of Macartney's visit was much harder to carry out than expected. The emperor himself was impossible to see as he kept to a very rigid routine. He rose every morning at three o'clock for prayers, then read official dispatches until his breakfast at seven. Afterwards he relaxed by walking in his palaces and gardens with his wives and eunuchs, before meeting with his prime minister and Cabinet. At 3 p.m. the emperor dined, and then went to the theatre or to other amusements before retiring to read privately. By seven in the evening he had invariably gone to his bedchamber attended by a eunuch whose duty was to fetch the lady of the emperor's choice. Thus all Macartney's attempts to discuss the reasons for his embassy either were turned aside affably by the mandarins or disappeared into the maw of Jehol's bureaucracy. Even when Macartney tried sending Li at the crack of dawn to catch Ho-Shen before he left his house, the plan came to nothing, and it became clear to Macartney that he was being ignored deliberately.

One black mark against Macartney had been his arrogance in refusing to kowtow, but his embassy as a whole was not really making much of an impression. A party of Chinese officials went down to inspect the British servants, and after rubbing touchstones on the tawdry gold braid of their livery, made it quite clear that they were scornful that it was sham. Next, Colonel Benson considerably damaged the embassy's reputation by the brutal court martial of one of the private soldiers for clandestinely obtaining a quantity of liquor from a Chinaman. The soldier was convicted and publicly tied to one of the pillars of the embassy's residence where he received sixty lashes before a crowd of disapproving Chinese.

Nor, when the imperial court left Jehol and returned to Peking, was the emperor's long-awaited visit to inspect the main presents at Yuen Ming Yuen much of a success. Ch'ien Lung went down to see the display at the old Summer Palace, but there was very little which caught his fancy. The officials refused to show him the two camera obscuras as 'too childish', and poor Dinwiddie was denied permission to try any of his beloved experiments although he had laid them out specially in a side room. The only imperial interest was when one of the palace eunuchs stupidly put his hand in the way of a large burning-glass and was scorched. This raised a few chuckles, but a senior mandarin then scornfully lit his pipe by the device, and the emperor was overhead to remark that the air-pump and other experiments were only good enough to amuse children.

Still, Macartney did not give up hope of achieving some diplomatic advance. In Peking he dutifully presented memoranda, wrote out formal lists of his requests, and badgered the senior mandarins incessantly. He moved into the large town house and was settling down for a hard round of diplomatic bargaining when, quite suddenly, he was apalled to receive a blunt communication from the Chinese secretariat telling him to pack up and leave China forthwith. Macartney could scarcely believe it. He had anticipated several weeks of negotiations, and none of his projects had been accomplished. But the mandarins were insistent. The emperor no longer considered it necessary for the embassy to remain in his country as there was nothing further to discuss. Stiffly the mandarins pointed out to Macartney that the water level in the rivers was falling, and if he was to travel by river

The elaborate process of hauling a junk from one level of the canal to another with huge capstans

junk he would have to hurry in order to reach the *Lion* which was waiting for him at Canton. In short, the sooner he left Peking, the better, and the Chinese authorities felt the British embassy was at an end.

Now began a hectic rush to pack up and leave. No one was more furious than Anderson the valet. Everything was chaos in his master's quarters. The mandarins rushed in and out pressing the visitors to hurry. The royal portraits were ignominiously unhooked, the state canopy literally ripped from the wall, and because there was no time to pack them, the elegant state chairs were given to the Chinese. Dinwiddie and his technicians were bundled out of Yuen Ming Yuen by urgent attendants who insisted that they knew exactly how to use the planetarium and other devices, although it was quite clear that they did not, and by Monday, 7 October 1793 the entire embassy was ready to leave Peking without even time to bury one of the guard who had died of fever. His body had to be carried along and buried in the countryside. In a quick final ceremony a mandarin, fifth class, wearing his transparent white button, knelt before the emperor's chief minister; two large scrolls containing the emperor's reply to King George and a list of presents to him, were fastened by broad yellow ribbons to the mandarin's back; and led by this strange scarecrow figure on horseback, the embassy was taken to Tungchow where their river junks were awaiting them. There the white-button mandarin knelt down again in the same humble posture; the ribbons were untied; and Macartney had received his formal answer.

The one consolation for the British was that their return route lay by a very different road to the one by which they had arrived four months before. To reach Canton in the south of China they had to travel almost the length of the country from north to south, first by the Grand Canal and then by a series of navigable rivers linked by short land portages. It was a stupendous journey which unfolded before them imperial China from the plains of the north to the paddy-fields of the south.

The greatest of its wonders was undoubtedly the Grand Canal linking Tungchow with Hangchow over seven hundred miles away. The canal was

Fishermen and their cormorants

part waterway, part reservoir, part flood-control device. Compared to the European canals of its time, it was designed along a relatively flat profile so that in places the waterway ran through a deep trench carved in the land, and all the travellers saw was the sky above their heads and the deep banks on each side. Elsewhere it was carried above the surrounding countryside as a massive aqueduct, held up by a tall embankment and hemmed in by buttresses of granite blocks riveted together with iron bands; or it marched across intervening lakes on series of arches flung across the obstacle. The Chinese controlled the flow of the current by sluice-gates of boards sliding up and down in grooves in the river embankment, and passing through these control points was an exciting business. The sluices were only opened at certain times in the day, and all the vessels in the area had to congregate there at the right moment. Then the planks were lifted and the vessels swirled through like flotsam on the sudden current while the sluice-keepers raced up and down holding fenders of leather stuffed with hair to stop the vessels from being smashed against the embankment wall. On the canal proper, instead of the usual paddle-locks, the junks were sledged bodily up slopes of dressed stone by vast capstans, and tipped out on to the next level of water like toys in a bathtub.

Everywhere the Grand Canal dominated its surroundings. In places it was as much as a thousand feet wide, towns and villages were built along its line, hundreds of thousands of peasants drew water from it by an ingenious variety of water-wheels and sluices and they even grew crops on it in floating barge gardens or on vines draped across poles driven in the water. Canal fishermen planted cage-traps, dragged nets in the canal, set trot-lines, and of course employed the famous tame cormorants to fish for them. Some stretches lay across lakes and meres, and here the junk captains could set their sails, but usually the waterway followed the lines of rivers, and the inevitable gangs of trackers were called into service to drag the junks along by brute force. In a high wind the slab-sided junks were uncontrollable and blown all over the water despite twin shore-lines. And in the teeth of even a mild breeze it was a tricky and sometimes dangerous business manœuvring a junk beneath the arch of a bridge. Underpaid and poorly fed, the trackers consistently stole their food from the embassy, and their plight contrasted sharply with the ease and comfort of the escorting mandarins. Wang and Chou were still with the embassy and had been reinforced by another mandarin who brought his travelling library aboard with him. After Hang-chow Dinwiddie had to cure two of them of syphilis caught in the city's brothels.

The British on the whole lived well. The Chinese authorities had thoughtfully provided a cow on shipboard so that the barbarians could have their fresh milk, and the gentlemen took it in turns to scan the countryside through a three-foot-long brass telescope which often caused consternation among the peasants who thought it was a gun and took to their heels in terror of being shot. The gentlemen went ashore to stretch their legs; the scientists made sketches of all the Chinese inventions which caught their fancy; and the gardeners busily picked samples of herbs and flowers, staggering back clutching young tea bushes with balls of earth round their shoots.

Crossing the Hwang-ho or Yellow river was a great adventure. The river current ran strongly, and before he dared embark upon it, each junk captain held a short ceremony. Taking a live cockerel he wrung off its head and sprinkled the spurting blood over the deck, mast, anchor, and cabin doors. Next several bowls of food were lined on the deck. The junk's brass gong was beaten loudly, and one by one the offerings from the bowls were thrown into the river while the crew lit coloured papers and set off fire-crackers. Only then did the junks venture on the Hwang-ho and cross to the opposite bank where they took up the Grand Canal once again.

Rumours had reached Macartney of the war between England and France and so he was heartily glad to find the *Lion* waiting for him in Canton on 19 December. He wanted to go home at once in order to escort the valuable Indiaman fleet with his warship, but first he gave a farewell dinner for Wang and Chou, of whom everyone in the embassy had grown extremely fond. It was a highly emotional affair and when the mandarins made their farewells, both had tears in their eyes. Later it was heard that Chou had returned successfully to the civil service, while the jovial soldier Wang was killed fighting rebels. Interpreter Li also said goodbye, intent on taking up his former status as a missionary, and on 17 January 1794 the fleet sailed for England without him.

At first glance it seemed that the embassy had achieved very little. At the cost of some £78,000 Macartney had not even managed to sign a treaty of friendship between Britain and China. Trade conditions at Canton, where Baring stayed on as a supercargo, were not improved, and Macartney had not been allowed to leave Staunton behind as a resident minister in Peking.

On the Chinese side, too, the embassy made scarcely any headway. Ch'ien Lung's mandarins were glad to see the last of Macartney, and the emperor himself composed a brief poem on the visit of the red-haired English which dismissed them with the lines:

Curios and the boasted ingenuity of their devices I prize not.
Though what they bring is meagre, yet,
In my kindness to men from afar I make generous return.
Wanting to preserve my good health and power.

Nevertheless, the appearance of failure was deceptive. In its own way the Macartney embassy was to have a very far-reaching effect, because it had cracked the brittle and distorted image of China which previously existed. When the *Lion* sailed, she carried aboard her the seeds of an extraordinary dissemination of new information about the country. From Macartney's own perceptive journal of his impressions to George Staunton's massive two volumes, the scientific notes of Dinwiddie and Barrow, and even the private diaries of Aeneas Anderson and trooper Holmes, there was a sudden new vision of Chinese culture. Their writings were soon to be printed, either privately or publicly, and reach an extraordinarily wide audience, while the authors were themselves to spread across the world like spores of thistle-down carrying their knowledge of China with them. Macartney, taking Barrow with him, went on to become governor of Cape Province in South Africa after he had reported at length on China to the British Government, and Barrow later became enormously influential as Second Secretary at the Admiralty, where for forty years he was a great advocate of world exploration. Many years later he would still be drawing upon his reminiscences of his China days, when telling young travellers how to behave and what to expect. Staunton tried to get a chair of Chinese established at King's College, London, and his son, young George, with his knowledge of Chinese affairs and language served as a Government adviser on China well into the next century. He helped to found the Royal Asiatic Society, and his former tutor Dr Huttner became a Foreign Office interpreter.

Yet the greatest index of the embassy's influence on contemporary thoughts was the advancement of Dr Dinwiddie. Flamboyant to the last, the worthy doctor-demonstrator did not return to England with the *Lion*, but left the fleet and went to Calcutta. There he deposited his samples of Chinese tea bushes at the botanical gardens and took to his old trade of giving lectures and scientific shows. So great was popular interest about China among the English merchants of Calcutta that advance subscriptions for his lecture course came to the extraordinary sum of £2250 – 'the greatest sum', as Dinwiddie happily put it, 'that probably ever was received for one course in any part of the world'. Later he repeated the lectures with equal success before the mercantile grandees of Madras and was chosen to take charge of the new Fort William College in Calcutta. Eventually Dinwiddie came to rest back in London worth £10,000, and he set up a comfortable office stuffed with various Chinese knick-knacks including a mandarin's gown which he had tailored from silk given to him in China, a conceit matched only by the new wallpaper at Coutts Bank in the Adelphi made from silk sent back by Macartney.

Equally influential, in a quieter vein, was the self-effacing draughtsman to the embassy, William Alexander. He had brought back nearly a thousand sketches and almost fifty colour-wash drawings of life in China and scenes of the embassy, many of them beautifully executed and of a very high accuracy. He became an assistant keeper of antiquities at the British Museum and many of his pictures were preserved there or at his native town of Maidstone where they were consulted and reproduced over many years by people interested in China, including Barrow, who used Alexander's paintings to illustrate his own popular book on the country.

Opposite Chinese engineering: a water-wheel on the Grand Canal

This new surge of interest in the Chinese empire was to bring an equally healthy change in the popular view of the Chinese and their country. The Macartney embassy had brought back a mass of genuinely fresh data about the Chinese empire – pioneer charts of its unknown north coast and its navigation, new calculations on the size and density of China's population, scientific and technological data of all sorts whether about the construction of water-wheels or the method of acupuncture. There were many mistakes, particularly over Chinese science which was vastly underrated, but the general effect of the embassy's reports was to give a more detailed and balanced understanding of the Chinese way of life. And there was also a new image of the Chinese peoples themselves. In place of the stylized Chinaman of the popular Jesuit accounts, all piety and self-control, Macartney's men told of a nation which was loquacious, cheerful, and good-humoured; yet capable of just the same quarrels and bad temper as any other group of men. Anderson recalled how flattered the Chinese women were when he approached them stammering out the Chinese word for 'beautiful! beautiful!', and Barrow left an amiable picture of the mandarin Wang calling out cheerfully across the water every day as he was rowed past Barrow's barge 'Pallo how do', for 'Barrow, how are you' – and receiving an equally kindly reply in broken Chinese from the former English maths tutor. Yet perhaps the greatest single result of the entire trip was the new understanding it brought of the Chinese empire itself, and an overall appreciation of the diligence and obedience of its peasantry, the declining morality and suspicion of its once-superb bureaucracy, and the fragile state of the Manchu regime.

It was Macartney who provided the most perceptive commentary of all when he wrote his famous summary that

> the empire of China is an old, crazy, first-rate man-of-war, which a fortunate succession of able and vigilant officers has contrived to keep afloat for these one hundred and fifty years past, and to overawe their neighbours merely by her bulk and appearance. But whenever an insufficient man happens to have command upon deck, adieu to the discipline and safety of the ship. She may perhaps not sink outright; she may drift some time in the wreck, and will then be dashed to pieces on the shore, but she can never be rebuilt on the old bottom.

Events were to prove that Imperial China could stay afloat for another century and a half, but in the end Macartney's judgment would be remarkably close to the fact.

COLONIAL COMMISSION

IN 1862 THE EMPEROR OF ANNAM, as Vietnam was then known, signed a treaty with the French recognizing their territorial rights over the three lower provinces of Cochin China, where France already possessed the city of Saigon. Five years later, in the neighbouring state of Cambodia, the most powerful man, except for its fat and conniving King Norodom, lived in a smart little French compound with its flag-pole and tricolour at a strategic position on the banks of the Mekong river where one arm of the great stream branched off to join the inland lake of Tonle Sap, and the other arm led deep into the Cambodian hinterland. Here, in a neatly thatched house which he had designed and built himself, dwelt Captain of Frigates, Ernest-Marc-Louis-de-Gonzague Doudart de Lagrée, veteran of the Crimea, holder of the Knight's Cross of the Légion d'Honneur, and effective controller of Cambodian policy by virtue of his appointment as French military representative to the court of King Norodom.

On most days the main instrument of the captain's power could be seen anchored opposite his home – a *canonière* or steam-brig whose guns were capable of smashing into matchwood in less than half an hour the flimsy cardhouse assembly of bamboo buildings on stilts which formed Norodom's brand-new capital at Pnom Penh, where the pigs and chickens strayed along its single main street. Only Norodom's private residence would have given genuine target practice, for in a fit of sycophantic enthusiasm the King of Cambodia had bargained with a glib French salesman to build him a new royal home and had chosen the totally unsuitable design of a French provincial villa, laboriously built in brick.

Throughout the whole of Indo-China the French were in a hurry. They intended to catch up with the British in the race for empire, and they remembered nostalgically the earlier colonies which France had lost in India and Louisiana. Now in Southeast Asia they were intent upon making up for that loss with a whirlwind campaign of colonial expansion which would bring as much as possible of that strategic corner of the Orient under direct French control. At first sight it was not too difficult a proposition. The patchwork of Southeast Asia – Annam, Cambodia, Laos, and Siam – was made of small puny countries which were so constantly at loggerheads with one another that it would be easy to prize them apart and swallow them one by one. Only Burma had to be avoided, because the British regarded it as their own preserve; and of course it was always wise to tread gently near the long border with China which overhung the area from the north. But China was less of a threat than formerly, because a full-scale revolt by Muslim rebels against the emperor was being fought in the western province of Yunnan, and word had reached the French authorities in Saigon that the

95 East of Greenwich · 100 · 105 · 110

INDO-CHINA

INDIA

CHINA

River Brahmaputra
River Chindwin
River Irrawaddy
River Salween
River Mekong
River Yangtze
Red River
Black River

Mandalay

BURMA

Hanoi
Haiphong
Gulf of Tonkin

VIETNAM

Luang
Prabang

LAOS

HAINAN

Vientiane

River Irrawaddy
River Salween

Rangoon
Moulmein
Gulf of Martaban

River Me Nam

SIAM

Ubon

Rapids of Khon

Hué

SOUTH CHINA SEA

Bay of Bengal

Bangkok

Angkor

Tonle Sap

CAMBODIA

Pnom Penh

River Mekong
Cataracts of Kratié

VIETNAM

Saigon

Gulf of Siam

Scale in Miles
50 · 100 · 150

Pointe de Camau

95 East of Greenwich · 100 · 105 · 110

Members of the expedition: from left to right, Garnier, Delaporte, Joubert, Thorel, de Carné and Lagrée

Chinese central Government was powerless to crush this rebellion. Indeed there seemed a very real chance that the province of Yunnan would break away from China to form a separate state of its own. If so, the French intended to be the first foreign power to establish friendly relations with it and derive the benefit.

So it was with a redoubled sense of urgency that the French decided in 1865 to launch a single decisive expedition of reconnaissance into the interior of Indo-China, organized by the French Government and acting directly as its agent. Nothing quite like it had been encountered before in the Oriental Adventure, for this was to be exploration harnessed directly to colonialism, with very little attempt at disguise. The purpose of the expedition was to spy out the land to see if it was fit to be claimed as a colony, to find ways of diverting all Indo-Chinese trade into French hands, and – almost as an afterthought – to clear up the geographical uncertainties of Southeast Asia. Fortunately, though, the French also brought Gallic style to the plan, softening its ambition and giving it more generous proportions. As explorers in Asia the French proved to have an appreciative eye for the colour and variety of the regions they encountered, a more indulgent view of the native cultures, and a sympathetic if less precise judgment of Asian subtleties. Yet, behind it all, it was difficult to forget that this expedition was a classic exercise in colonial policy.

The composition of the French expedition illustrated its dual character very well. First of all there was its transport: *Canonière No. 27* of the French colonial forces which was to carry the expedition as far as the upper limit of steam navigation on the Mekong river, wherever that might be, and put them ashore. Next there was the military escort which was to accompany the expedition. It comprised two French marines armed with carbines, two French sailors, two Tagals or Filipinos left behind in Saigon from the days of the Spanish, a native sergeant, and six Annamite militiamen, all of them armed with muskets and bayonets, besides a revolver for every man on the expedition, and a special rifle which fired exploding bullets. In local terms this armament was invincible. By contrast the officers of the expedition, who with one exception held naval rank, seemed positively non-belligerent.

Their leader was the French Resident in Cambodia, whose unwieldy name
was shortened for convenience to Doudart de Lagrée and who, despite a
hawk face, fierce hedge of whiskers, and his martial record, preferred the
study of archaeology and Oriental languages to military science, spoke
fluent Cambodian, and was one of the earliest students of Cambodian history.
His second-in-command, Francis Garnier, was a naval lieutenant, a fervent
believer in France's colonial destiny and the author of a recent fiery pamphlet
on the topic which he had signed with the shallow pseudonym of G. Francis.
Now, however, Garnier was charged with the full-time task of taking all the
expedition's meteorological and astronomical observations, as well as
keeping a precise survey of its route, and this would keep him too busy for
colonial politics. Junior to Garnier were two more naval men, both of them
surgeons, Dr Joubert and Dr Thorel who were respectively the expedition's
geologist and anthropologist-cum-botanist. And then there was Ensign
Delaporte, also of the navy and officially in charge of the expedition's
discipline but really its artist. His job was to sketch all the landscapes and
peoples the explorers met, and to help Garnier with his maps.

It was almost inevitable, therefore, that the expedition's most sinister
member should be its only civilian. He was Louis de Carné, son of the
Count de Carné and on special detachment from the French Foreign Office.
His instructions were so secret that although he was placed under Lagrée's
command, de Carné was told not to report to Lagrée but to keep in touch
directly and by special letter with his Foreign Office superiors in Saigon.
Since de Carné was a colonial specialist, it took little imagination to guess
that it was his job to evaluate the new-found territories for their potential as
colonies and, in particular, to decide whether or not they should be acquired
by France and how best to exploit them.

The French authorities in Saigon lived in hope that the Mekong river
would prove to be the key to the whole control and development of Indo-
China. So the exploration of the river was to be the expedition's paramount
objective. Lagrée's official letter of instruction told him that no matter how
long it took him, or at what cost to other research, he was to follow the
Mekong into the interior as far as humanly possible and report whether it
could be used as an avenue of communication, possibly with China. To do so,
he was told, would be 'for the general interest of civilization, and more particularly our infant colony', and Louis de Carné put it rather more aptly
when he claimed that one day the Mekong could be another Mississippi, and
that Saigon would be its resplendent New Orleans. Others even dreamed that
Saigon would thus rival Shanghai as a trade emporium; and there was one
grandiose plan that the vastly increased shipping which would soon result
from the opening of the Suez Canal then under construction (where de
Carné's brother was working) could be diverted up the Mekong into China
and so avoid the typhoons of the China Sea.

The expedition was loftily called 'the Commission for the Exploration of
the Mekong', and it left Saigon in the summer of 1866 to assemble at Lagrée's
compound near Pnom Penh. Among the first to arrive was de Carné, and he,
Lagrée, Garnier, and the other officers made a lengthy detour by elephant and
bullock-cart to visit the magnificent Khmer ruins at Angkor Wat in order
to complete Lagrée's earlier studies of its unique relics. This detour was

Overleaf *One of the magnificent gateways of Angkor Thom*

another example of the Commission's conflicting nature. Equipped and intended for deep penetration into unknown territory, the Commission in fact spent its first week scrambling carefully about the fantastic buildings of Angkor Wat, running tape-measures over the tumbled remains, sketching views, copying inscriptions, and in place of colonial ambition generally substituting a scholarly and often romantic view of their role. It was an interlude which brought out the best in them, and the site itself was worth any amount of attention they could give it.

Angkor Wat had been known to outsiders including the Portuguese for centuries, but had only recently been brought to public attention by the efforts of the French naturalist Henri Mouhot. He had stumbled upon it during a trek through the jungle five years previously, and the excitement among Orientalists caused by Mouhot's discovery was intense. Here, abandoned in the jungle, were the ruins of an Asian civilization whose scope and artistic achievement surpassed anything that had been guessed at. No one had yet worked out precisely what the remarkable stone structures at Angkor Wat had been meant for, though a mysterious symbolism was recognized in the long flights of steps leading up to the great pagoda domes, so heavily ornamented that they looked like huge pine cones rising above the surrounding green of the forest, the symmetry of the long palace galleries flanking the pagodas, and the constantly repeated symbols of grotesque heraldic beasts dominated by the motif of the many-headed sacred cobra, the Naga, with its five to eleven heads, each with the hood distended.

In these strange surroundings the Frenchmen plunged with their note-books and pencils, jotting down the precise measurements and details of Angkor Wat which Mouhot had neither time nor facilities to gather. De Carné had only just finished re-reading Mouhot's original description of how he found the place, but even so, the hard-headed young Foreign Office expert was stunned by what he saw as he approached across the flagstones of the great ceremonial causeway, wide enough for a parade of elephants, leading over the ancient moat and into Angkor Wat's main buildings. 'In spite of all, I felt overcome', he wrote;

> I had, as it were, a shock of astonishment. I had hardly cleared the gate of the central pavilion when a second paved avenue, about 200 metres in length, opened before me a huge building, the style of which is different from any of our Western forms of architecture as the Chinese fancies, of which I had already studied some examples. Wearied with the journey and overcome by the heat, I thought I saw an incredible number of towers of strange outline dance before me, nothing supporting them in the air, and another higher tower rising above them. This kind of hallucination soon passed and gave way to a just admiration.

An air of desolation added to the grandeur of Angkor Wat. The only sign of recent occupation were four rather mediocre statues of Buddha which the local priests, the *bonzes*, had placed beneath its great central pagoda tower, which rose a couple of hundred feet above the ground. Otherwise the buildings had been totally shunned by human beings. Bats infested the two miles of palace corridors which stank of their droppings and almost over-powered the Commission as they patiently examined the intricate wall-

Performance of a Cambodian ballet in honour of the Commission at the court of the lecherous King Norodom, whose servants crawl on hands and knees

engravings depicting scene after scene in the power and majesty of the Khmer Dynasty, their battles and parades, the gods they worshipped and claimed themselves to be, and the great epics of Indian legend which they had adopted. On the outside the buildings were literally being torn apart by the advancing forest vegetation. Windblown plants had taken root in the nooks and ledges of the astonishing profusion of stone-carvings which covered every exterior surface like a great lace net and produced an orgy of decoration. Even the foundation-blocks, great iron-clamped slabs of laterite, were being forced apart by the roots of trees, and of the ancient roadway which had once joined Angkor Wat to its adjacent city of Angkor Thom scarcely a trace remained beneath the advancing carpet of jungle.

Finally, on 1 July Lagrée regretfully ordered his party to leave Angkor Wat and return on their elephants to the rendezvous with *Canonière No. 27*. They then steamed down to Pnom Penh to pay a courtesy call on King Norodom and stock up on trade goods. Several varieties of cotton check cloth, which the Cambodian merchants assured them were in great demand up river, were added to the collection of items already bought from Saigon, the trinkets, cutlery, rifles, watches, revolvers, and telescopes which were intended as presents for the river peoples. For cash the Commission had been given a grant of twenty-five thousand francs by the French Government of which ten thousand francs were held in the convenient currency of Mexican pesetas and the rest in gold-leaf and gold bars and in Siamese currency. For luxuries the expedition had chosen to take along twenty-three cases of varied conserves, mostly jams and tinned delicacies; and in an indisputably French touch they also allocated thirty-two of the total 140 packages of the baggage-train to liquor: twenty-four barrels or 766 litres of wine and eight barrels or 302 litres of eau de vie, plus sundry private bottles of table wine packed carefully in their personal effects.

163

Opposite *A Chinese comedian.*
Overleaf, bottom left *Emperor Ch'ien Lung arriving to give audience to the British embassy (see p. 146).*
Overleaf, top *Indo-Chinese natives wear a selection of Siamese, Annamite and Cambodian costumes in an illustration, after Delaporte, to Garnier's Atlas of his travels.*
Overleaf, bottom right *The firework display in Bassac*

In their honour King Norodom threw a truly royal feast, culminating with a Cambodian ballet performed by a selection of the prettiest dancers on his court payroll. Norodom sat the members of the Commission in a line next to him beside the stage, and while a Cambodian orchestra struck up a tune, the royal women danced and mimed before them only a few feet away. King Norodom was a notorious philanderer and he was delighted with the show, as one after another of the dancers stopped before him and gave him a special salute, squatting on the ground and then slowly and sensuously raising their arms above their heads while arching back their bodies in time with the drummer so that their costumes showed off their figures, before suddenly dropping forward on their knees and remaining there for an instant with their breasts bent forward. Norodom was ecstatic, and he kept on turning to Lagrée to ask him whom he thought was the prettiest of the girls, a question which the interpreter diplomatically relayed by glancing towards the royal favourite of the day.

On 7 July the Commission finally got away from Pnom Penh and its hospitality, though not before Norodom unsuccessfully tried to press into Lagrée's hand a gold bar as a gift to mark his stay at the court. The French commander's refusal to take the gold astonished Norodom, though to mollify him *Canonière No. 27* fired off a full royal salute as she hauled out into the river and, turning upstream, headed towards her serious exploration.

The cataracts of Kratie, some 280 miles above the mouth of the Mekong, formed at that time the limit of French knowledge of the interior. This was the highest point which their gunboats had reached, and it was a comparatively unimpressive distance since at Kratie the effect of the tides could still be felt. Yet Kratie was an important boundary, for it was not only the first set of rapids on the river which threatened to block steam navigation, but it was very close to the boundary between Cambodia and Laos, and almost the limit of King Norodom's authority. Lagrée intended that *Canonière No. 27* should try to work her way up through the rapids, but her captain was unwilling to press the attempt too closely as his vehicle was old and fragile, her hull shaky, and her boilers nearly worn out from six years of almost continuous service on the river. He feared, quite rightly, that if she was deflected by the current, she was likely to be smashed on the rocks. So at Kratie a disappointed Lagrée led his Commission off the gunboat and transferred to a flotilla of eight native river-boats which King Norodom's local governor had been asked to provide for them.

The Commission knew that they would be travelling nearly all the way up the Mekong on native boats, either by hiring them or as official Government guests, and so they took a close look at this new form of transport. Each vessel was a long slim dug-out canoe, varying between ten and eighteen metres in length, and covered for the most part by a low semicircular canopy made of bamboo hoops thatched with palm leaves, so that the passengers could shelter in a long tunnel-like cabin. The whole craft, in fact, looked rather like a weaver's shuttle. One curious feature about them was that they were neither sailed nor paddled, but literally hauled along by their crews. Round the sides of each boat ran a narrow ledge, terminating in a small platform at bow and stern. Each crewman was armed with a long bamboo pole which had a metal hook at one end and a spike at the other. Standing on

London Published Aug.t 13.th 1801. by G. and W. Nicol Pallmall.

W. Alexander fec.t

the bow platform, he would take his turn to hook his pole on to some convenient tree or rock on the bank, and then haul back on it as he walked slowly down the catwalk, literally dragging the boat forward while his place in the bow was taken by the next man in the chain returning by the opposite catwalk. The crewmen could keep up this exhausting progress for up to eight hours a day which made de Carné compare them to 'the blind horses used to turn wheels', and he was astonished that although their overseers did nothing but threaten them with beatings if they slacked, yet they remained 'sweet tempered and resigned, often almost mirthful; yet they are men mostly dragged away from their rice fields, sent far from their families and their interests, and they have no right to any wages; for in Cambodia every free man is liable to forced labour from eighteen to sixty, and we are provided by the king's orders. I was', he concluded sadly, 'leaving civilization behind, and entering on a savage country.'

Canoe-handling required careful judgment. The dug-outs had to nose their way up through the long series of rapids just above Kratie where the Mekong came boiling in full flood through a maze of islets and rocks which formed the barrier. The river was also bringing down dangerous masses of flotsam, huge dead trees like battering-rams and rafts of broken vegetation which threatened to dash against the canoes and overturn them. The boats found their way upstream like returning salmon, wriggling a path through side channels and using the back eddies, while their crews hooked and heaved on half-submerged rocks and the overhanging branches of trees. The steersmen kept the craft hovering delicately balanced against the current, hanging at that crucial point where progress could be made upstream and yet guarding against the current striking the canoe on its landward bow so that the craft was sent spinning helplessly down-current losing precious advantage until the boathooks could grapple again with the land.

It took almost six days of this hard work to clear the zone of rapids, an area virtually uninhabited by reason of the dense virgin forest and the difficulties of the river, and thus the effective buffer zone between Cambodia and Laotian territory, which the Commission finally entered on 20 July. Here the fifty Cambodian boatmen and their canoes were sent back downstream, while the explorers began negotiations with the local Laotian governor for a new flotilla of boats and fresh crews to take them up river. It was a long wait. The governor was stupid and opium-sodden – his most prized foreign possession was a trade knife with an obscene picture stuck in the handle – and he was uncertain as to whether he should help the explorers. He insisted on sending to his Siamese overlord to check the Commission's credentials, and in the meantime, Lagrée had to busy himself with side trips up the local tributaries of the Mekong to see what he could find, while his companions began taking notes on the notorious Laotians, who were so feared by the Cambodians downstream that the expedition's original interpreter had refused to come with them and jumped ship at Pnom Penh. Garnier thought the Laotian face exhibited 'a singular combination of cunning and apathy, benevolence and timorousness', and it seemed that they were great thieves, for the expedition was constantly being pilfered of small items. Yet the Laotians were also lighthearted and devil-may-care in a way which the Cambodians lacked, and they were certainly far more

Opposite *A silk temple-banner from the Caves of the Thousand Buddhas representing the Bodhisattva Kuan-yin (see p. 222).*
Overleaf *The end of a dream: the expedition members negotiating the Khon rapids which, they discovered to their dismay, made steam navigation of the Mekong impossible*

flamboyant. The Laotian men shaved their heads except for a single tuft of hair, and they were always beautifully dressed in bright waist-cloths or *langoutis* of brilliant colours and if possible made of silk so that they set off their copper-coloured skin admirably. Each *langouti* was complemented by a small vest, gorgeously worked in matching colours, and a bright cummerbund or a neckscarf to heighten the effect. The Laotian women made a match for their husbands. Their *langoutis* were longer and worn like stiff petticoats, and over this a second piece of coloured cloth was wrapped across the bosom and thrown back over one shoulder. They tied their glossy black hair up in a chignon, adorned it with a few flowers, and their arms, necks, and legs were a shop-window of rings, bracelets, and bangles of gold, copper, and silver.

Despite these bright surroundings this was not a happy interlude for the Commission. They were already learning that Southeast Asia came uncomfortably close to the popular image of jungle Asia, with its inhospitable forests, miserable climate, diseases, and insects. One of the officers caught fever and was delirious, and Francis Garnier contracted typhus so badly that his life was despaired of. Also the expedition's morale suffered a profound shock when in a single night a swarm of wood-boring insects chewed their way into the barrels containing the expedition's precious supply of liquor. By morning not a single drop was left, and the travellers were reduced to using their last few bottles of wine to wash down the massive doses of quinine which they were swallowing daily. Their stock of flour was ruined by a flood, and their diet soon reduced to an occasional scrawny chicken or whatever fish they were able to catch from the Mekong. Hunting excursions along the banks of the river, in the hope of shooting a wild peacock for the pot, proved to be so unproductive that they were quickly abandoned, and the weather deteriorated daily. Every afternoon brought thunderstorms accompanied by vivid displays of lightning and torrential rain so that it was no longer possible to camp out at night. And when the expedition finally got under way again on 14 August, the Frenchmen had to sleep aboard the Laotian canoes, whose palm-leaf roofs failed to keep out the rain so that they lay half in a steady drip of rainwater and half in the slop of the bilges which was periodically baled out by a crewman using a large leaf as a scoop.

An even worse scourge was the insect life. On their second night in the wilderness the Commission learned that it was impossible to get any sleep unless they rigged mosquito-nets, and they were constantly being visited by armies of leeches which crept beneath the heavy frock-coats of blue serge which the commissioners were still wearing. On an island in the rapids of Khon, Garnier, now fully recovered from his typhus, had a most unpleasant experience when he attempted to land in order to find a vantage point to make his survey of the rapids. He was puzzled when the boatman who agreed to guide him, stopped to roll up his *langouti* tightly about his waist and then plastered his bare legs with a thick sticky mixture of lime and areca juice. The Frenchman learned the reason for this precaution as soon as they set foot on the island. The soil was literally covered with thousands of leeches. Some, he reported, were no bigger than a needle, while others were as much as two and a half to three inches long. As the strangers came ashore, the

Garnier measuring the angle of the sun before an admiring audience

insects could be seen literally rearing up at the scent of their prey, and almost every leaf and blade of grass began to tremble as they started to converge with their loathsomely determined march on the two men. Protected by his plaster coating, the Laotian was scarcely troubled by the leeches, but Garnier was quickly overwhelmed. For every leech he plucked off, two more took its place, and within a few moments a living tide of the predatory suckers was wriggling up his legs and crawling into his clothing. He was forced to run to a tall tree and climb it as a refuge, and there take off all his clothes and pluck the blood-swollen leeches, flinging them to the ground like ripe plums. Even in that short time one leech had managed to work itself as high as his chest.

The Khon rapids were a major setback, because they finally shattered any hope of using the Mekong as a single, continuous waterway. At Khon the Mekong tumbled over a series of cataracts which were impossible for any steamboat to surmount. A ridge of sandstone cutting across the line of the valley had created a number of magnificent falls, the largest of which was seventy feet high, and here the Mekong slid in a spectacular sheet of water a thousand yards wide to burst into huge gobbets of foam and with a roar like the sea beating against the shore in a storm. It was an impressive sight, even if a disappointing one, because below the falls the river opened out into a beautiful lake, rich with aquatic birds and large fish, and round the falls

173

themselves the trees came down so close to the river that their branches overhung the racing water. Only by unloading their canoes, portaging the baggage, and then hauling the boats up the quietest channel on rattan cables was the expedition able to get past the obstacle and enter the calmer water upstream, where the Mekong now flowed as a single river, twelve to fifteen hundred metres broad and at last unencumbered by rocks and floating masses of vegetation.

On 11 September the expedition arrived at the pleasantly bucolic town of Bassac whose fifteen pagodas were strung out in a line along the bank of the river and its neat bamboo houses set elegantly beneath a splendid forest-clad hillside. Bassac was by far the most congenial town the expedition encountered, as well as the healthiest. It received a pleasant breeze off the river, and Garnier, no doubt to make up in part for the disappointment of the Khon rapids, had no hesitation in recommending it as a future convalescent station for invalid Frenchmen serving in Indo-China. The expedition itself decided to take time off to enjoy Bassac's healthy situation, and convalesced there for more than two months while the wet season rained itself out. On clear days the officers climbed the near-by hills to admire the view, got on with the task of compiling a glossary of the local dialect, and went for muddy walks in the near-by forests. They uncovered yet more Khmer ruins, less impressive than Angkor Wat but instantly recognizable by the same characteristic style of architecture with its heavily sculptured columns half submerged by the forest, a ruined sanctuary with its statue to some forgotten Khmer king, and the great bulk of a stone platform buried by the undergrowth and showing only the outlines of its balustrades beneath which, after hacking back the clinging plants, one could still read the carved inscriptions to its builder.

Bassac's ruler was an amiable and rather timid young man, about twenty-five or thirty years old, and the Commission made a great impression on him by presenting him with a double-barrelled gun. Eager to please his generous visitors, he invited them to attend the annual ceremony in which he pledged his allegiance to the Siamese Crown. As the timing of this ceremony coincided with the end of the rainy season, it was a great occasion for the country people to visit Bassac and celebrate the occasion with singing and feasting. The highlight of their day was an energetic regatta on the Mekong between racing canoes owned by the rival pagodas. The teams of paddlers were men from the wilder outlying tribes who were seldom seen in the town, and clad only in tiny strips of cloth, they drove their craft along at considerable speed, the paddles striking up at a terrific rate, while two or three cheer-leaders, dressed in red cowls and cloaks like court jesters, danced aboard each vessel, grimacing and shrieking at the tops of their voices to urge their team to victory. Later there were bouts of wrestling and boxing by trained fighters whose enormously developed chests gave their heads a shrunken look; and at dusk the ceremony concluded with a firework display held at the waterfront. Sky-rockets were shot over the river; short lengths of bamboo stuffed with gunpowder were tossed into the fire and exploded with loud bangs; and on the Mekong itself, elaborate fire-rafts were pushed out to descend the current, wheeling and bobbing in erratic circles as the eddies caught them.

The political structure of Laos was a subject which the Commission had particularly been instructed to study, and they found that although the bulk of the territory was formally claimed by Siam, the up-river chieftains were so isolated that they were virtually independent kinglets. At Ubon, the next province the French entered after Bassac, they found a local dignitary who regarded himself as its independent sovereign. The Frenchmen arrived just at the moment when this chief was preparing to move into a new palace he had built for himself on the outskirts of his capital. In front of a huge throng of his subjects he made a spectacular entry into Ubon, riding on a war elephant and dressed in a tunic of green velvet. On his head was an extravagant crown which reminded de Carné of a Prussian helmet, and a gang of attendants held over him a state parasol worked with gold threads on a long pole. Making a tremendous noise, a band of drummers and gong-players led the royal elephant up to the elevated platform of the new palace, and there the king was greeted by his royal *bonzes* who clothed him in a white mantle in place of his tunic. He was then escorted to a wooden trough, intricately carved in the shape of a sacred dragon and held up on trestles. Stooping beneath this trough, the king took a public shower-bath in sacred water while a *bonze* simultaneously released two doves to fly out over the heads of the watching crowd as a symbol of universal happiness. Then the king changed back into dry clothes; gave a great banquet of rice, pork, cucumbers, eggs, bananas, and rice wine to his supporters; and the usual firework display rounded off the evening's festivities while bands of musicians and singers wandered through the streets singing popular local songs.

From Ubon all but one of the Commission's European escort was sent

Showering in holy water, the self-styled King of Ubon prepares himself for the final stage of his investiture

175

back downstream to Cambodia. Partly this was because it had been found that they were not really necessary among the peaceable river folk, and partly because Lagrée wanted to cut down the size of his expedition as his funds were beginning to run dangerously low and he needed to economize on the cost of hiring canoes and paddlers. Also some members of the escort had disgraced themselves. After the loss of their wine supply, there had been a lot of grumbling about the food and the lack of drink, and at Bassac there was a mutiny. When Lagrée was out of the camp, one of the French soldiers and a sailor stole weapons and went on the rampage, terrorizing the natives, smashing open doors to enter their homes and steal food, and had eventually run away with a group of Laotian women. Ensign Delaporte, who had been left in charge of the French camp, was obliged to go to the young king and arrange for a posse of twenty Laotians armed with clubs to track down the mutineers. Luckily they took the trouble-makers by surprise and over-powered them without bloodshed so that they could be brought back in irons.

The expedition's morale was sagging for other reasons as well. Delayed by the need to be tactful with native chieftains and by the difficulty of obtaining canoes, the Commission was already far behind its schedule. By the time it left Ubon, the better part of the dry season was already wasted, and Lagrée had to hurry forward, keeping an eye on the gathering rain clouds while hoping to reach Luang Prabang before the rains broke once again. De Carné in particular was dispirited. The numerous cataracts on the Mekong had destroyed his hopes for using the river, and his disappointment showed quite clearly in his opinion of the Laotians. He thought them brutish, unreliable, and dull, and he was revolted when their Laotian interpreter, a renegade *bonze*, suddenly felt the call of his old religion and in his remorse sacrificed half of the upper joint of his forefinger to Buddha. The local priests performed the operation with a chopper and a footrule.

In de Carné's opinion the country needed a dose of French colonial rule to put it right, and he was not even impressed by the expedition's Laotian boatmen who remained uniformly polite and cheerful, even when obliged to jump overboard into the water to heave the canoes off mudbanks, which was happening more frequently, or when taking care of their passengers, which they did with considerable devotion. The boatmen had made careful notes of each commissioner's preferences in food, and tried hard to prepare suitable menus. Once, when travelling on land, they accidentally spilled a box of pins and insisted that the whole column should halt while every single pin was picked up and returned to its rightful place.

Nevertheless the Commission was steadily gathering useful information. On the way to the recently devastated town of Vientiane, where they arrived in April 1867, they found that the Mekong took a two-hundred-mile bend to the west, a diversion which no one had previously known. And near Vientiane itself they stumbled across more classical ruins buried by the jungle. It was another of those romantic interludes when a sudden glimmer of light reflected in the undergrowth led them to a cluster of abandoned pagodas whose Siamese and Laotian craftsmen had mingled glass plates in the gilding of the roofs to make them more showy. Every surface of the destroyed temples was covered in the same profusion of carved arabesques and fantastic animal figures which had been seen at Angkor Wat, and the excitement of discovery combined with the absolute silence of the surrounding forest to make the ruins all the more impressive, as they lay prematurely aged by the festoons of lianas which grew up the sagging columns, the bright green lines of grass sprouting through cracks in the broken pavement, and the trees soaring up through shattered cupolas. And yet, like Vientiane itself, the place could not have been abandoned long, for in one pagoda, better preserved than the rest, the Frenchmen found a priest's library, its books still lying scattered on the floor, narrow pages cut from the leaves of palm and gilded on the edges, and the lines of writing still plainly legible.

Luang Prabang, another three weeks up river, brought the expedition a special duty to perform. It was here, six years before, that Henri Mouhot, the French pioneer explorer, had died of fever. Trying to extend his archaeological survey of the ancient Khmer kingdom, he had spent his last days in a lonely hut in the forest, unaccompanied by any European. The Commission had been specially charged by the French governor in Saigon to seek out Mouhot's last resting-place and leave a suitable monument. This they did, and it spoke well of Mouhot's memory with the local population that the ruler of Luang Prabang, a wizened betel-chewing old dignitary, whose courtiers and bodyguard were obliged to stay kneeling before him holding up their muskets and swords like knights at vigil, contributed at his own cost the materials for the monument which the Commission erected in the depths of the forest, while the local natives kept on bringing specimens of plants and insects to the strangers' camp, imagining that they too had Mouhot's love of natural history.

Above Luang Prabang the Mekong entered territory claimed by Burma, and once again there were frustrating delays as the Commission waited for permission to proceed. It was time they could ill afford to waste because their travelling money was now almost gone, and the explorers themselves were severely debilitated by recurrent attacks of dysentery and malaria. They had been taking such massive doses of quinine that they were suffering from dizziness and a ringing sensation in their ears. Already the whole aspect of the countryside had changed. The Mekong itself was now so shallow that in many places their boatmen were able to punt their dug-outs, and instead of a broad open plain, there were now forest-clad hills closing in round the valley. Tributary streams were smaller but more numerous, and the terrain was broken and confused. The human landscape, too, was noticeably different. All along the upper river the Commission began to find small scattered villages, inhabited by natives who sported magnificent body tattoos, extending from their waists downwards in a mass of indigo whorls and patterns, a device which had earned them the name of 'Blue Bellies'; and almost every bend in the Mekong brought into view an isolated pagoda standing on its terrace cut out of the hillside, or a Buddhist shrine in honour of some revered *bonze* and placed at his favourite meditation spot on the river bank.

By June, after a few more miles' travelling, Lagrée was finally forced to admit the failure of his primary objective, and he gave orders for the expedition to turn aside from the Mekong, dismiss the canoe-men, and strike out for China on foot. Quite simply the Mekong's importance had petered out. The Mekong no longer dominated the region, and many of the minor chieftains had located their villages away from its banks. Few of them had

The Commission visits a local chief, the King of Muong You

ever seen a white man before, and they insisted that the French should visit them. So Lagrée led his party on a painful last lap through Upper Indo-China, zigzagging from village to village and knowing that they must be very close to their goal of the Chinese border. Crippled by lack of money to hire porters, they were forced to throw away most of their remaining equipment and rely on native hospitality. They sold their clothing and tools for food, suffered the miseries of jungle fever, mosquitoes, and leeches, and spent many nights on the trail huddled together in crude shelters made from tree branches. When possible, they were no longer loathe to camp overnight in empty pagodas. Fortunately the countryside was pleasant enough, gentle valleys divided by irregular lines of hills, and they had gained sufficient altitude for the temperature to have moderated comfortably.

The ethnography of the area was its main fascination. It was the home of obscure and primitive hill tribes with their own dialects, dress, and customs. The women of one group called the Mou-tsen wore extraordinary hats made from layer upon layer of bamboo rings covered with straw. From the edge of the brim dangled a fringe of silver balls, and above them a double ridge of white glass beads. On the left side of the hat emerged a tuft of cotton thread from which hung a loop of many-coloured pearls, and the whole contraption was lavishly embellished by bunches of leaves and flowers. If this was not enough concoction, the Mou-tsen women also trimmed the sleeves and edges of their bodices with pearls, sewed rows of pearls on their leggings under a knee-length petticoat, draped themselves with ear-rings, bracelets, collars, and two embroidered shoulder-belts crossed like a grenadier; and on top of all still managed to balance a bizarre cloak shaped like a half-open book which was fastened at the neck and in rainy weather could be brought up over the head like a portable roof.

This exotic garb was a last touch of barbaric splendour before the expedi-

A display of regional fashions, including elaborate hats and a 'book cloak'

tion finally re-emerged into Oriental civilization as they knew it. On the afternoon of 18 October 1867, after sixteen months' travel from Saigon, the Commission crossed a final mountain ridge and saw China spread out before them. To Garnier the moment of transition from the savage to the civilized was when he saw his first properly engineered bridge since leaving Cambodia, and the mark that he was really in China when he saw a woman with bound feet. Not that Yunnan, the province they had finally reached, was exactly the mainstream of Chinese progress. When the expedition called on the local mandarin to present its passport and compliments, the mandarin was so excited by the gift of a revolver that he began to pull the trigger there and then. Bullets went flying all over the audience-hall, and if an attendant had not knocked up the mandarin's arm, someone would certainly have been shot.

The Commission's condition on arrival in Yunnan was pitiable. Their clothes and equipment were worn out, and their health badly shaken. Lagrée himself was in such a poor way that he needed constant medical attention from the two surgeons, and only Garnier and de Carné were fit enough to carry out the last part of their mission and contact the rebel Muslims. Leaving Lagrée with the two doctors, they set out for Talifoo, the rebels' stronghold. But it was a wasted journey, for they were regarded as foreign devils and only escaped arrest by shooting in the air to frighten the mob and galloping as fast as possible back to their rendezvous with the rest of the Commission. There they found that Lagrée had died of a liver disease and exhaustion. A Chinese undertaker made up a travelling coffin for their leader's body which they then carried across country to the Upper Yangtze, and took ship via Shanghai for their original starting point in Saigon.

Back at Saigon they buried Lagrée with full honours. Virtually the whole

of the city's French population turned out to follow his cortège, and the funeral oration was given by the French governor. To some the funeral was a fitting conclusion to the mission of exploration of the Mekong, for undoubtedly it had been a disappointment to its official sponsors. The Mekong had proved that it was not the avenue to China; the up-river territory had not offered an outstanding prospect as a future colony; and the Muslims of Yunnan were hostile. Yet the Commission had made important and unexpected contributions to the story of Southeast Asia. It had shown that France possessed the spirit to take the initiative in Asian exploration, and her official expedition had charted a great deal of new territory. Garnier's map of the twists and turns of the Mekong and the Commission's land route was a major advance: it provided a firm base line, 4176 miles long, on which later surveys and travels could be planned. The travellers had also gathered book upon book of valuable notes on the Mekong's major tributaries, on the peoples and the native politics of Laos and the border country, and on a host of botanical, linguistic, and geological topics. Perhaps even more important was the opportunity the French Government now gave to Garnier to prepare a massive official account of the Commission. With full financial and technical support from the French authorities who saw the book as a publication to enhance French prestige, Garnier returned to France to prepare the report. And under his direction there appeared for the first time a precise account of the fantastic ruins at Angkor Wat, based on Lagrée's long and meticulous work and it was this description which led in turn to further research into Khmer history by other scholars.

Opposite *'The last lap'*

Certainly the public did not feel that the Commission had been a failure. Despite her troubles in the Prussian War, France trumpeted the achievement, comparing it favourably with anything the British had achieved in Burma. Everywhere he went, Garnier, who now assumed Lagrée's mantle, was showered with prizes and medals by all the leading geographical societies. Yet the real effect of the Commission was something which could have been foreseen much earlier, even when it was being planned. Born out of France's colonial ambitions and her wish to participate more profitably in the Oriental Adventure, the disappointment of the Commission's report only served to deflect French ambition towards an adjacent target. Garnier and de Carné both came back to Saigon recommending vehemently that although the Mekong was of limited use, the next major river system towards China – the Red river flowing past what would later be Hanoi and Haiphong – would surely prove to be the sought-after avenue into China. So France turned her attention there and began expanding into future North Vietnam. Ironically, both Garnier and de Carné themselves were martyrs to the colonial dream they had supported and reinforced. De Carné paid the price of his Oriental travels when, in 1870, soon after going back to France he went into a fatal decline brought on by illness which his wasted constitution could not withstand. Soon afterwards Garnier, who was sent back to Cochin China at the head of the euphemistically named 'Mission of Enquiry' to help in the military conquest in the north, was killed near Hanoi in an ambush by Chinese guerrillas. He was just thirty-four years old, and one of the first to be sacrificed in that region to colonial ambition.

CHAPTER NINE **THE GREAT TRIGONOMETRICAL SURVEY**

IN THE SAME YEAR, 1792, THAT CHINA opened her front door in the east to Lord Macartney and the first British embassy, she also firmly shut a back door in the west by closing the Tibetan frontier with Nepal and India. The reason for this apparent perversity was a short-lived and foolhardy invasion of Tibet by the Ghurkas of Nepal. Imagining – quite wrongly – that Tibet, which the Chinese regarded as a protected state, was too far from Peking to receive any practical help, Ghurka troops crossed the Himalayan ranges and occupied the southern part of the country. They looted the great monastery at Tasilhunpo, home of the Teshu or Panchen Lama, second only to the Dalai Lama in the church hierarchy; and before withdrawing had the effrontery to demand a large ransom in silver.

In Peking Emperor Ch'ien Lung reacted with characteristic vigour. He ordered one of his ablest generals to lead a special expeditionary force of Mongol cavalry and crack mountain troops into Tibet and chase the Ghurkas back to their own territory. The man he chose achieved the near-impossible feat of delivering his entire army in fighting trim across the bleak Tibetan plateau, and dealt the Ghurkas such a series of smashing blows that they reeled back to Nepal, and instead of collecting ransom, found themselves paying it to prevent the Chinese and Tibetans from sacking Katmandu. Henceforth, the Chinese decided, the best way of preventing a resurgence of Nepalese territorial ambition was to close the frontier. They left a permanent Chinese garrison in Tibet under two Chinese Residents known as *ambans* who virtually acted as provincial governors; and because they suspected the British in India of encouraging the Ghurka invasion – the matter was discreetly raised with Macartney while he was in Peking – the Chinese warned the Nepalese Government to reject all British connections in future. They themselves then supervised a strict blockade. Anyone coming to Tibet from the south had to have a special passport, which was checked and double-checked at the frontier, and such passports were rarely granted. In effect, Tibet was now a forbidden territory.

The blockade was remarkably successful. The geography of Tibet helped, because any visitor tended to enter by one of a few passes, which could be policed very effectively by the Tibetan *djongpons* or district officers who were often appointed with the *amban's* approval. Furthermore travel across the mountains was usually limited to those months when the passes were not blocked by snow. Every year one or other of the *ambans* went on a tour of the frontier, accompanied by an escort of Chinese regular troops and Tibetan levies, and he checked that the system was in good order. Passports were issued only to bona fide pilgrims on their way to visit Buddhist and Hindu shrines in Tibet, to recognized traders from border states like Bhutan,

KAHANUK

Kashmir, and Sikkim, and to the occasional caravans of noblemen and officials from these minor kingdoms. The only European of consequence to succeed in evading the blockade did so in disguise. He was a heavily bearded Sinophile, Thomas Manning, who managed the trick by posing as a doctor and attaching himself to the entourage of a Chinese general. Manning was so mad about anything Chinese that, ignoring the advice of his friends, he had already spent three years in Canton learning the language. He arrived in Calcutta in 1804, dressed as a Chinaman, and announced that he proposed to visit Tibet. To everyone's astonishment he fulfilled his boast and became the first Englishman to enter Lhasa, but his description of the place was so eccentric and subjective – he spent much of his time complaining about the villainy of his ragbag attendants – that his story was of personal rather than geographical value. Manning was luckier than his next compatriot to get across the border: a veterinary surgeon named Moorcroft, who was superintendent of the East India Company's stud-farm. Moorcroft visited the holy lake of Manasarowar just inside Tibet in 1811–12, and on his way back was arrested by the Nepalese authorities. He was badly treated, and had it not been for the intervention of two influential hillmen who spoke on his behalf, he could well have ended his days in Nepal. As it was, Moorcroft vanished on his next expedition behind the mountains and it was later established that he had been murdered.

Thus the secrecy of Tibet was still standing firm in the mid-nineteenth century, a fact which was a source of considerable frustration and occasional alarm to the British in India. British rule had expanded right into the

Left *An Indian army patrol probes the Kahanuk Pass across the Northwest Frontier.* **Overleaf** *Moorcroft and his companion, Hearsey, riding yaks on their way to Lake Manasarowar*

183

Himalayan foothills. The important Maharaja of Kashmir had recently placed his border state under British protection, and British Territory, as it was known on the maps and in the memoranda, abutted directly on to Tibet in several places. Yet the whole of the mountain wall, the great Himalayan arc extending from the Pamirs in the west to Upper Burma in the east and including the great bulk of Tibet was scarcely known at all. The Himalayas made an imposing flank for the Indian Empire, logical on the map and neat in international politics. But on the ground it was raggedly defined and not so easy to defend as it might appear. The generals of the Indian Army fretted that they did not have enough accurate information about the passes through which an invader might descend upon the lowlands, and the gatherers of political intelligence were all too aware that it was here in the Asian heartland that the three great Asiatic empires of Britain, Russia, and China, converged upon one another. With the Russians advancing steadily into central Asia on the one hand, and the Chinese empire withering away at the edges on the other, the region was acquiring a totally unexpected strategic importance as it fell into political vacuum.

A second, and equally good, reason why the British made up their minds to explore the Himalayas, was that the mystery of Tibet and the mountains threw down a challenge to their imperial sense of scientific achievement. On the plains of imperial India enormous changes were in hand: canals were being cut, dams built, an educational system set in motion, and all the substructure of a modernized state put under way. Yet the engineers who planned to throw barrages across India's great rivers did not know where those rivers rose, except that they all took their sources beyond the forbidden mountains; and the officials busily designing a river transport network for India had no notion of the upper reaches of their waterways. Commercial departments were aware that Tibet's market was tied illogically to China when it was five times quicker to reach the sea via India; and some people had seen the tantalizing samples of gold-dust which hill traders regularly carried out of Tibet. Intellectuals, too, were frustrated that the Indian Empire's considerable Buddhist population should revere a high priest whom no British official had yet met; and that no British scholar had obtained Tibetan scriptures at first hand. A whole generation of the new scientists, including botanists, geologists, and zoologists, hungrily regarded the unknown Himalayas as a storehouse waiting to be inventoried. In 1848–9 Joseph Hooker, of the famous botanist family, made a lightning dash into the saddle of one of the Tibetan passes to collect some new plants before he was bundled out. But Hooker's companion, a Dr Campbell, had the indignity of being roughly handled by the Sikkimese for his curiosity.

Only one group of people in British India really knew anything scientifically precise about Tibet and the adjacent uplands, and these were the officers of the Great Trigonometrical Survey of India, because they could gather their information at long range without ever entering the forbidden areas. Of all projects launched by the Raj, the Great Survey was perhaps its most ambitious and certainly the most painstaking. It was nothing less than the precise mapping of every significant geographical feature within the Indian Empire, from the Khyber Pass to Rangoon, in order to draw a master plan for the imperial dream, and it was considered to be so vital to British

*A caricature of a Royal
Engineer, Lieutenant Lake,
surveying in unhelpful
conditions*

interests that even during the worst of the Indian Mutiny, the Survey was
never told to stop work. The Royal Engineers had been given this colossal
task, and teams of their surveyors were taking their sextant angles and
chain measurements in the most extraordinary locations. They discovered
previously unknown Stone Age tribes still living deep in the Indian jungles,
learned to stand waist-deep in the quaking mire of mangrove swamps while
trying to hold their sighting-poles on firm bottom, and in Assam would find
themselves erecting bamboo towers to raise their theodolites above wild
'grass' which grew eighteen feet high, each stalk as thick as a young sapling.
Nowhere was their task more arduous than in the Himalayas. One by one
the mountain peaks within British territory had to be climbed; thermometers
boiled and aneroids consulted to find the correct heights of the summits; and
by squinting through their telescopes, the engineers identified and located
on their co-ordinates every major mountain peak in sight across the border
in Tibet, even when their flanks were many miles inside foreign territory.
Each peak was then marked on the blank map and usually given an identify-
ing number instead of a name, because it was an agreed principle of the
Survey that it would be presumptuous to add new European names to
Himalayan peaks which were already known and revered by Asians. The
major exception was the highest mountain the Survey had yet found, and
they called it Everest in honour of a superintendent of the Survey. But even
this was a measure of general ignorance about Tibet, because it was strongly
rumoured that an even higher mountain lay inland out of view, beyond the
next range.

It was an engineer with the Trigonometrical Survey who devised the
plan to open up the secrets of the farther Himalayas. Captain T. G.
Montgomerie had exhibited all the marks of a first-class officer. He had been
a brilliant student at training college, passing out first in his class, and
within a year of joining the Bengal Engineers he had been posted to assist

187

Colonel George Everest (with stick, far right), after whom the world's highest mountain was named, supervises the erection of a survey mark on the Chur Mount

the Survey. He had already made an outstanding map of the area round Attock, and gone on to supervise the complicated task of mapping Kashmir under the suspicious eye of its maharaja. Montgomerie had clambered up and down many of the Kashmiri mountains, several of them fifteen thousand feet high and some over eighteen thousand feet; and he had suffered severely from cold, exposure, and the constant danger of rock falls. More than anyone, he was aware that as soon as any of his surveying parties came too near the sensitive Tibetan frontier, a watchful Tibetan patrol would appear as if by magic and keep pace with the surveyors until they had left the area. In 1862, therefore, he wrote a letter to the Asiatic Society of Bengal, suggesting that as Europeans were not allowed past the mountains, the answer was to train native agents and send them in disguise to do their survey work for them. As he solemnly put it,

a European, even if disguised, attracts attention when travelling among Asiatics, and his presence, if detected, is nowadays often apt to lead to outrage. The difficulty of redressing such outrages, and various other causes, has, for the present, all but put a stop to exploration by Europeans. On the other hand, Asiatics, the subjects of the British Government, are known to travel freely without molestation in countries far beyond the British frontier . . . without exciting any suspicion.

So was born Montgomerie's team of native agents, sent in disguise across the frontier to travel specific routes laid down for them by the officers of the Survey, and when they returned to India, they handed over their notes to the Survey which then worked them up into maps.

In many ways it was remarkable that no one had formally suggested this idea before. Native spies were an obvious solution to the problem, and the Indian Government was easily able to put the idea into practice. Moreover, such agents had obvious precedents. The Jesuits in China, for example, had used Chinese surveyors while preparing their great map of the Chinese empire, which was still the most accurate map of Tibet available. And much more recently the ill-fated Moorcroft had relied on an Indian assistant to help him survey the route to Lake Manasarowar. The Indian had measured the distances of their road by the simple expedient of counting off the number of paces he took at each stage of the march, and multiplying the sum by the length of his stride. Even among Montgomerie's own colleagues there were Indian Army officers responsible for gathering intelligence about the frontier tribes, who were regularly using what they called 'correspondents', reliable native travellers who could circulate freely among the hill tribes in their usual way of business and pick up snippets of useful information which they then relayed to the British. Montgomerie's contribution was really to blend these two types of agents, the fully trained surveyor of the Jesuits and the part-time spy. He saw his native surveyors as direct agents of the Survey; paid, trained, and equipped by the Survey rather than casually employed, yet incapable of producing a map on their own. The agent's job was merely to record data from which the Survey's staff would produce the actual maps, working at their headquarters in the pleasant little north Indian town of Dehra Dun. In short, Montgomerie's men were to be creatures of the Survey, and thus they became a curiosity of the Oriental Adventure as native-born participants, working on their own, yet as a direct part of the European plan.

Montgomerie's scheme was welcomed so enthusiastically by the Government that the following year the first of his agents, code-named 'the Munshi', set out for his target, the city of Yarkand on the old Silk Road. The Munshi reached it without great difficulty and managed to survey his route without being detected. He also fixed the precise location of Yarkand by sights with his sextant, and showed it to be a good deal farther west than the Jesuit maps had marked. But while re-entering British territory, the Munshi died in mysterious circumstances. The exact cause of his death was not recorded, but some officers of the Survey thought it sinister that they should be robbed of a first-hand account of all that their agent had seen. Even more abrupt were the fates of the next two agents Montgomerie used in this sensitive area. The first, known as 'the Pathan Sapper', Montgomerie borrowed from the local Colonel of Miners and carefully trained for a whole year in survey technique before sending him across the border. But it was a wasted effort. The Pathan was involved in a blood-feud and survived only six weeks before he was identified and killed. The third agent, another sapper, also disappeared though it was never decided whether he had deserted or been killed. When last seen, he was going off in the company of a retired English officer named Hayward who had volunteered to explore the caravan trails and passes round the Pamirs. After some initial success Hayward was indelicate enough to try to force a way through the territory of a very tough chief named Mir Walli, and the Englishman made himself vastly unpopular by forcing the villagers into serving him as porters and seizing their food stocks to feed his column. When Mir Walli objected to this behaviour, Hayward was very high-handed and insulted the chief, refusing even to dismount from his horse while speaking to him. Hayward was allowed to proceed, but Mir Walli and a party of about sixty tribesmen galloped ahead and lay in wait for him. That evening Hayward camped on the edge of a wood where, suspecting some kind of attack, he sat up all night in his tent, his pistols ready. But his enemies waited until he fell asleep at dawn, and in the early light took the entire camp by surprise. Hayward was seized, bound, and

190

led out among the trees where his throat was cut. A British patrol later recovered his corpse from where it had been buried under a pile of rocks.

Hayward's grisly end was reported to Montgomerie by the Survey's third, and most successful, recruit among the Pathan tribesmen serving with the Indian Army. This was a very cool native engineer sergeant code-named 'the Havildar', who succeeded in following up the story of Hayward's death and actually met Mir Walli at a tribal gathering. Mir Walli was proudly carrying one of Hayward's rifles and openly boasting of his murder, so that the Havildar had to keep one hand on a revolver hidden beneath his clothing throughout the meeting in case Mir Walli suddenly guessed the identity of his colleague. The only comfort that Montgomerie drew from the Havildar's report was that Mir Walli's leg had recently been broken by a kick from a horse, and 'when the Sapper left', Montgomerie noted malevolently,

> Mir Walli was still in great agony from his broken leg, and as he could actually hear the bone grating when he moved, and as it was then more than a month since its fracture, there is little doubt but that this scoundrel may hereafter be recognized by his lameness, which is likely to be permanent, and which may yet perhaps assist in bringing him to justice, and to the fate he so richly deserves.

Mir Walli was typical of the cut-throats who controlled the areas which Montgomerie's agents had to penetrate. It was a recognized practice among the hill tribes for traitors and suspected agents to be thrown alive into mountain streams so that their bodies were broken and battered by the torrent until unrecognizable. In the little state of Chitral, the ruler executed out of hand a *subedar* or native company commander and two sepoys from a British Native Regiment who were caught passing through his territory disguised as fakirs, only on suspicion that they had been taking notes. And yet, curiously enough, Montgomerie never found he had any difficulty in finding volunteers for his dangerous work. His original notion had been simply to search the bazaars of Peshawar, looking for natives from the areas he proposed to explore and to recruit them as his agents. But this happy-go-lucky approach was singularly unproductive. 'Any number of men are willing to volunteer for such a service,' he noted wryly,

> and if their own accounts are to be believed, they are all well fitted for the task. But a very little enquiry, however, reduces the number of likely men nearly down to zero; many cannot write, others are too old, and have no ideas beyond those of trade, and nearly everyone has special ideas as to what pay and rewards they are to get, and generally have special stipulations to make; all, however, apparently thinking nothing of the risks and exposure involved.

In fact Montgomerie's bazaar-hunting came close to finding only one agent, an itinerant silversmith who regularly made a circuit round northern Afghanistan to repair and make jewellery for noblemen and chiefs. But by the time Montgomerie got wind of this man, the silversmith had already left Peshawar on his circuit and was out of reach beyond the frontier.

So, virtually by default, Montgomerie settled on his replacement, the agent known as 'the Mirza', who turned out to be the most energetic of all his surveyors in the western sector. The Mirza's father was a Turkish trader from Meshed, his mother was a Persian, and his education had been partly English because he had served a spell as a native assistant with the Survey. Thus the Mirza spoke fluent Turkish and Persian, knew the rudiments of survey, and – most important – had already travelled in the Pamirs with his father's trading caravans. Montgomerie decided that it was worth training such an unusual recruit very carefully, and the Mirza was sent to Survey headquarters and put through the general course. Then, accompanied by three or four native assistants, he was dispatched across the Northwest Frontier with instructions to follow a route which would take him in a great curve over the crest of the Pamirs and down their eastern flank into the edge of the desert before making his way back to India.

This route was nearly the same trail that Marco Polo had taken in the thirteenth century, and like Marco Polo the Mirza found the physical difficulties disheartening. Following Montgomerie's instructions, he and his party struggled up the valley of the Oxus until it brought them out on the Roof of the World, where they plodded across the snows of the plateau, often losing their way in the deep snows and suffering dreadfully from cold and mountain sickness. Even their mountain ponies began to feel the effects of the extreme altitude and had to be bled from the nose to relieve them, while the men huddled in the lee of their animals and chewed handfuls of sugar and dried fruit to sustain themselves. When a pony kicked off its load and bolted, the travellers were obliged to divide the load between them and carry it the rest of the way on their backs. All the men suffered from snow-blindness, and several were in torment from their footwear which was unsuitably made from soft leather, so that their boots soaked up the moisture like sponges and then froze solid until they stumbled along in boots of solid ice. Yet somehow the Mirza and his men kept up their observations, counting their steps to measure the distance they covered, and took compass bearings of prominent features. There was one terrifying moment when a suspicious Kirghiz chief asked what the Mirza was doing and demanded to see the compass the surveyor was hiding in his hand. Luckily the Mirza was able to switch compasses without being noticed, and exchanged his best prismatic compass for a crude, gaudily painted instrument of the type sold by the Russians for the Muslim trade. This gadget, the Mirza explained, helped him to know the precise direction towards Mecca, and the Kirghiz chief was delighted to be given it as a present.

Several times the Mirza's party was fired on by robbers and once the Mirza was singled out by a mysterious stranger who joined the caravan and insisted on staying close to Montgomerie's agent. This stranger was dressed as a native, but he had an uncommonly fair complexion, and all the other travellers were sure that he was a European in disguise. The Mirza was on the point of revealing his own secret identity to him when something about the stranger's complete fluency in Persian led the Mirza to suspect that perhaps he might be an *agent provocateur*. In the end he decided it would be better not to trust him, and later it was Montgomerie's opinion that the fair-skinned stranger had been deliberately planted on the Mirza's group as a spy.

Travelling in eastern Turkestan was particularly dangerous at that time because the collapsing authority of the Chinese empire was encouraging the local chieftains to fight viciously among themselves as they tried to seize the shreds of power. In several towns on the flanks of the Pamirs the Mirza was put under house arrest; and in one place, to his horror, he encountered a man who had actually seen British surveyors at work on the Indian frontier. Until he got clear of this dangerous acquaintance, the Mirza did not dare take any observations for fear that the man should recognize the instruments he was using. His final test was to get past an engaging ruffian called Atalik Ghazi, who had recently driven the Chinese garrison out of the city of Kashgar. Atalik Ghazi was always armed to the teeth for fear of assassination by rival chiefs, and he had a notorious temper. To the Mirza he was courteous enough, but he had been known to fly into such a rage that he chased one unfortunate man around his audience-room trying to hack him to death, while the poor man dodged behind a pile of muskets to save his life. Atalik Ghazi's Cabinet meetings were understandably nervous occasions, because all his ministers preferred not to risk discussing matters of state in case they gave offence, and instead sat with their eyes cast down, only answering when he put a direct question to them. When the Mirza met him, this robber-baron was busily consolidating his boisterous rule and already commanded an army of twenty thousand men, his infantry rigged out in long black boots and red quilted uniforms in Russian style. They were armed with home-made brass cannon and matchlocks, some of them so long that it took three or four men to work them, while his *sowars*, or irregular cavalry, were a wild-looking assembly of nomads on mountain ponies, every man slung with a huge knife and a tinder-pouch.

The Mirza's report of this new despot had direct political results, because the Government of India decided to recognize Atalik Ghazi as the official ruler of Kashgar and sent a British mission to open formal negotiations with him. Montgomerie took his chance to attach two more secret agents to the mission in order to augment the Mirza's earlier reports, but the Mirza's success had really answered the main questions about the area and Montgomerie's interest in the Northwest was done. The Survey itself continued to send occasional agents across the border, but more and more Montgomerie turned his attention directly northward towards Tibet which was a more delicate and intriguing problem for a spy master-cum-surveyor.

CHAPTER TEN   # THE PATIENT SPIES

THERE WAS A SHARP CONTRAST BETWEEN the sort of men Montgomerie sent across the Northwest Frontier, and the recruits he picked for missions into Tibet. Rather than use ex-soldiers and former assistants of the Great Trigonometrical Survey, Montgomerie chose his best spies for Tibet, rather unexpectedly, from the Indian Education Service. Indeed the most successful of them was a former village schoolmaster. Montgomerie's method of recruiting was to apply direct to the Indian Education Service or to the district officers posted to northern areas, and ask them for suitable candidates whose families either had relatives living on both sides of the Tibetan border or themselves had some experience of trading across the frontier.

Traditionally these trading links were very close. For instance, it was a time-honoured custom between trans-border trading partners to split a large pebble into two halves, each man keeping one half which he would send with his trade goods so that his partner could match the two halves together on receipt. Montgomerie particularly was interested in what the Survey called 'semi-Tibetans', meaning natives of partially Tibetan stock, and since suitable men of this background were rare, one result of his research was that his detachment of Tibetan agents became virtually a family team. The first two agents he selected for Tibet were cousins; both were related to the two Nepalese hillmen who had spoken up for Moorcroft when he was arrested; and the next of his agents to shine in Tibet was again a member of the same family.

The two cousins came to Montgomerie with the first batch of eight recruits offered by the Education Department. Most of the eight failed to pass Montgomerie's strict training programme for 'Intelligence Workmen' as he liked to call them. But Nain Singh and his cousin Mani Singh mastered the course after two years' work. The core of their training, besides learning the use of compass and sextant and knowing what features to look for when making a survey, was to learn to take an absolutely uniform stride as they walked. A precisely measured step was vital to Montgomerie's plan, because it was the only way the agents could measure distance in hostile territory without being discovered. So during training sessions Montgomerie repeatedly took measurements of the length of his men's stride, and afterwards, when they returned from a mission, double-checked their paces over a measured distance. To help them keep count of their paces and memorize the totals, the Survey's workshops at Dehra Dun made up specially modified rosaries of the type which every pilgrim in Tibet carried. A normal Buddhist rosary numbered 108 beads which the pilgrim counted off as he recited his sacred prayers, but the Survey's rosaries had only 100 beads, made of cheap imitation coral, and with every tenth bead slightly larger and made from a

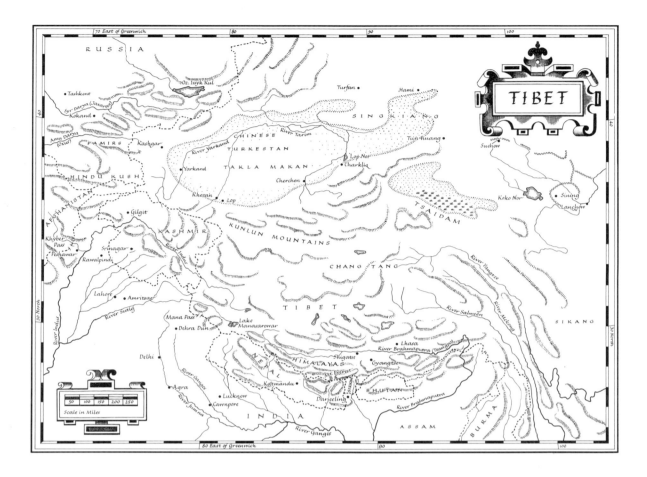

Map labels (from the map):

70 East of Greenwich · 80 · 90 · 100

RUSSIA

Oz. Issyk Kul

Tashkent

Syr-darya (Jaxartes)

Kokand

Amu Darya (Oxus)

PAMIRS

Kashgar

CHINESE

River Tarim

TURKESTAN

SINGKIANG

Turfan · Hami

Tün-huang

Suchow

HINDU KUSH

Yarkand

River Yarkand

TAKLA MAKAN

Lop-Nor

Charklik

AFGHANISTAN

Khotan

Cherchen

TSAIDAM

Koko Nor

Sining

Lanchow

Gilgit

Lop

Khyber Pass

Peshawar

KASHMIR

KUNLUN MOUNTAINS

CHANG TANG

River Yangtze

Srinagar

Rawalpindi

Lahore

Amritsar

River Sutlej

TIBET

River Salween

River Mekong

SIKANG

River Indus

Mana Pass

Lake Manasarowar

HIMALAYAS

Shigatse

River Brahmaputra (Tsangpo)

Lhasa

Gyangtse

Delhi

Dehra Dun

NEPAL

Mt Everest

Katmandu

Darjeeling

BHUTAN

Agra

Lucknow

Cawnpore

River Ganges

River Jumna

INDIA

ASSAM

River Brahmaputra

BURMA

River Ganges

Scale in Miles

50 100 150 200 250

TIBET

80 East of Greenwich · 90 · 100

30 North · 40

dried berry of a different colour. Montgomerie's agents were taught to walk separately from the rest of the caravan, ostensibly reciting their prayers in private, but in fact concentrating on counting their steps properly and measuring their stride. At every hundred paces they moved one bead along their rosary, and every thousandth pace was represented by a large bead. Whenever they were unobserved, they were to make a note of the figures.

To protect these secret notes from suspicious eyes Montgomerie's workshops also adapted the ordinary portable prayer-wheel carried by devout Buddhists. Normally this prayer-wheel was like a child's toy merry-go-round. An enclosed barrel about four inches high rotated freely round a spindle, one end of which the pilgrim held, while he used his other hand to spin the barrel. Inside the barrel was wrapped a long paper scroll on which were written sacred Buddhist rubrics, and each time the pilgrim whirled the device, the rotating prayers gained him merit. Montgomerie's prayer-wheels were made so that the barrel could be opened by a secret catch, and inside was a store of many long, thin slips of paper on which the agents jotted down their bearings and distances and any other valuable information they acquired. Hidden within the wheel, too, was a compass so that the agent could take his bearings while pretending to be at his devotions.

Above *Tibet and her border states.*
Overleaf *A* kafila *on the move*

195

Nain Singh, the Original Pundit

Montgomerie's technicians also worked on concealing the large cumbersome sextants which were a standard part of each agent's equipment. Their solution was to construct for each man a special strong-box, sometimes rigged out as a pharmacist's stock-box or as a container for trade valuables; and into this box they built a secret compartment of precisely the right size to hide the sextant and keep it firmly in place so that it was not damaged in transit. Hidden in the shafts of hollow walking-sticks, the agents also carried boiling-thermometers for calculating altitudes, though these thermometers were notoriously fragile and were often broken in falls. And the problem of setting an artificial horizon when taking sextant readings was solved by a very simple device. Mercury was the material most commonly used for the artificial horizon, and when Nain Singh set out on his first mission to Tibet, he was given a supply of mercury hidden in a coconut shell sealed with a stopper. When he needed to make an artificial horizon, instead of using the normal mercury trough, he found it quite satisfactory to half bury his hemispherical pilgrim's bowl of polished wood in the ground, and pour in his mercury. Provided he chose a spot well sheltered from the wind, he found he had a perfectly usable artificial horizon.

Nain and Mani Singh left Survey headquarters in January 1865 with instructions to tackle the first of Montgomerie's Tibetan objectives: the secret survey of the main road which led through Nepal into Tibet and on to the capital at Lhasa. This was the main artery of communication between Tibet and India, and although the route was known in general terms from the reports of travellers like Manning, there were no reliable maps or precise details suitable for military or political use. Nor had the exact position of Lhasa been defined accurately.

The two agents set out with the idea that they should either work in Tibet together or, if circumstances demanded, travel separately. So they were burdened down with two sets of instruments – two large sextants, two box sextants, spare prismatic and pocket compasses, pocket chronometers, common watches, and a battery of air- and boiling-thermometers. All this paraphernalia had to be taken first to the Survey's trigonometrical station at Bareilly to be checked and correlated, as Bareilly had been selected as the reference point from which their route survey would start, and it was from there that the two men began to plod northward, carefully counting paces, clicking their rosaries, and making notes of compass bearings. They travelled in disguise, assuming the clothes and character of Bisahari horse-dealers from Upper Kashmir on their way to trade horses across the border in Tibet. This disguise was good enough to get them through the comparatively easy control points in Nepal, but it failed them at the Tibetan border. At the frontier district of Kyirong, they were stopped by the Tibetan guards, questioned about their intentions, and their baggage was searched. The guards failed to find their survey instruments hidden in the secret compartments, but the Singhs' cover story did not satisfy them. The *djongpon* of Kyirong was a prudent and careful official, and when his men reported on the strangers, his suspicions were aroused because it was the wrong time of the year for the Bisahari horse-dealers to be entering Tibet, and the two men were taking an unusual route for their business. He refused permission to enter, and Nain and Mani Singh had to fall back into Nepal.

Mani Singh was disheartened by the rebuff, and to make matters worse, learned that the *djongpon* was a man who had previously been stationed near his home village in Kumaon and had actually met Mani Singh in person. Under the circumstances there seemed no point in Mani Singh trying to bluff his way through the border or risking a different disguise. So the two cousins agreed to split up: Mani to find another route into Tibet; Nain Singh to have a second attempt at getting past Kyirong. But Mani's heart was no longer in the venture, and he wasted a good deal of time in Nepal, complaining of bad health and poor travelling conditions before scouting the frontier rather unenthusiastically. Nain Singh, on the other hand, began to show that extraordinary tenacity for which he was to become famous in the Survey. First of all, he switched his disguise. Abandoning the pretence of being a Bisahari, he dressed up as a minor Ladakhi trader dealing in *nirbisa* root, a spice plant with a sweet scent which grew in Tibet, and even pinned a pigtail to the back of his head under his cap. Next he found a prosperous merchant who was already known to the Tibetan guards and, by ingratiating himself with this merchant, Nain Singh went on ahead of him to the frontier with a small *kafila* or caravan claiming to be the merchant's colleague. He succeeded in getting past the frontier guards and into Tibet, though they made him swear on pain of death that he would stay with the *kafila* all the time it was inside the country.

This restriction presented a real problem, because the *kafila* was not bound for Nain's true destination at Lhasa. So the agent stayed with the *kafila* only as far as the junction with the road leading to Lhasa, and there he deliberately fell out of the convoy, pretending to be sick, and waited by the roadside until picked up by another caravan, this time bound for Lhasa. This in itself was a courageous act: a lone traveller in Tibet was taking a considerable risk, for he was likely to be set upon and robbed either by the professional bandits who infested the country or by hostile villagers who often turned to robbery if it offered easy pickings. Nain Singh found that nowhere in Tibet was travel entirely safe or comfortable. At times the night temperature fell so low that the traveller woke up with his cheek frozen to the pillow, and sometimes the road was no better than a ledge scraped out of the sides of the mountains. A false step could send a man plunging hundreds of feet, and even the main roads occasionally crossed bridges so rickety that all passers-by prayed before using them. The bridges themselves were extraordinary contraptions – two immense iron chains slung across the gap and anchored at each end with enormous billets of wood sunk under piles of rock. A shaky arrangement of wooden slats hung on short ropes between the chains and the traveller had to step carefully from slat to slat. If the chains were not regularly smeared with yak butter, they often became badly corroded, and sometimes the bridge had been reduced to a single cable along which the traveller was obliged to swing by hands and feet like an ape. To cross the Tsangpo river Nain Singh's *kafila* preferred to use little skin-covered coracles which served as ferries in Tibet, and the Indian agent saw three of his companions swamped and drowned before his eyes.

Nain Singh was lucky enough to be picked up by a Lhasa-bound caravan almost at once, but the new *kafila* had decided to travel part of the way by boat along the Tsangpo and so the agent was obliged to stay on the bank, keeping pace with his companions and counting his footsteps for the sake of his route survey. He had the additional worry that he had very little money, and by the time he reached the town of Shigatse he was forced to stay over and make extra cash by tutoring the local shop-keepers in the Hindi method of book-keeping. This in turn meant that there was no way of avoiding the customary visit to the huge Tasilhunpo Monastery near by and being blessed by the Panchen Lama. Nain Singh dreaded the interview, because although he was a Brahmin he had been brought up among Buddhists and could not help wondering if they were right when they claimed that the Panchen Lama could see into men's hearts and penetrate their every duplicity. In the event, the Lama turned out to be an amiable boy of about eleven, dressed up in his High Lama's robes and seated on a raised platform while batches of pilgrims were shuffled past in front of him and blessed with an air of quiet disinterest.

A few weeks later at Lhasa Nain Singh had to endure a similar audience with the Dalai Lama which was conducted with much the same formality. This time, however, the Lama was a thirteen-year-old boy, obviously being kept under tight control by his attendants and advisers who stood about him in reverential attitudes, and the real power as Nain Singh observed, seemed to lie with the chief minister or *gyalpo* who was closely connected with the two Chinese *ambans*. Lhasa did not impress him either. Most of the houses were built of clay or mud, though a few of the richer merchants had built in brick, and the place had an unkempt, rather menacing atmosphere. Packs of savage dogs roamed the streets after dark; and informers were rife, reporting any unusual circumstances back to the Chinese authorities or to the abbots of the rival monasteries. What law there was, was brutal and swift. A Chinaman accused of fomenting trouble between two monasteries while Nain Singh was in town, was immediately led out into the street where his head was lopped off.

In such dangerous surroundings it was little wonder that Nain Singh preferred to stay indoors in his Lhasa lodging-house as much as possible, taking his sextant sights out of the window so as to fix the true position of the city. Even so he twice had a bad scare: once when a pair of Kashmiri traders saw through his disguise and took him quietly on one side to tell the unhappy agent precisely who he really was (luckily they had no intention of betraying him to the authorities). And the second time was in the street one morning when he encountered the entourage of the *djongpon* of Kyirong who was on a visit to Lhasa. Remembering that he would be executed for disobeying the *djongpon*'s prohibition on leaving his first *kafila*, Nain Singh ducked back out of sight before he was recognized, and hurried back to his hostel where he picked up his belongings and changed to another lodging-house, scarcely venturing out again until he left the city and began his return to India.

Nor was it easy to escape from Tibet undetected. When Nain Singh arrived back at the border, early snow had blocked the passes, and there was a scare among the frontier guards that a British officer was in the area. Nain Singh personally met the special squad of four Tibetan guards waiting to intercept the officer, and because of the tension the authorities refused him permission to cross out of Tibet. Undeterred, Nain Singh doubled back on his tracks,

and leaving the main trail, found a small path which brought him out safely, so that he was able to be reunited with his cousin Mani and arrive back at Survey headquarters on 27 October 1866.

Lapchas (prayer cairns) in the Donkia Pass, overlooking Tibet and Cholamoo Lakes

From his very first interview with Nain Singh, Montgomerie knew that he was on the right lines and that his initial Tibetan mission had been a major success. Nain Singh's notes and verbal report were carefully matched against all existing information about Tibet and found to be entirely consistent. The agent had managed to maintain an astonishingly accurate stride on his walk through Tibet, averaging thirty-one inches each step or approximately two thousand paces to the mile, even when marching up and down the mountains or over rough ground. His compass bearings of the route were not only very accurate but he had worked out a new method of taking them. Along many sections of his road Nain Singh had found *lapchas*, the Tibetan stone cairns which signposted the trail and could be spotted at a distance by the clusters of prayer-flags which pious travellers stuck into the rocks. By keeping a sharp look-out, the surveyor had been able to identify *lapchas* at a distance and take their precise compass bearings, so plotting with unusual clarity the twists and turns of the trail. His sextant readings, too, were reliable and he had managed to take thirty-one of them in secret, including the vital readings which located Tasilhunpo and Lhasa on the Survey's map to an accuracy of one minute. His sextant work was all the more creditable because much of it was done in the dead of night with the air temperature well below freezing, and the observer hidden away out of sight of his companions. Nain Singh had been issued with a plain bull's-eye lantern so that he could read his sextant surreptitiously, but even this simple lamp had attracted unwelcome attention. At one monastery some lamas had admired it so much that Nain Singh was obliged to make them a present of it, and afterwards he had to rely on the light from a single oil-wick to read his sextant, shielding the flame from view. When this feeble light had been too much, he had been forced to take his star sight and then carefully put his sextant on one side, not moving the micrometer screw, until he could read it by daylight in the morning.

The net result of this first Tibet foray by the cousins was a huge advance in Tibetan knowledge. Montgomerie now had in his hands accurate data about the most important routeways into Tibet and the great east–west road behind the mountains to Lhasa, as well as a stage-by-stage account of the trail, the heights of the passes, and a certain amount of political intelligence about conditions within Tibet. But this knowledge also highlighted the gaps in Montgomerie's information, and even as the cousins were taking a well-earned rest, Montgomerie planned their next secret expedition, drawing on their experience from the trip just completed. This time their target was to be the headwater region of the Indus and Sutlej rivers, which the Survey had long desired to investigate but had been barred from doing because the rivers rose well inside Tibet. Coupled with this problem, Montgomerie also wanted more information about the near-by gold-producing area of Tibet which had been known by hearsay to Indians for many generations. According to these reports the Tibetan gold-fields were very rich in alluvial ore but the Tibetans themselves saw little point in working them, arguing that it was too much effort to obtain material for which they had little use.

So Nain Singh went back across the Tibetan frontier in July 1867 to investigate these fabled mines, and this time he travelled under a strict code-name as Montgomerie was dismayed to learn that however hard he tried to keep his agents' activities secret, reports were already circulating in Tibet that the Survey had successfully put one agent into Tibet and was planning another mission. The code-name which Nain Singh was given was 'the Pundit', a word which meant a man of learning as well as having other, more precise, Indian connotations, though the Survey preferred to see it as recognition of their agent's peculiar command and knowledge of his job. So admirably did this code-name fit, that Montgomerie took to calling his entire team of Tibetan agents 'the Pundits', and deliberately shaped them in Nain Singh's image, eventually using Nain himself as their chief instructor.

Besides his cousin Mani, rather unfairly described by Montgomerie as 'somewhat lacking in nerve', Nain Singh had a new companion in 'the Third Pundit', a giant of a man who, when one of the native porters was set upon by two robbers in a lonely spot, seized one attacker by his pigtail, whirled the astonished bandit right off the ground, and frightened him so much that he gasped out an apology and ran off with his companion.

Nain Singh was now experienced enough to prepare his cover story in depth, and Montgomerie provided him with more money than before, enough to buy a dozen asses and a pony, lay in a considerable stock of trade goods, hire servants, and engage as guides three men who knew the gold-fields region. So it was a well-organized little party which presented itself at the Tibetan border post of Mana, once more in the guise of Bisahari traders, and, after a search which failed to locate the hidden surveying instruments, was allowed to proceed into Tibet after paying the usual traders' tax. Such an auspicious beginning was abruptly reversed when to Nain Singh's dismay the headman of an important village on the Upper Indus refused to believe his story, and calmly proceeded to establish with absolute accuracy the precise identity of each man in the Pundit's party and the exact district he came from. Only by leaving Mani Singh in the village virtually as a hostage was Nain Singh allowed to continue, and he thought it prudent to hurry his plans. So while the Third Pundit struck off independently to survey the Indus, Nain Singh went ahead to the famous gold-mines.

He found them to be an even odder place than rumour had suggested. The actual diggings were a huge trench about a mile long and up to two hundred paces wide, which meandered over the desolate, windswept plateau along the line of the gold deposits. In this trench at a depth of twenty-five feet laboured hundreds of Tibetan miners, digging away with long-handled shovels and cheerfully singing in unison as they hoisted out the loose earth, so that the approaching traveller had an eerie sensation of hearing their chorus floating out across the barrens while he was still some distance away and could not see a living soul. On the bleak flank of the mountain slopes behind the diggings the sacred words 'om mani padme hum' had been picked out again and again in white stones, and of the camp itself, almost six thousand tents in winter, scarcely anything could be seen because the black yak-hair tents were sunk in pits below ground-level to escape the bitter winds which moaned across the plateau. According to Nain Singh, he had never been so cold in his life. At sixteen thousand feet altitude, there was neither wood for fuel nor natural shelter for a camp site, and the water was so brackish that it had to be frozen and rethawed before it was drinkable. The miners themselves existed on an unbroken diet of yak meat, buttermilk, barley cake, and tea. Yet they were remarkably happy. They found enough gold to pay their expenses and on a lucky day had a chance of turning up a large nugget – one weighing two pounds was found while Nain Singh was there. Nain Singh had to admit that no one else was likely to operate the mines more efficiently under such cruel conditions. At night the cold was so intense that the miners and their families slept face downwards to the earth, their knees drawn up close to their heads and resting on their elbows and knees with every scrap of clothing they possessed heaped on their backs. According to Nain Singh this was the only way they could keep their stomachs warm and exclude all the cold external air.

The chieftain of the mining camp clearly did not believe Nain Singh's story any more than the village headman; and it was only by bribing him with the best Indian tobacco and giving his wife a present of coral, that Nain Singh won grudging permission to stay. Yet the chieftain obviously welcomed Nain Singh's presence as a diversion from the monotony of his job, and the surveyor spent much of his time talking to the man in his tent, half buried like the others but bigger and laid out with a small Buddhist chapel at one end. Near the entrance lay a huge black guard dog which had the deep jowls and white chest mark of the breed the Tibetans called their 'Royal Dogs'. Sipping cup after cup of tea in the tent, Nain Singh endured a never-ending cross-examination by his host whose curiosity was particularly drawn by Nain Singh's special box for hiding his instruments. Such a box, the chief pointedly observed, was a very grand object for an ordinary trader to carry about with him on his travels, and it was obviously foreign made. The Pundit hastily explained that he had bought it in an auction given by the British in India, and that it served him well as a strong-box for his valuable stock of coral. Fortunately, though the chief examined it carefully, he failed to detect the sextant's secret compartment.

The rest of the gold-fields' reconnaissance passed off smoothly. When Nain Singh had acquired his data, he returned to collect Mani Singh and the Third Pundit and the reunited party got back to Montgomerie at Dehra Dun without incident. There they presented him with enough information to draw up 850 miles of new route survey, a topographical synopsis of more than 18,000 square miles of previously unknown territory, eighty altitude points

checked by thermometer, and seventy-five astronomical fixes. A good part of this material had even been cross-referenced by taking back bearings on the higher peaks already mapped and recorded by the Trigonometrical Survey from across the border.

Montgomerie, of course, was delighted, and it was on his recommendation that Nain Singh, 'the Original Pundit' as he was now known, was eventually awarded the Gold Medal of the Royal Geographical Society for his explorations, an unusual honour for a native schoolmaster in the days when African explorers like Henry Stanley were more likely to be commanding the headlines. But the Pundits and their adventures in Tibet had caught the imagination of their British sponsors, and the British were coming to regard the Pundits as symbols of their own imperial achievement. They were seen as the natives who had been trained to serve a higher cause of scientific civilization and as exemplary figures of loyal service to the Raj. So there arose the curious paradox that while the British were very proud of the Pundits and wished to reward them publicly, at the same time they did not want the Tibetan authorities to learn what was happening and so put a stop to future exploration. Of course there was no real solution to this problem, and apart from keeping each Pundit's real identity hidden beneath a code-name until he retired, the best that the Survey could manage was to delay the official publication of the results of any journey for two or three years in the hope that Tibetan memories would fade. In practice, however, the Tibetans continued to show an uncanny knack of divining the Pundits' activities, even before they had got back to Dehra Dun, and the system of code-names really served only to heap glamour on the explorers' adventures.

The most devious of Montgomerie's Pundits, the man who evaded the Tibetan authorities more often than anyone else and brought back the most information, achieved the distinction of having two code-names, being known both as 'A-k' and 'Krishna', one being the reversal of the first and last letters of the other. He was the nephew of Nain Singh and he took over from him when the Original Pundit was forced by failing eyesight to retire from active exploration, and went to live on a well-earned land grant awarded to him by the Indian Government. By that time Krishna, whose real name was Kishen Singh, was already a seasoned surveyor-in-disguise with two short Tibetan missions to his credit, and had shown that he was even more of a perfectionist than his uncle. Once when he was not satisfied with his thermometer readings, Krishna had gone back alone into a snow-filled pass to retake the figures. By the time he rejoined his companions at the camp-fire, he was half dead with exposure. On another occasion, he was robbed and left destitute by bandits, but plodded stubbornly on with his rosary, still counting his paces and remembering to allow for a shorter stride because he was so weak from hunger.

It was in 1878, two years after Montgomerie's retirement as a colonel, that Krishna, his star pupil, started out on the immense journey that really established the legend of the Pundits. It was a journey that Montgomerie never lived to hear about, because the spymaster's health had been broken by his own surveying climbs in Kashmir, and he died soon after returning to England. So Krishna received his instructions from a new chief, General Walker, who told him baldly to pass right through Lhasa and keep on marching until he came to Mongolia and the far border with China. He could, said the general optimistically, return to India by sea if he felt that was more convenient. As it turned out, this 'journey' lasted four and a half years before Krishna was seen again at Survey headquarters, and yet his calculations and pace counting never faltered in all that time, so that after walking twenty-eight hundred miles across the highest mountain lands in the world, Krishna's position by his own reckoning was only nine and a half miles too far south and two and a half miles too far west when compared to the Survey's master-map. It was a feat of perseverance and accuracy which stunned the most exacting cartographers.

As before, Krishna set out disguised as a trader and accompanied by several native assistants. He had to wait almost a year in Lhasa before he found a caravan going northeast, and he used this delay to improve his knowledge of Tibet and read up the Buddhist scriptures. Finally on 17 September 1879, he and two companions left Lhasa with a *kafila* of about a hundred men, mostly Mongolians and a few Tibetans. Everyone was scared of bandits, and so the *kafila* kept strict discipline with mounted scouts riding three or four miles ahead to search for ambushes and two horsemen well behind to warn of any strangers approaching from the rear. Krishna walked along with his clicking rosary among the Tibetan contingent, most of whom were on foot and burdened down with a fearsome array of spear, matchlock, and sword. On the whole Krishna preferred the mounted Mongols whom he thought a cheerful happy-go-lucky lot, always friendly, always prepared to wait for stragglers to catch up, and, of course, superlative horsemen. It was quite remarkable, he observed, how a Mongol rider even when totally drunk, as he often was, still managed to stay upright on his pony and never fall off. Each day's march would begin at sunrise and, after a teabreak at ten o'clock, continued through to the afternoon when the *kafila* stopped for the night. The diet was tea made with water and melted yak butter, boiled yak meat when available, and dough cakes of flour and powdered milk, all prepared on a small fire of animal dung with a minimum of flame, smoke, and noise, for fear of attracting robbers. At night the ponies were tethered in the middle of the camp, the travellers slept in two long lines on each side of them, and a double guard of two Tibetans and two Mongols was posted.

His route took Krishna right across the tableland of the Chang Tang, an area never previously described in detail and three and a half times as large as the entire British Isles. The Chang Tang lay at an altitude of fifteen thousand feet, and only its southern portion was inhabited, mostly by *dopkas*, the dwellers in black tents who were professional bandits. The rest of this immense area was open rolling countryside which supported a stupendous number of wild animals, yak, sheep, and deer. Unmolested by predators except for a few wolves and jackals, these herds of grass-eaters multiplied to vast numbers until a freak snow-storm or a really severe winter suddenly cut down the population. The surface of the plateau was littered with the skeletons of thousands upon thousands of animals which had died in these mass disasters, and the survivors were still so numerous that their droppings provided an inexhaustible supply of fuel for the travellers. Wild yaks were found in such profusion that they resembled the herds of North American buffalo and 'they were seen in such considerable herds',

Krishna's official report put it, 'that some three or four thousands beasts were visible at short distances and *at the same time*: handsome, black brutes without a speck of the white which appertains to domestication and bondage, and with long hair trailing so low as to conceal their legs, they presented to view the remarkable, great, dark moving masses of animal life.'

From the plateau Krishna and his party descended into the unpleasant saltlands of the Tsaidam where a white powder of salt covered rocks, shrubs, and the earth, and whenever a breeze blew, a whirling salt cloud reduced visibility to a hundred paces or less, and drove sharp grains of salt into the travellers' eyes. Here they were finally found by bandits. A shrilling war-cry at dawn heralded the charge of two hundred mounted raiders of the Chiamo Golok nomads who swept through the encampment. The Mongol travellers simply jumped on their ponies and scuttled for safety, leaving their tents and belongings to be plundered, while Krishna and the wretched Tibetan foot travellers fled to a makeshift redoubt and blazed away at the nomads as they ransacked the camp before riding away with their booty. Krishna saved his precious survey instruments, but he lost most of his baggage, and to compound the disaster, his servant ran away soon afterwards, stealing nearly all the rest of his horses and gear. He told Krishna that it was foolish to continue the crazy route survey when it was far better to desert now and lead a life of one's own far out of reach of the British.

But Krishna persisted. With his last remaining companion, he pushed right up to the Chinese frontier at Sachu, and only turned back when the governor of the city put him under house arrest until a Tibetan lama agreed to take Krishna back southwards with him. To survive, Krishna and his colleague worked as pony-herders on the *kafila*, and though the Mongols laughed at him, he turned down the offer of a riding-horse and instead volunteered to be a bullock-driver, walking beside his animals while his rosary clicked in his sleeve. Quite deliberately he chose to return by a road different from his outward journey, swinging in an arc through the east of Tibet until he arrived at the great emporium of Darchendo on the Tea Road between China and Tibet. There Krishna went secretly to see an outpost of the Jesuit fathers and borrow a little money before struggling on for Assam.

It was an incredible trek, traversing the headwaters of the Mekong, Salween, and Irrawaddy rivers through the tangled mountains, and by paths so narrow that the only traffic was an occasional pilgrim and the files of tea-porters striding along with bricks of green tea strapped in panniers on their backs. Just thirty miles from British territory in Upper Assam, Krishna finally had to admit defeat. The intervening area was the home of Mishmi tribesmen who raided Assamese villages for girl slaves and sold them in Tibet, and they killed anyone who tried to pass. Two French missionaries had recently been murdered attempting to get through, and the Tibetans themselves had designated the adjacent area as a convict colony. Wearily, Krishna turned away and headed back via the much longer route through Lhasa. For his travelling expenses he went from village to village reciting holy texts for alms, and on 12 November 1882 finally walked into the Survey office in Darjeeling to report his return. He and his companion were both destitute, emaciated, and in rags.

Months earlier the Survey had given up hope of seeing Krishna again.

From Tibet there had been a gruesome rumour that Krishna had been caught, and to stop him exploring again, the Tibetan authorities had chopped off his legs. Now their agent produced for their inspection an astonishing route survey, covering territory which had been completely unknown. In four and a half years' travel Krishna had scarcely missed a single chance to take his readings, even when working as a servant. He had compiled an unbroken series of compass bearings and distances, and during a short spell when his employer insisted on travelling fast on horseback to avoid bandits, the surveyor had counted his horse's steps and measured the average length of the animal's stride. His prayer-wheel, too, was packed with notes, and the journal of his adventures filled several tiny volumes which were hidden in his clothing. He had even brought back all the instruments the Survey had originally provided, though his sextant now lacked its box and was carefully wrapped in felt and wadding. Krishna's accolade was the map which the Survey drew from these notes. It was a beautifully meticulous piece of work, and across its surface Krishna's trail, precisely picked out by a neat red line, showed the immense scope of his walk, longer than any of his predecessors' journeys for the Survey, deeper into Mongol and Chinese territory, and penetrating through some of the worst terrain in Asia. It was only fair that after such an effort Krishna should be fitted up with a new set of clothes and sent in triumph to Calcutta to meet General Walker who congratulated him and presented him with a medal issued by the International Geographical Congress at Venice in 1881 on the understanding that it was to be awarded to an outstanding Asiatic explorer. More practically, the Indian Government gave Krishna a land grant, and the Survey gave him long leave.

There now remained one last problem to be solved from Montgomerie's original programme of exploration, and that was the question of the source of the Brahmaputra river. To a generation which had just witnessed the race to find the source of the Nile in Africa, the mystery of Asia's great rivers was almost as intriguing. Nearly all of these rivers rose in the Tibetan uplands, but their sheer profusion had led to a considerable muddle. The mountainous country between China, Tibet, and Upper Burma was so broken that it was difficult to make any theoretical sense out of its drainage; and of all the rivers which passed through this area the Brahmaputra was the greatest puzzle. By far the largest tributary of the Ganges, the Brahmaputra was also the most volatile and impressive waterway in the whole of India. It regularly flooded thousands of square miles, drowned entire villages and destroyed crops, and yet provided the main artery of communication with the whole of the fertile Assam valley.

The Brahmaputra came bursting out through the Himalayan wall into Upper Assam as a series of fully fledged rivers, the most important known as the Dihong, which united to flow down Assam as one great stream. Several military parties had tried to penetrate up these tributaries from British India but had always been stopped short by cataracts, thick vegetation, and the hostility of the wild tribes. What made the Upper Brahmaputra even more intriguing for geographers, though, was the possibility of a connection with the Tsangpo river inside Tibet. The Tsangpo was the main river of Tibet, but no one knew exactly what happened to it after it flowed south of Lhasa.

Opposite *A camp on the bank of the Brahmaputra river as far upstream as British survey parties could get*

209

Instead of emerging directly through the Himalayas to find its way to the sea, the Tsangpo stayed behind the mountains, running in a trough parallel with the main ridge and collecting its run-off like a huge rain-gutter. If, in fact, it did join the Brahmaputra, then the Tsangpo needed to make an extraordinary right-angle bend in its course and slice through the Himalayan rocks by a gorge so deep that it was theoretically almost impossible. In the last 120 miles of its course the river also needed to drop more than nine thousand feet, either in a series of cataracts, or over a fantastic waterfall which would far exceed Niagara or the Victoria Falls in grandeur. Every Survey agent who had ever gone into this area of Tibet had been asked to report on the problem of the Tsangpo, and all those who returned said that the Tibetans themselves believed that the Tsangpo became the Brahmaputra. But no one was completely sure, and in its quest for accuracy, the Survey had to have scientific proof. The method of obtaining this proof was finally suggested by the new officer in charge of the Trans-Himalaya Section, Captain Harmer.

Harmer's idea was a straightforward one, but it required careful timing and co-ordination. He proposed to send a disguised native surveyor into Tibet with orders to go as far as he could downstream along the Tsangpo. When he could get no farther, the agent was to throw into the river a number of specially marked logs. The logs would be swept downriver and out through the Himalayas, where the Survey would post corps of observers to watch the river tributaries to see if any of these logs appeared. By calculating the speed of their appearance and the volume of water in the right tributary, surveyors hoped to pinpoint any connection between the Brahmaputra and the Tsangpo.

The first attempt to put Harmer's theory into practice was a dismal failure: the agent was unmasked before he could get far downstream, arrested by the Tibetans, and deported. The next trial also nearly came to grief, though the Survey had no knowledge of it. They selected for their agent a Sikkimese whom they code-named 'K-p', from the first and last letters of his real name which was Kintup. Their man was much less educated than many previous Pundits, but this was not considered important as his task was mostly mechanical. He was provided with an auger for boring holes in the logs, and a number of special metal tubes to slip into these holes before dropping the logs into the river at a specified time. That was the extent of his mission, and he was to return as fast as possible to India.

But Harmer's plan turned out quite differently. On 7 August 1880, Kintup crossed into Tibet disguised as the servant of a genuine Mongolian lama who was returning from a visit to India. The lama was a heartless character who broke his promise to the Survey that he would look after Kintup, and once inside Tibet sold Kintup as a slave to a Tibetan official, and then went on his own way with the money. For seven months Kintup had to work as a household drudge for his master before he saw an opportunity to escape. Then, instead of fleeing back to India, he decided to head for the Tsangpo to try to complete his mission. His former master sent men to catch him, and to save himself Kintup sought refuge at a monastery, claiming to be a pilgrim who had been betrayed. The head lama, nothing loath, prevented Kintup's pursuers from seizing him and after deciding the agent's market

value, paid them fifty rupees and took Kintup as his own slave. The wretched Pundit's ill-luck only made him more tenacious. For four and a half months more he laboured at the monastery to establish his credentials, and then asked permission to go on a pilgrimage to a shrine on the Lower Tsangpo. When this was granted, he made his way to the river, found a cave hidden in the forest, and laboriously cut fifty specially notched logs, each about a foot long which he cached in a cave. As he had lost his auger, he broke up the marker tubes and tied the metal pieces to the logs with strips of bamboo. But it was long past the allotted time for dumping the logs in the river and so Kintup needed to warn Captain Harmer when he would do so. This meant that he first had to return to the monastery to work as a slave for another two months; then ask permission to make a pilgrimage to Lhasa; and finally trudge all the way to that city where he wrote out a note and sent it by *kafila* to another Survey agent living on the frontier. In his note Kintup explained his new schedule and asked the Survey to post its river watches once again. Finally Kintup returned to the monastery for another nine months' slavery, where the head lama was so astonished by all these repeated pilgrimages and by Kintup's loyalty to his master that when Kintup asked for a third leave of absence to go again to the Tsangpo, the lama granted him his freedom in recognition of his religious devotion.

The heartbreak was that after Kintup had got back to his secret cave and thrown the logs into the river, he returned to the Survey in India only to find that his warning message had never been received. His agent contact had died, and the logs must have floated past unnoticed, eventually washing out into the Bay of Bengal. To make matters worse, several of the Survey officers could scarcely believe that their semi-literate agent had stayed at his post for so long and endured his slavery. So poor Kintup received only an *ex gratia* payment of one thousand rupees, and to the indignation of some Survey officers he was refused either a pension or a land grant. He disappeared into the streets of Darjeeling where he became a humble tailor, occasionally visited by kindly British officers who believed in and admired his extraordinary fortitude.

On this sad note retired from view the most stubborn of the Survey's intelligence workmen at a time when Montgomerie's successors in the Survey had to admit that the romance of their Pundits was fading. They had done their main job well, and pierced Tibet's defences often enough to rob her of most of her earlier mystique. No longer was it possible for Tibetans to fend off the cultural influences filtering across the border from the south, and when the Bengali headmaster of the Bhutia Boarding School, a special college set up in Darjeeling by the Survey and the Department of Public Instruction to educate boys of semi-Tibetan families, visited Tibet in person, he found that the chief minister already possessed a stereoscopic viewer in which he enjoyed looking at slides of Paris and the French countryside. The minister's dearest wish, he told the headmaster, was to own a modern printing-press, and to know how to develop his own photographs.

Of course the map of Tibet still had enormous blank areas on it, but these were, for the most part, of little or no strategic or commercial interest to the Government of India. It was felt that for practical purposes Tibet's secrets had been found out, and the proof of this was to come in the winter of 1903–4

when Francis Younghusband, himself a Himalayan explorer, led an expedition composed of Indian Army units to Lhasa using maps based on the work of the Pundits. This time, by a curious reversal, it was an invasion of Tibet from India which finally destroyed the atmosphere of secrecy which had been created by the earlier attack of the Ghurkas. The interval had produced the Pundits, whose record of exploration was perhaps best expressed by one of the Survey officers given the task of interviewing the agents after they returned to Dehra Dun. Writing of Kintup, the enslaved explorer, he respectfully drew his superior's attention to 'the strange persistency with which the native explorer will stick to his work. Time is nothing to him, and the same characteristic of dogged obstinacy which distinguishes the Mongolian character in general, and the Tibetan in particular, has been turned to most excellent account by those who train explorers for Asiatic research in India.' Patronizing though the judgment may have been, it was honest praise for the brilliant involvement by Asians themselves in the Oriental Adventure.

Sarat Chandra, Principal of the Bhutia Boarding School, crosses the Donkia Pass on a yak

213

CHAPTER ELEVEN

SAVANTS AND SURVIVORS

BY THE LAST DECADE OF THE NINETEENTH CENTURY much of the momentum had been exhausted from the progress of the Oriental Adventure. There were several reasons for this, not least the fact that most – though not all – of Asia's land mass had been satisfactorily explored and mapped by Europeans. Moreover, vast areas of the continent now lay under direct colonial rule which gave such regions a comforting familiarity. And it was evident that whether one intended to go to the Orient as a merchant or a missionary, as a soldier or a colonialist, or just as a tourist, the traveller was likely to be repeating a journey or a role which had been accomplished long before him. In short, the Oriental Adventure was losing most of its glamour and nearly all its novelty and, like a meteor decelerating as it encounters the thicker atmosphere of earth, the Oriental Adventure began to break into smaller fragments. Many of these fragments were spectacular in their own sudden blazes of fire, as mountaineers, botanists, or anthropologists each went to Asia to pioneer his own speciality. But the overall effect was of less consequence. Europe's image of Asia had already been set in broad outline by the earlier travels, and it required a quite exceptional new talent if any one man was to stand out among his fellows and alter the Asian image.

But such talent did exist. The last decade of the century had the unexpected bonus of producing two men who could both have been fairly described as 'the last great Asian explorer'. Both men demonstrated that it was still possible to develop a new and unique style in the Adventure, and to make substantial contributions to Western knowledge of the Orient. What was perhaps more unexpected was that these two men represented opposite poles in the whole manner and aim of their work. They formed, as it were, the two largest and most brilliant fragments hurled in opposite directions by the disintegrating Adventure before it finally burned itself out.

Marc Aurel Stein, Knight Commander of the Indian Empire, was the intellectual aspect of the Oriental Adventure brought to its ultimate pitch. He was the scholar-traveller *par excellence*, a field archaeologist whom many considered to be the paragon of all experts on Asian history. A Middle European by background, Stein came to the Adventure in a roundabout way. He was born in Budapest in 1862 into a well-to-do family. Younger by nineteen years than his only brother, he had received lavish care from his parents. He was brought up speaking Hungarian and German, tutored in four other languages and unstintingly encouraged in all his budding interests. When he began to show an inclination for Eastern studies, he was sent to a succession of universities to pursue his researches, and then sailed to England which at that time was recognized as the centre of Oriental research. There he worked in the library of the British Museum to prepare a learned, if obscure, monograph on Asiatic coin inscriptions, and in 1886 was rewarded with the offer of the job of principal of the Oriental College at Lahore and registrar of the Punjab University.

Up to this point Stein had all the makings of a painstakingly earnest and potentially very dull Orientalist. But his arrival in India seems to have wrought a remarkable change in him. It was as if his physical presence on the continent he had so long studied and thought about charged him with a superabundance of energy for digging into Asia's unknown history. It also revealed a store of enthusiasm within him, which had previously been known only to Stein's close friends and tutors. For the rest of his life Stein was to give, as one colleague later put it, the impression of a man constantly straining at the leash in order to get as much work done in as short a time as possible; and there was scarcely a moment in the rest of his career (and he studied and travelled until 1943) which he did not devote to his life's work.

Marc Aurel Stein

Sheer enthusiasm was not enough to explain Stein's phenomenal success. As a Hungarian employed by the Indian Education Service, it would have been natural for Stein to have been swallowed up by the bureaucratic process and vanish from view. But Stein had a quality which was rare among the great Asian explorers: he was a superb manipulator of the official machine. He had the knack of persuading the full power of colonial authority to support his own plans for research, and, although he was a full-time employee of the Education Service, he somehow got for himself a succession of special postings which enabled him to go on lengthy archaeological expeditions inside and outside the Indian Empire. He coaxed the Survey of India into lending him trained surveyors as his assistants; the Political Service gave him permission to enter sensitive frontier areas for his work; the Indian Army allowed Stein to march along in the rear of their expeditionary columns; and the viceroy himself, Lord Curzon, gave him leave to cross the Himalayas by a route normally forbidden to anyone but the most special Government envoys. Quite how Stein managed to assemble such widespread help is a mystery. Partly it was because he had a very engaging personality and made many friends in high places. But partly, too, it was because Stein was a bureaucratic expert in his own right. He knew exactly what official to approach on what subject, the right time to do so, and in the correct manner. Furthermore, he was a ferocious writer of letters and dispatches. He had a positive mania for written communications and was known to have written between two and three thousand letters to a single correspondent. Stein thought nothing of marching thirty-five miles across country during the day, then pitching his tent and sitting up until four in the morning writing letters by the light of his portable lantern. As he penetrated deeper and deeper into unknown territory, he always took care to organize a complex system of runners and mail-carriers to maintain his postal links with his base, so that he was never out of touch with his sponsors; and he wrote so many notes and memoranda that one has the suspicion that Stein cowed officialdom by grinding it down, and defeating it at its own game.

Stein imposed on himself a programme of antiquarian research which could well have broken a lesser man. He began with a succession of archaeological digs in India itself, and in 1898 got permission to follow the Malakand Field Force, making an archaeological survey in its wake like some erudite scavenger. Two years later he obtained Curzon's authority to march across the western Himalayas and enter the great desert of western China by its back door, so to speak, and it was here, near Marco Polo's desert of Lop, that Stein began to make the archaeological finds which astonished his contemporaries. All along the former line of the Silk Road he began excavating lost towns which had formerly flourished as trade centres until their water supplies had failed, and they had been buried under the drifting sand-dunes. Uncovering these sand-buried ruins was an eerie experience. The ghost towns lay several days' journey out into the empty desert and the archaeologists had to take with them galvanized tanks of drinking water to supply themselves and their camels. On the sites the sand usually lay in such a thin blanket that the timbers of the ancient houses could usually be seen at some distance, poking up through the dunes like bones. This sand and the other accumulated debris was usually so loose that it could be casually scraped aside with a boot heel, revealing the floorboards of a room which might not have been used for perhaps a thousand years. The desert people shunned these ruined towns for fear of offending the ghostly spirits, and, apart from an occasional pilferer, left them undisturbed. Several times Stein returned to particular sites, after an interval of two or three years, to find that no one had visited them in his absence. At one ancient ruined watchtower, he immediately recognized the only footmarks in the dust as the ones that he himself had left, with his dog, on a previous visit several years earlier.

The core of Stein's work was the ancient network of trade routes which had once criss-crossed all over Asia, linking peoples and cultures, and stimulating an extraordinary transfer of ideas and goods. In the Western Desert he stood, in a sense, at the crossroads of this vast interlocking system, and by digging into the sand he was able to prove that civilizations as far apart as classical Greece and China had once met and mingled in the caravan towns. He found letter-seals and Buddhist paintings which were influenced by Hellenistic art; clay tablets written in long-vanished Indian languages and scripts; hundreds upon hundreds of Chinese artefacts left behind from centuries of Chinese dominion over the desert; and even the swatches of silk and brocade which had been clipped as samples from the bales paid as tax by the silk-merchants passing through the desert. In places Stein was so close to the ancient way of life that it seemed as if the previous inhabitants had only evacuated their towns a few years before him. On the outskirts of one town he exhumed a number of native corpses which had been buried in late medieval times. Their bodies had been perfectly mummified by the dry sand of their graves and, on unrolling their shrouds, the dead men's facial features were still visible. One day, walking across a stretch of stony desert, he caught sight of an old Chinese coin lying exposed. Picking it up, he identified it as a coin minted in Roman times, and noticed another coin, exactly the same, lying father on, then another, and another. One by one he collected them as he went forward, picking them off the ground in a neat line where they must have dropped, coin by coin, from a hole in a badly packed baggage-roll, over a thousand years before as a Chinese supply caravan jogged across the desert to visit the trading towns. Until Stein saw them, the coins had lain unnoticed and undisturbed on the ground, not even covered by the sand drift.

The Western Desert was a superb place for Stein to work, because the sand, after it had choked the ancient civilizations to death, then preserved them as carefully as a museum collector packing his specimens in sawdust. Yet it took a man of Stein's exceptional imagination to know exactly where to dig and what to look for, otherwise the desert would have been no more than a vast treasure hunt, demanding generations of search. Stein, however, reinforced his academic knowledge with an almost magical knack of locating the right spot for his digs. He had a sixth sense in his ability to reconstruct exactly where the ancient inhabitants of an area would have located their settlements and laid out their towns. It was as though Stein could transport himself in his imagination back to the heyday of the Silk Road. Walking for the first time through the ruins of a half-buried town, he would go straight to its most important site, and show his men precisely where to commence digging in order to produce the best results. He also developed the technique of stationing himself at dusk on a particular vantage point from where he could watch the shadows lengthen and change on the sand-dunes. By watching the patterns and shapes of the shadows, he could deduce the lines of the long-lost Chinese defence walls, whose foundations ran for miles across country beneath the windblown sand which had buried them. By following these lines, Stein located the ruined Chinese watchtowers and garrison posts, and even found the piles of firewood neatly stacked where Chinese sentries had once guarded the desert frontier, keeping a look-out for desert marauders and ready to light signal fires to pass their messages to the high command.

Thickset and short, Stein had the stamina to match his enthusiasms. On two separate trips to the Western Desert he walked a total of twenty-five thousand miles and brought back more than four hundred packing-cases of specimens, enough to keep an army of museum specialists busy classifying and cataloguing his finds for the rest of his lifetime, and to bequeath outstanding central Asian collections to both the British and the Indian national museums. In 1908, while climbing in the Himalayas, he lost all the toes on his right foot when they had to be amputated after a severe case of frostbite. And in 1914 while travelling in central Asia, his horse reared back and fell on him, badly crushing the muscles of his left thigh. Undeterred, Stein ordered his party to march on, while he was carried in a litter until he could walk again.

To keep up with such a demanding prime mover required exceptional qualities from Stein's assistants in the field, and it was typical of Stein's unorthodoxy that he much preferred to work with a small team of Asiatics, although he could easily have assembled and led large expeditions of European scholars. Stein always tried to cut his field team down to the barest minimum. His ideal team consisted of one or two native surveyors, a personal assistant, a 'handyman' who also acted as cook, and his favourite dog. With such companions Stein would penetrate hundreds of miles into tribal territory, recruiting local porters and guides if he needed them, and usually reappearing with a long line of hired pack-animals laden with his archaeological treasures. His native assistants either broke down early under the gruelling pace and begged to be sent home, or they stayed on with Stein and became his devoted companions. One native surveyor whom Stein

asked to stay behind in the desert and salvage some decaying wall-paintings, stuck at his lonely post until he went blind in the effort and yet still continued with his task, using local labour.

One single coup, however, established Stein as an archaeological explorer of world status, and would have assured his reputation even if he had made no other discoveries. In 1907 he visited the oasis town of Tun-huang, which was still a thriving place near China's western frontier. Several European archaeologists had already visited Tun-huang before Stein, and they had examined the strange place known as the 'Caves of the Thousand Buddhas'. This was a dried-up river valley whose sides were riddled with caves, some of them natural and some hollowed out artificially. In these caves had formerly lived a very large colony of Buddhist priests and monks. They had opened up the caves, and converted many of them into small temples, in many cases covering the cave walls with sacred paintings. For centuries the Caves of a Thousand Buddhas had been a well-known place of pilgrimage, attracting pilgrims from all over central Asia and, as it lay just off the Silk Road, diverting pious travellers on their way to and from China to call at the valley and offer their prayers.

Opposite *One of the Tun-huang cave-temples.* Overleaf *Claimed as the world's earliest printed book, the Diamond Sutra, which Aurel Stein found at Tun-huang, was made in AD 868 from six blocks, each two and a half feet long and nearly a foot wide*

By Stein's time, the valley had the decayed look of an abandoned termite colony. Most of the Buddhist community had left, and whole slabs of rock had dropped away along the sides of the valley to reveal the cavities in which the monks had once prayed and meditated. A handful of priests still guarded the place and tended the shrines, and piously attempted to restore the former glory of the valley. But they were suspicious of any intrusion into their holy places, and it was one of these priests, a Taoist named Wang Tao-shih, who had been cleaning up the walls of a cave when he stumbled across a crack in the plaster. Exploring further, he had opened up a hidden chamber, literally stuffed with ancient documents. The discovery frightened the priest, who was scared to investigate anything so old or to risk attracting the attention of the local authorities. So to keep his secret, he carefully walled up the chamber with new bricks and refused to reopen it. Stein, however, heard rumours of the discovery and arrived at the valley determined to investigate the hoard and, if it proved worth while, to try and save the documents for study by scholars.

There now occurred one of those inexplicable strokes of good fortune without which even Stein's great tact and patience would have been useless. The problem was to persuade Wang Tao-shih to reopen his jealously guarded secret chamber, and Stein tried explaining his interest in the hidden documents by telling the priest how he himself had devoted his life to tracing the Buddhist links between India and China by retracing the trails and visiting the age-old shrines. His patron and hero in these travels, he told the priest, was the saintly figure of Hsüan Tsang, the great Chinese pilgrim who had crossed the desert in the seventh century to go to the founding centres of Buddhism in India and bring back original Buddhist texts and scriptures to China. Now, Stein said, he too was travelling like Hsüan Tsang in a great pilgrimage for scholarship to collect the old documents. Wang Tao-shih was sufficiently impressed by Stein's reputation to be coaxed into reopening the sealed chamber, but he would only do so in secret, plucking out a few manuscripts at random and taking them under cover of dark to Stein's

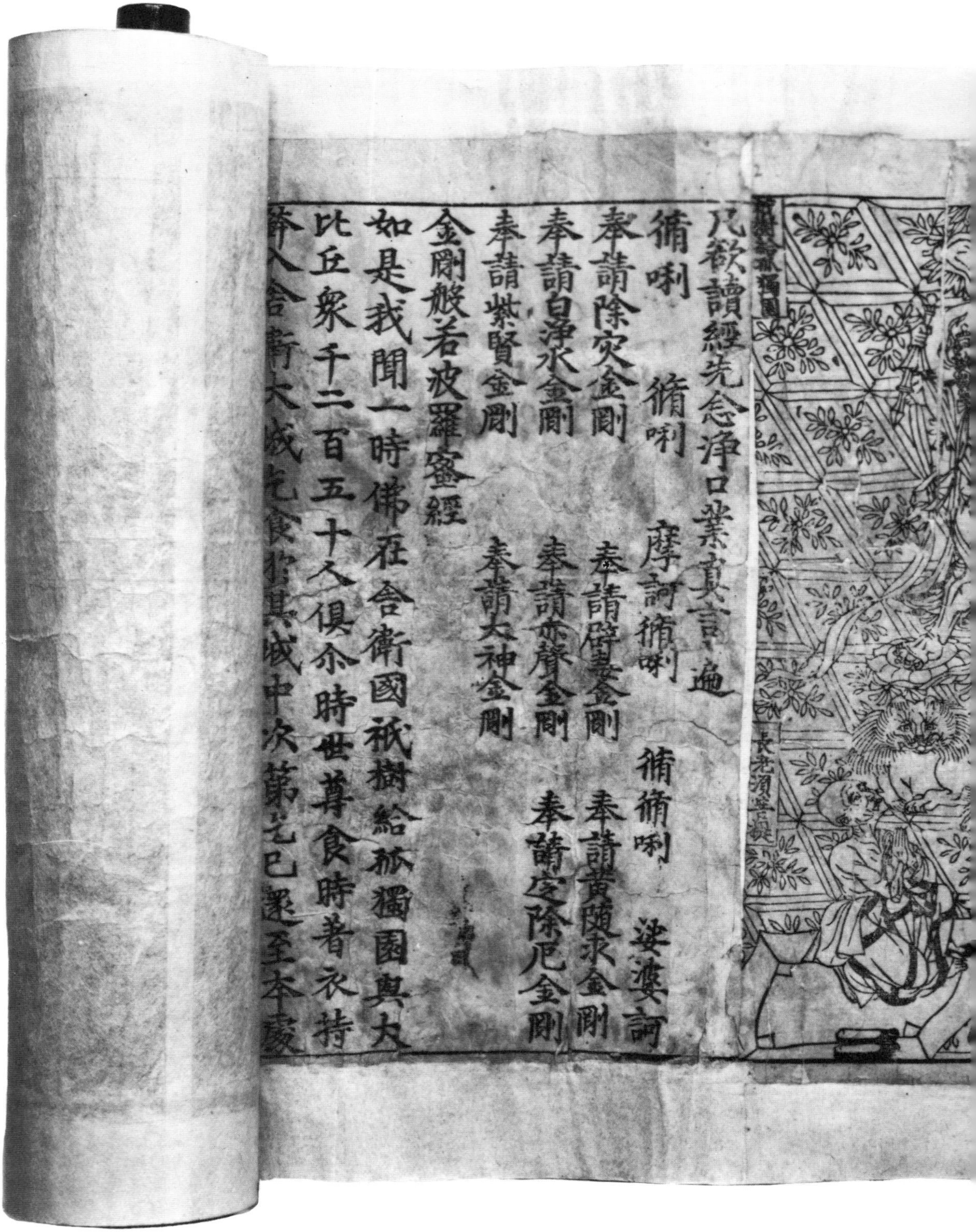

凡欲讀經先念淨口業真言一遍

唵　修唎　摩訶修唎

修唎　修修唎　婆婆訶

奉請除穢金剛

奉請辟毒金剛

奉請白淨水金剛

奉請赤聲金剛

奉請黃隨求金剛

奉請紫賢金剛

奉請定除厄金剛

奉請大神金剛

金剛般若波羅蜜經

如是我聞一時佛在舍衛國祇樹給孤獨園與大

比丘衆千二百五十人俱尓時世尊食時著衣持

鉢入舍衛大城乞食於其城中次第乞已還至本處

Chinese secretary. Almost unbelievably, one of the first scrolls to be opened was a collection of Buddhist canonical texts known as Sutras which, according to the inscription on the manuscript, had been first brought out of India by Hsüan Tsang himself and translated by the great pilgrim. Such a remarkable coincidence was enough to overturn Wang Tao-shih's reluctance, and he gave permission for Stein and his secretary to visit the secret chamber and make a rapid survey of its contents.

The sight which greeted Stein's eyes as he peered into the gloomy rock-cut chamber was something which he had never dreamed he would find. The secret chamber was literally heaped from floor to ceiling with a great stack of neatly rolled documents and relics, which made a solid mass of material rising to a height of nearly ten feet. There was only just enough room for two men to stand in the space left by this amazing pile of documents which, it was later calculated, occupied five hundred cubic feet. Indeed there was so much weight of material that Stein was genuinely worried in case Wang Tao-shih, as he scrambled about tugging out samples, should topple the structure and be buried beneath the collapse of the pile of documents. The frail and superstitious priest proved to be a difficult person to work with. He alternated between fits of enthusiasm and suspicion, sometimes encouraging Stein to examine whatever he wanted, and at other times threatening to brick up the chamber again for fear of angering the authorities. Under these difficult conditions Stein and his secretary had to work at a frantic pace, examining and cataloguing as much of the material as possible, before Wang Tao-shih finally lost his nerve and expelled them from the chamber.

In five days of unremitting work Stein was able to calculate that the secret chamber must have been walled up sometime early in the eleventh century, and that documents had been stored there since the ninth century, though several of the scrolls were much older and dated right back to the third century. The chamber also seemed to have been used both as a storehouse and as an archive, for it contained old silk temple banners and scraps of cloth left as offerings in the Tun-huang temples, as well as thousands upon thousands of scrolls. There were at least nine thousand scrolls in Chinese, but as Stein was not a Chinese scholar he concentrated on the material relevant to his study of the ancient cultural links of central Asia. The results were stupendous. He identified texts written in Indian, Turkish, and Uighur, in Iranian-based languages, Tibetan, and several previously unknown languages of central Asia. In just one example, Stein unrolled a huge manuscript, seventy feet long and a foot wide, which was covered in Indian Brahmic writing and interspersed with one of the unknown central Asian scripts so that it was possible to translate and recover the 'lost language'. Just as important were the collections of temple banners he found, folded up and stored away in the chamber by the Tun-huang monks centuries before. Some of these banners were so badly crushed by being on the bottom of the pile of material that Stein dared not open the brittle fibres for fear of ruining them. But others, from nearer the top, were still soft and supple. Unfurled, their superb workmanship was immediately visible, their colours still vivid, and the scenes they depicted so animated when held so that the sun shone through the gauze-like silk as intended, that they looked as impressive as when they had once fluttered in the shrines of medieval Tun-huang.

Even selecting only those items from the hoard which interested him most, Stein soon accumulated an embarassingly large pile of items which he wanted to purchase. Luckily those scrolls and banners which Stein valued most, the priest usually regarded as worthless rubbish, and he was pleased to receive from Stein five hundred rupees in silver in return for sack upon sack of material which was secretly carried out at night. There was so much weight of material that it became a physical problem to move the stuff by hand, Stein's Chinese secretary staggering back to his tent every night under the repeated loads (for Stein dared not be personally involved in case he was seen), until twenty-four cases of manuscripts and another five cases of embroideries, paintings, and art relics were ready for shipment. Wang Tao-shih, it seemed, was well pleased with his bargain, because the following year when a French Orientalist visited the Caves of the Thousand Buddhas, Wang sold him a quantity of the remaining Chinese scrolls; and when Stein himself returned to Tun-huang some years later to make additional purchases, he found that Wang had kept back a nest egg of six hundred manuscripts for him. The local authorities then heard about the amazing cache of material, and Wang was ordered to deliver it to the regional authorities. The remaining contents of the secret chamber were loaded on to carts, and were never seen again except for isolated items which were occasionally offered for sale to private collectors.

Stein's most brilliant contemporary in central Asia, the Swedish explorer Sven Hedin, would never have contemplated the patient and tactful technique used to coax Wang Tao-shih into parting with his treasures. But then Sven Hedin, the other genuine claimant to the title of the last great Asian explorer, had his own, equally successful methods. Hedin was blunt where Stein was diplomatic, flamboyant where the Hungarian scholar was self-effacing, and brazen and daring where Stein was cautious and restrained. If Stein was the epitome of the Oriental traveller in search of intellectual satisfaction, Hedin galloped headlong against the physical challenge of unknown Asia as though he were entering the lists of a tournament. He was the sort of man who was drawn irresistibly by the blank on the map. He craved to be the first European ever to set foot on any particular spot; and he exulted in defeating all competition. Nowhere was this contrast between Stein and Hedin more evident than in their attitudes to the Great Desert. Stein, the scholar, valued the desert for the chance it gave him to study the dried and mummified relics of ancient civilizations, but to Hedin, the adventurer, the parched wasteland was the last frontier, a supreme challenge to be tackled and conquered at no matter what cost, provided that Sven Hedin proved to himself that he had succeeded. It was a difference of which Hedin was well aware. Criticizing Stein's decision on one of his expeditions to turn his caravan back from the dangers of the desert, Hedin flatly stated, 'In a similar situation I should never have made such a decision. I should have continued through the desert. It might have been the death of me and my men . . . but the adventure, the conquest of an unknown country, and the struggle against the impossible, have a fascination which draws me with irresistible force.'

This statement was not mere bravado. Hedin could, and did, expose him-

self quite deliberately to terrible hardships, and as a result he suffered desperate privation. One of his earliest desert journeys was when he cold-bloodedly set out to cross a section of the desert never before attempted, even by the local camel-men. His only chance of survival was a rumour, impossible to check in advance, that water could be found on the other side of the crossing. The journey proved to be a nightmare for Hedin, his four hired camel-drivers, and the eight picked camels. They lost their way and ran out of water; in places the sand was so loose and treacherous that a passage had to be dug for their camels; and one by one the animals began to falter and die. Even Yoldash, Hedin's pet dog, lost its senses and ran off into the wastes to perish. Two of the camel-men in their desperation tried drinking camel's urine mixed with sugar and vinegar; they suffered terrible cramps. Finally only Hedin and one of the guides were left on their feet, and they made a desperate sortie to try to fetch water. Hedin realized that they could only hold out for another two or three days at most, and in one last gesture he changed into his only remaining suit of clean clothes so that if he should die in the desert, he would at least be decently dressed. For two days the pair struggled on, marching by night and resting by day, buried up to the neck in sand to escape the fierce sun. Finally the guide collapsed, pleading that he could continue no longer, and it was left to Hedin to stagger and crawl forward on his own. Semi-delirious he bumped into some bushes and chewed their sap to give him the strength to make one last spurt, which brought him, stumbling and falling, to the long-awaited river. There he filled his boots with water and carried them back to his companion. One of his camel-men was miraculously picked up alive by nomads, but two had died in the desert, and only one of the eight camels survived the fearful ordeal.

This ghastly episode convinced many people that Hedin was a dangerous menace as an explorer. With some justification they pointed out the astonishing mortality that occurred among the pack-animals used on any of Hedin's expeditions. In Tibet, for example, Hedin's terrific pace killed ten out of his twelve horses and four of his seven camels, and he lost yet another native guide, dead of exposure. Equally, it was easy to criticize Hedin for being so brash. He scorned diplomatic niceties, and if he wanted to go exploring on central Asian routes which took him across international frontiers, he simply set off on his journey, whether or not he had been given permission, and snubbed the outraged officials on his return. Nor did he have much regard for local feelings. As a young man he heard that the Stockholm Museum of Craniology was interested in measuring the skulls of members of the Parsee sect settled in Persia. So he boldly equipped himself with some climbing rope, and went off to burgle one of the sacred Towers of Silence where the Parsees exposed the bodies of their dead. When no one was looking, Hedin scrambled up into the tower, stole three skulls, and carried them back to his lodgings where he boiled them in milk to clean them. When he got back to Sweden, he jauntily delivered them to the museum.

But those who condemned Hedin as a dangerous fraud, overlooked the fact that Hedin himself believed he had done nothing to be ashamed of, or that circumstances had not demanded. He had a thoroughly romantic view of his life, and was acting out the role of professional adventurer which he had always imagined for himself, and for which he had always prepared. As a

Opposite *Sven Hedin, in heroic pose and surrounded by native colleagues and dogs in Tibet in 1908*

One of Hedin's own sketches
of his porters and
pack-animals crossing a river
on an early expedition

child, he deliberately toughened himself by rolling in the snow and sleeping by an open window in harsh Swedish winters. And totally lacking in experience or proper equipment he had tackled his early feats with tremendous personal bravery. In the Pamirs he tried climbing a notorious mountain known locally as 'The Father of Ice', even though it was the height of the avalanche season and he lacked supplies and professional help. He was driven back by constant snowfalls and was lucky to escape with his life, but he did not complain even when he was so badly stricken by snow-blindness that his native porters had to lead him by the hand away from the mountain, his eyes covered in bandages. On another occasion he had the nerve and schoolboy optimism to try to enter Lhasa disguised as a native. He shaved his head, coloured his skin, and wore tinted blue Tibetan glasses to cover his eyes, and for several weeks successfully acted the part of a native servant in his own baggage-train, before his disguise was finally penetrated by an astute Tibetan official. Hedin was let off with a warning, but he could just as well have been imprisoned or even executed.

Nor could Hedin's enemies deny that the Swede was phenomenally successful in opening up unknown territory. At the peak of his form Hedin crisscrossed the Gobi Desert in a series of spectacular expeditions, locating lost cities of the old caravan roads, exploring enormous areas of unknown country, and bringing out masses of new information about the social and physical features of the Asian heartland. He was also a vivid and exciting writer. His publishers, the German firm of Brockhaus, had a great success with his books which sold in large numbers, winning him thousands of devoted readers and making Hedin a popular hero in Germany and Scandinavia.

Like Stein, Hedin was also on easy terms with men in high places. The King of Sweden was his staunch patron, and Hedin was entertained by the

Tsar of Russia and the Kaiser, who both took a personal interest in his escapades. Hedin used his influential contacts ruthlessly to obtain passports and other special rights, but eventually these privileges demanded repayment. During the First World War Hedin was invited on an official visit to the German armies, and he wrote a book about his impressions which were, on the whole, favourable. Enraged, the Royal Geographical Society in London, who had awarded Hedin their Gold Medal, took the unprecedented step of denouncing the explorer as an enemy of the king, and by a special resolution the Society's Council struck Hedin's name from their role of Honorary Members. Increasingly pro-German as he grew older, Hedin damaged his reputation still further in the 1930s by siding openly with the Nazis, partly because he saw Germany as a bulwark against the 'Asiatic Hordes' and partly because of his friendship with many of the German leaders, including Goering, and his long-standing reliance on the German publishers and banks who had supported him.

Whatever the reasons for Hedin's pro-Nazi sympathies, the real pity of his political bias was that it overshadowed the finest achievement of his entire career. After a lifetime of being castigated as a showman and a lightweight, Hedin successfully led in 1928 the largest and most complex scientific expedition ever to have worked in central Asia. The expedition was so big and so diverse that the Press nicknamed it 'the Travelling University', and when it set off into the desert, its camel column was the largest in living memory. For six years this huge undertaking, mostly staffed by Swedes and Chinese, maintained a series of research stations extending most of the way from the Great Wall to the Caspian Sea. In each station one might have found visiting geologists and meteorologists, philologists collecting Asian vocabularies, zoologists collecting plants, palaeontologists hunting fossils, and Hedin himself patrolling between the isolated outposts, smoothing down local difficulties, grappling with officialdom, and bringing much-needed supplies, money, and encouragement. It was a colossal task for a man then in his sixties, especially since Hedin was suffering from gallstones and from terrible pains in his back so that he needed morphine injections to keep him on his feet. A tumour on his spinal cord was suspected, and he had to take time off to visit a surgeon in Boston. But fortunately an operation was not necessary and Hedin was allowed back in the field where his exceptional talents of leadership and his unquenchable energy were at last channelled into a worthwhile project. His Travelling University gathered up sufficient central Asian data to fill fifty-six volumes of learned commentary, and still leave so much material that to this day it has not been analysed for want of qualified experts to do so. If that was not enough, Hedin himself returned to the desert at the age of sixty-nine to lead a convoy of trucks and cars along the Silk Road and test its potential as a motor track of the future.

It made a neat conclusion to the Oriental Adventure that its last two great participants, Hedin and Stein, should have brought the Adventure back to precisely the same place where it had begun with Marco Polo's original caravan. Across the gap of six hundred years the connection was still so close that nearly every European on Hedin's Travelling University, however limited his baggage allowance, chose to bring with him a copy of Marco

Tevi dortie. Kebiane. 36 ai.   Tamding angal. 19a. Kebjay

S.Hn.
1908

Polo's *Description of the World*, and Hedin himself carried no less than four different editions. They found that Marco Polo's book was not only the most convenient fixed point of reference in central Asian history, but the best surviving description by any European of conditions in the Gobi. Indeed the Oriental Adventure had achieved a unity which managed to embrace all the men of vastly different backgrounds who had come out of Europe to visit Asia for a whole variety of reasons. Whatever their differences, the travellers had all contributed – and often were aware of the contribution – to a single, interconnecting image of Asia which they inherited, augmented, and then handed on to their successors. Hedin the twentieth-century Swede consulting Marco Polo the thirteenth-century Venetian for guidance on conditions in the Gobi was an extreme example of this continuity, but it existed equally between the reports of the Jesuits in China which influenced the preparations for Macartney's embassy, between the reports of the traders in India and the hopeful soldiers of fortune who went to serve the Great Mogul, and even, with immediate effect, between news of Yermak's conquests in Siberia and the stampede of Russians to reap the fur harvest of the north Asian forests.

This dream of Asia which bewitched all these men, was never quite the same from one group to the next. Sometimes it changed so slowly that the differences were scarcely perceptible, but it often altered with dramatic speed as the result of new discoveries by the travellers themselves. Yermak, for example, broke down the notion of the invincible Tatar hordes as quickly and effectively as Marco Polo built up the picture of the Great Khan of China with his millions of subjects, his immeasurable wealth, and his efficiently ruled empire. In fact it could be claimed that no single travel book ever had so profound an effect on Europe's knowledge of the outside world as Marco Polo's *Description*, and yet even Marco Polo's image of Asia was to provide only the central core of a theme which would be extensively modified as the Oriental Adventure progressed. His glittering figure of the Great Khan became in turn a target for the Jesuits' missionary zeal, a foil for Lord Macartney's diplomatic effort, and a waning despot to be ignored by the Commission for the Exploration of the Mekong, more interested in establishing contact with the rebels who rejected the Chinese emperor's authority.

Yet, despite this changing Asian image, it is strange just how often, when reading the accounts of the early travellers, one is struck by the aptness of their remarks to modern circumstances. When Lord Macartney commented on the vast state machine of China centred on the emperor in Peking, or Manucci sweated in the dust of Delhi and wrote of the peculiar mixture of tawdriness and pomp that is so characteristic of India, or Garnier pronounced his judgment of the little Southeast Asian kingdoms as ripe and slightly rotten fruit, they seemed to have such uncanny prescience that one is left wondering whether the early writers were peculiarly shrewd observers, or whether Oriental conditions have really not changed fundamentally in the interval, or whether the travellers fixed their Oriental images so firmly in our minds that one is still swayed by them.

Perhaps it is because the European travellers in the Orient were seldom arrogant in their attitudes towards the Asians that their experiences have endured so well. Very few of them behaved with the self-confidence and superiority which now seems to be so out of place in the early reports of the

Opposite *Two Tibetans by Hedin.*
Overleaf *Sven Hedin and part of the 'Travelling University'*

229

first travellers in the New World, in Africa, or Australasia. Instead, the Orient was a unique experience for the Europeans. No other continent made them so aware that they were only touching the hem of great places and events. In the Orient there was so much to observe and to learn, and so much to record, that few of the visitors dared claim that they had grasped the complexities of even their own small area. This led them to adopt a healthy and cautious attitude, and it explained why so many of the returned travellers offered their experiences as straightforward reports on their journeys, with very little attempt at commentary.

And for the same reason the story of the Oriental Adventure remains best appreciated as the chapter-by-chapter endeavours of the individuals who were directly involved. Asia was 'discovered' with equal validity for its religions, its geography, its social customs, and its commercial potential. Occasionally a traveller's tale had direct historical merit when it presented an outsider's view of historical events that either went unrecorded by Asiatics themselves or were coloured by local prejudices. But usually the travellers and their reports must be seen in their European context, as examples of how Europeans were behaving overseas, and how the image of the Orient was created by them. In the last analysis one is left with the feeling that the sheer bulk and diversity of the Orient both rewarded and awed the men who took part in the Oriental Adventure. It repaid them by giving them ample opportunity to succeed and flourish in their chosen courses whether as scholar, merchant, soldier, or civil servant. And however cynical, disappointed, or uncomfortable the traveller might become, every visitor to the Orient could not avoid being touched by some episode in his wanderings, some moment when he felt that he was uniquely privileged in his experience. On the other hand the Orient also hedged every traveller about with such novel and inexplicable events and scenes that he was always obliged to remember the limits of his own competence. In short, if there was one feature common to every participant in the Adventure, it was that the Orient, to the end, commanded not so much his affection or his fascination as his respect.

ACKNOWLEDGMENTS FOR ILLUSTRATIONS

The following abbreviations are used in the text:

Bibl. Nat. – Bibliothèque Nationale, Paris

Brit. Lib. – British Library, London

Brit. Mus. – Courtesy of the Trustees of the British Museum, London

Freeman – John R. Freeman & Co. (Photographers) Ltd, London

I.L.C.O. – Institut des Langues et Civilisations Orientales, Paris

I.O.L.R. – India Office Library and Records, London

Nat. Pal. Mus. – Collection of the National Palace Museum, Taipei, Taiwan, Republic of China

R.G.S. – Royal Geographical Society, London

S.H.F. – Sven Hedin Foundation, Etnografiska Museet, Stockholm

Page numbers marked with an asterisk* indicate colour illustrations

ACKNOWLEDGMENTS
FOR ILLUSTRATIONS

rary and Records, London. Photo: R. B. Fleming & Co. Ltd

112 Mogul miniature, 1658, from a manuscript of the *Shah Jahan-nama*, folio 115 v. Royal Library, Windsor Castle. Reproduced by gracious permission of Her Majesty Queen Elizabeth II. Photo: A. C. Cooper Ltd

116 Indian drawing, commissioned by Manucci. MS Od. 45. Bibl. Nat.

119 Indian drawing, commissioned by Manucci. MS Od. 45. Bibl. Nat.

121 Double portrait by Lemuel Francis Abbott, 1784. National Portrait Gallery, London

123 'From myself, done at sea'. Pencil and Indian ink, tinted with watercolours, *c*. 1792. Royal size LBI, 1897.8.13.2. Brit. Mus.

127 P. 70 of William Alexander's watercolour drawings made on his journey in Lord Macartney's embassy to China 1792–4. LB22. 198.c.l. Brit. Mus.

129* 'An Imaginary View of an Entertainment at the Mughal Court' by W. Schellinks, Dutch School, late 17th cent. Indian Section 30-1892. V. & A. Photo: Derrick Witty

130–1* Watercolour by William Alexander, *c*. 1792. Royal size LB13. Dept of Prints and Drawings, Brit. Mus.

132* From *The Costume of China* by William Alexander, London, 1805. Photo: Freeman

134 Alexander, p. 5 (see credit to p. 127)

136 Watercolour by William Alexander, *c*. 1793. Royal size LB9. Brit. Mus.

138 Alexander, p. 20 (see credit to p. 127). Brit. Mus.

142 The Kessu Tapestry. National Maritime Museum, London

145 Alexander, p. 1 (see credit to p. 127). Brit. Mus.

149 Alexander, p. 2 (see above). Brit. Mus.

150 Alexander, p. 45 (see credit to p. 127). Brit. Mus.

153 Alexander, p. 25 (see above). Brit. Mus.

155 Alexander, p. 76 (see above). Brit. Mus.

158 Plate facing p. 26 of *Voyage d'Exploration en Indo-Chine* by Francis Garnier, Paris, 1873. R.G.S. Photo: Freeman

160–1 Garnier, plate VIII (see above). R.G.S. Photo: Freeman

163 Garnier, plate facing p. 156 (see above). R.G.S. Photo: Freeman

165* From *The Costume of China* by William Alexander, London, 1805. Photo: Freeman

166* Watercolour by William Alexander, *c*. 1792. Atlas size LB19. Dept of Prints and Drawings, Brit. Mus.

166–7* Plate X of *Atlas du Voyage d'Exploration en Indo-Chine* by Francis Garnier, Paris, 1873. R.G.S. Photo: Freeman

167* Garnier, plate XV (see above). R.G.S. Photo: Freeman

168* Painting on silk. Brit. Mus.

170–1 Garnier, plate facing p. 294 (see credit to p. 158). R.G.S. Photo: Freeman

173 Garnier, plate on p. 101 (see above, 1885 edition). Bibl. Nat.

175 Garnier, plate on p. 248 (see credit to p. 158). R.G.S. Photo: Freeman

178 Garnier, plate on p. 418 (see above, 1885 edition). Bibl. Nat.

179 Garnier, plate on p. 442 (see above). Bibl. Nat.

180 Garnier, plate facing p. 366 (see credit to p. 158). R.G.S. Photo: Freeman

183 Watercolour by Sir Edward Durand. I.O.L.R. Photo: Freeman

184–5 Drawing by Hyder Young Hearsey, 1812. I.O.L.R.

187 Pen and ink drawing by Herbert Edwardes, 1845. I.O.L.R.

188 Drawing by Godfrey Thomas Vigne, 1834. I.O.L.R.

190 G. W. Haward in Indian dress. R.G.S.

ACKNOWLEDGMENTS
FOR ILLUSTRATIONS

196–7 Plate facing p. 64 of *Across Thibet* by Gabriel Bonvalet, 1891. R.G.S.

198 Photograph of Nain Singh. R.G.S.

201 Plate facing p. 376 of *Himalayan Journals* by Sir Joseph Dalton Hooker, London, 1905. R.G.S.

204 Plate facing p. 208 of *Tibet the Mysterious* by Thomas Holdich, 1901. R.G.S.

208 Plate facing p. 178 of *The Mishmee Hills* by T. T. Cooper, 1873. R.G.S.

211 Photograph from the Turkestan box of Colonel F. M. Bailey's slide collection. Royal Society for Asian Affairs. Photo: Freeman

213 Plate facing p. 48 of *Journey to Lhasa and Central Tibet* by Sarat Chandra Das, London, 1904. R.G.S.

215 Drawing by W. Rothenstein, 1920. National Portrait Gallery

218 Plate 196 of *Serindia* by Sir Aurel Stein, Vol. II. By kind permission of The Clarendon Press, Oxford, and the Office of the High Commission of India

220–1 Diamond Sutra. Brit. Mus.

224 Photograph of Hedin. S.V.F.

226 'Crossing the Conche Darya, 1896' by Sven Hedin. S.V.F.

228 'Two Tibetans from a camp in Tibet, 1908' by Sven Hedin. S.V.F.

230–1 Hedin at the camp of Belimiao, November 1929. S.V.F.

INDEX

Numbers in *italics* indicate illustrations